Solar Energy Applications
in the Design of Buildings

Solar Energy Applications in the Design of Buildings

Edited by

HENRY J. COWAN

Department of Architectural Science,
University of Sydney, Australia

APPLIED SCIENCE PUBLISHERS LTD
LONDON

APPLIED SCIENCE PUBLISHERS LTD
RIPPLE ROAD, BARKING, ESSEX, ENGLAND

British Library Cataloguing in Publication Data

Solar energy applications in the design of buildings.
1. Solar heating—Congresses
2. Architecture and solar radiation—Congresses
I. Cowan, Henry Jacob
697'.78'02472   TH7413

ISBN 0–85334–883–9

WITH 13 TABLES AND 164 ILLUSTRATIONS
© APPLIED SCIENCE PUBLISHERS LTD 1980

Printed in Great Britain by Galliard (Printers) Ltd, Great Yarmouth
Photoset at Thomson Press (India) Ltd, New Delhi

Preface

This volume contains the papers presented at a symposium on solar energy held at the Department of Architectural Science of Sydney University from 29th to 31st August 1979. The authors were asked to confine themselves to applications presently useful in the design of buildings and to take account of the economic limitations of solar energy at this time. I think we would be doing a disservice to the promotion of solar energy if we gave too much attention to applications which may possibly at some future date become economical. These more spectacular, but presently unrealistic, uses of solar energy would distract attention from a number of immediately useful, if less dramatic, applications, which will be discussed in this symposium.

Since the economic potential of solar energy is still so limited, one might reasonably ask why there is such a great interest in the subject at present. Information on solar energy and solar energy appliances has been available for a quarter of a century. Ralph Phillips' *Sunshine and Shade in Australia,* which is still in print, was first published in the 1940s. Solar water heaters have also been commercially available since the 1950s.

Furthermore, there is no energy crisis as such at present. Some people consider that there is an oil crisis. The price of oil has already increased sharply, and there are shortages of petrol and heating oil in some countries. But as far as we can predict it is likely that there will be a severe crisis during the 1980s and 1990s. The houses we now build, and even the houses we now renovate, must take account of the altered situation which we can now foresee.

The term 'passive solar energy' includes a number of building techniques which we have employed for centuries, such as the use of sunshading, natural ventilation and thermal inertia. Many were put on a scientific basis before there was an energy problem. Some add little or nothing to the cost of a building. These techniques should be immediately introduced into the design of all new buildings. Others may not be economical now, but will become so during the life of new buildings. The buildings should be designed so that the necessary modifications can be made.

Active methods of solar energy employ solar collectors and the interest charges on their cost must be balanced against the solar energy collected. At present these are not economical in Australia's major urban centres, but they are worthwhile in more remote locations where the cost of electricity and of hydrocarbon fuels is high. As the cost of energy rises, active methods will become more attractive even in metropolitan areas. Most of the houses we now build will still be inhabited when the energy crisis becomes a reality and it is sensible to give some thought to the possible installation of future solar collectors in considering the design of a roof for a new building.

We have, however, excluded from this symposium the generation of electricity directly from the sun, because this is a development for the more distant future, except for regions with a low population density. The solar-powered telecommunications link between Alice Springs and Tennant Creek through more than 400 km of the Australian desert is a great technical achievement, a great convenience to the people who live there, and it is more economical than a link powered with conventional engines; but it does not save much hydrocarbon fuel.

HENRY J. COWAN

Contents

List of Contributors

R. M. Aynsley
Senior Lecturer in Architectural Science, University of Sydney, Sydney 2006, Australia

J. A. Ballinger
Lecturer in Architecture, University of New South Wales, Kensington, New South Wales 2033, Australia

H. J. Cowan
Professor of Architectural Science, University of Sydney, Sydney 2006, Australia

K. G. Dunstan
Senior Research Assistant in Architectural Science, University of Sydney, Sydney 2006, Australia

B. S. A. Forwood
Lecturer in Architectural Science, University of Sydney, Sydney 2006, Australia

J. S. Gero
Associate Professor of Architectural Science, University of Sydney, Sydney 2006, Australia

J. J. Greenland
Senior Lecturer in Architecture, New South Wales Institute of Technology, Broadway 2007, Australia

E. L. Harkness
Senior Lecturer in Architecture, University of Newcastle, Newcastle, New South Wales 2308, Australia

R. K. Macpherson
Formerly Professor of Environmental Health and Principal of the School of Public Health and Tropical Medicine, University of Sydney, 3 Melbourne Road, Lindfield 2070, Australia

L. F. O'Brien
Architectural Physics Group, Division of Building Research, C.S.I.R.O., Highett, Victoria 3190, Australia

R. O. Phillips
Faculty of Architecture, University of New South Wales, Kensington, New South Wales 2033, Australia

A. D. Radford
Formerly Department of Architectural Science, University of Sydney, Sydney 2006, Australia

A. M. Saleh
Department of Architectural Science, University of Sydney, Sydney 2006, Australia

P. R. Smith
Associate Professor of Architectural Science, University of Sydney, Sydney 2006, Australia

1

Is there an Energy Problem in the Design of Buildings?

H. J. Cowan

*Department of Architectural Science,
University of Sydney, Australia*

1.1. IS THERE AN ENERGY PROBLEM?

It was known long before the energy crisis of 1973 that there is a limited supply of the hydrocarbon fuels, namely coal, oil and natural gas; but there had not since the 19th century been any shortage of energy in any industrialized country, except temporarily in the USA during a hot summer. The events of 1973 produced a shortage in North America and Europe, although not in Australia, and a great increase in the price of oil. This in turn produced an economic crisis.

The energy crisis of 1973 drew attention to two facts which were known before, but had been largely ignored. First, the price of hydrocarbon fuels, and especially oil, will increase as supplies become scarcer. This will make more attractive a number of alternative sources

TABLE 1
AVERAGE GROWTH IN PRIMARY ENERGY CONSUMPTION
(% per annum)

Country or region	1960–70	1970–73	1974
Australia	5·4	5·5	5·4
Japan	12·3	7·2	−1·4
USA	4·3	3·5	−2·8
Western Europe	5·2	4·5	−1·6
World	5·0	4·7	0·8

Source: Information provided to the Ranger Inquiry by Miss J. C. Miller, Senior Statistician, Joint Coal Board (From Ref. 1, p. 3).

1

Table 2
FORECAST AVERAGE GROWTH IN PRIMARY
ENERGY CONSUMPTION
(% per annum)

	1974–80	1980–85
European Economic Community	2·4	3·6
OECD Europe	3·2	4·0
Japan	5·8	5·9

Source: World Energy Outlook, OECD, Paris, 1977.
(From Ref. 1, p. 4).

of energy which are at present not competitive. Secondly, the rate of energy usage was increasing at a rapid rate, and buildings were a major consumer of energy. The rate of increase in the use of energy prior to 1973 was about 5% (Table 1). In 1974 there was a decrease in energy usage, although not in Australia which was not greatly affected by the energy crisis; but the Organization for Economic Cooperation and Development (OECD) expected energy usage to increase again, even if not to the same extent (Table 2).

Let us examine what this increase implies for the future. If the rate of increase in the demand for energy is $r\%$ each year, the demand for energy increases after n years by a factor $(1 + 0 \cdot 01 \ r)^n \cdot$ This means that we may expect energy consumption in Australia to double again before the year 2000 if the present trend continues.

At the present rate of consumption Australia has proven reserves of black coal for 250 years, of brown coal for 1050 years, and of natural gas for 125 years; but at the present growth rate in consumption the supply

Table 3

Percentage increase in energy demand each year r	Number of years required to double energy consumption n
0·7	100
1·4	50
2·8	25
3·5	20
4·7	15
7·1	10

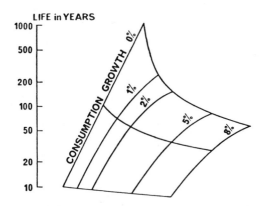

Fig. 1. Resource life as a function of consumption growth rate. (From Ref. 2, p. 89.)

is far less than a century for both black and brown coal, and about 30 years for gas (Ref. 2). The reason for this is evident from Table 3 and Fig. 1.

The rate of growth is therefore a bigger problem than present energy consumption. The rate of growth is more rapid in countries in the process of industrialization, such as Japan (Tables 1 and 2) than in countries which are already industrialized. Since energy consumption is roughly proportional to gross national product (Fig. 2), we may expect the demand for energy to grow even faster as countries in Asia and South America increase the pace of their industrialization.

There is, therefore, undoubtedly an energy problem. Why then are we doing so little about it; for example, by encouraging the greater use of solar energy? Contrary to popular belief, solar energy is not free. At the present time in Sydney and Melbourne, where about 40% of the people live, solar energy is generally more expensive than conventional energy generated from hydrocarbon fuels. This could be overcome by a subsidy, which would have to be paid from taxation, or by changes in the tariff for conventional energy, which would increase its cost to the general public. Increased taxes and prices are unpopular measures and the energy crisis is not at present sufficiently serious to persuade governments and energy authorities of their need. Even in the USA, where the position is less favourable than in Australia, a shortfall of energy is not expected until the early 1980s (Fig. 3).

In the meantime, however, some useful measures can be taken at negligible cost by conserving energy in buildings, which are a major

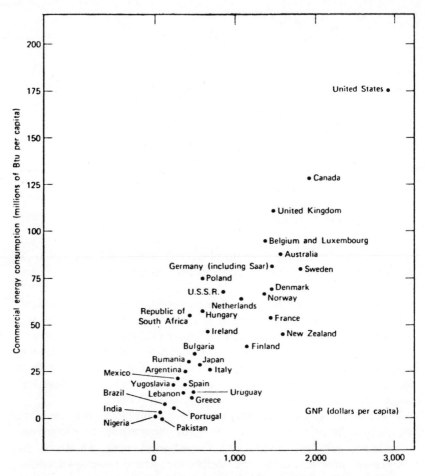

Fig. 2. Variation of commercial energy consumption with gross national product. (From Ref. 3, p. 23.)

source of energy consumption. In Britain buildings account for about 50% of the total, in the USA for about 40% and in Australia for about 20%. This difference is partly due to climate and partly to the extent to which private cars are used. However, even the temperate climate of the densely populated part of Australia offers scope for conservation. If the present rate of increase in energy consumption could be slowed down, the problem would become much easier. Moreover, a re-examination of our present usage of energy may actually increase our comfort.

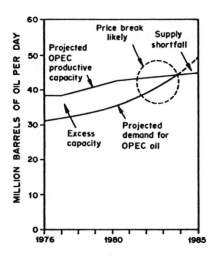

Fig 3. Possible development of supply and demand for OPEC oil in the USA
(From Ref. 4, p. 10.)

1.2. CRITERIA FOR THERMAL COMFORT

One possible method of energy conservation is a revision of our criteria of thermal comfort. It has been axiomatic for at least a century that a greater expenditure of energy invariably improves thermal comfort. Until comparatively recently this was in fact true. Prior to the 19th century one could only heat a room with one or two fireplaces or stoves and consume a certain amount of fuel in each. Available methods of cooling did not consume fuel. Many traditional methods of construction made ingenious use of thermal storage in both cold and hot weather, and of shading, ventilation and evaporative cooling from ornamental ponds in hot weather. These methods are now being revived in a more technological and efficient form under the name of passive solar energy.

During the late 19th century heating technology advanced to an extent which made it possible to increase the indoor winter temperature above the level of comfort, and in my opinion this has in fact happened in North America and in some parts of Europe. In the mid-20th century the same result was achieved for air conditioning. Excessive cooling of buildings in summer presents greater problems than excessive heating in winter. Air conditioning is often excessive in North America, but the problem exists also in developing countries where it is hardest to justify.

In some parts of Africa the temperature is set according to the rank of the person occupying the room. The unimportant person has an office without air-conditioning. Provided the room has (in the hot-humid zone) a suitable sunshade and correctly placed fans, it may be quite comfortable, except in the early afternoon. The slightly important person has air conditioning set to a temperature only slightly below that of the outside air; his visitor is the most fortunate because the room is just comfortable wearing a short-sleeved shirt. The more important person has a lower temperature in his office and he wears a lightweight coat; his visitor will be chilly unless he has himself brought a coat. The very important person has a room cool enough to enable him to wear an English suit; if his visitor walked to call on him, his short-sleeved shirt is slightly damp from perspiration and, if he did not bring a coat, he may catch a cold if the interview takes too long. It is to the credit of India that its government and universities have tended to build in accordance with an established architectural tradition well suited to the climate and requiring very little expenditure of energy.

Excessive heating and cooling, at first impression, conveys a feeling of luxury. The hot air in winter and cool air in summer at the doors of a department store attract customers who may feel too warm or too cool once they are inside; but they stay nevertheless. Offices which are not air-conditioned are difficult to let and the level of heating and cooling is presumably what the occupants prefer. However, tastes can be changed. We no longer eat the five-course meals which our great-grand parents, if they belonged to the middle class, considered essential for prestige and there have already been reductions in winter and increases in summer temperatures in air-conditioned buildings since 1973. In my opinion these changes have not gone far enough.

A more important question is the use of a fixed temperature for the interior environment. The ASHRAE Handbook (Ref. 5) and Fanger's research in Denmark (Ref. 6) are built around the question "at what temperature are you most comfortable?". This is a reasonable basis for a person who travels from his air-conditioned home to his air-conditioned office in an air-conditioned car and never goes outside. In Australia the house and the car or bus are probably not air-conditioned, only the office. In the circumstances the relation between the indoor and the outdoor temperature assumes some importance. It may well be that people would be more comfortable all day long if the indoor temperature moved closer to the outdoor temperature on days when the latter is either very high or very low. This would also save energy, and it would bring nearer the day when solar air-conditioning becomes economically feasible.

1.3. THE INFLUENCE OF MODERN ARCHITECTURE

Another possible method of energy conservation is a re-examination of architectural design. Several architectural critics have written books on the passing of Modern Architecture (for example, Refs. 7 and 8), and it is no coincidence that articles on Post-Modern Architecture started to appear shortly after 1973.

When the modern style of architecture came into existence, the scientific basis of environmental design received little attention. The technical emphasis was on the structure and the materials. Le Corbusier, Gropius, and Mies van der Rohe were all concerned with the lightness of the structure made possible by the invention of skeleton frames built from steel or reinforced concrete and with the use of glass-curtain walls to emphasize that lightness. Ludwig Hilbereimer, an associate of Mies van der Rohe first at the Bauhaus and later at the Illinois Institute of Technology, claimed that in Mies's buildings

"the disunity between architecture and engineering has been overcome; the engineer, once the servant of the architect, is now his equal". (Ref. 9, p. 21).

But this applies only to the structure. The environmental design of Mies's buildings is subordinate to the visual effect of the glass-curtain wall. An early pair of his glass-walled· buildings, the Lake Shore Apartments (860–880 North Lake Shore Drive, Chicago) built from 1949 to 1952, had no air-conditioning; but they proved to be too hot due to solar radiation through the glass walls, and individual air-conditioning units were subsequently installed, which ruined the appearance of the buildings. The glass-curtain-walled buildings of the 1950s and 1960s would, in fact, have been impossible without air-conditioning.

The technologies of lighting and of air-conditioning both made great progress in the 1940s and 1950s (Ref. 10), and the perfection of the interior environment became a principal objective of architectural design in the late 1950s and the 1960s. The pipes and ducts required for building services became a visual feature in some buildings, culminating in the design for the Centre Pompidou in Paris.

Energy was cheap and plentiful and energy conservation was

considered only insofar as it affected the overall cost, if it was considered at all. This trend has been reversed during the last few years, but the question whether full mechanical-electrical control of the environment is desirable for all important buildings in the temperate climate of Sydney and Melbourne remains to be answered. There have not been sufficient social surveys to establish whether the complaints one hears from time to time about the excessive use of artificial light and the absence of natural ventilation represent the grumbling of a few or the views of a majority. There are two alternatives for improving the interior environment, while conserving energy; one employs more technology, the other less. Computer-operated controls could be used to adjust the interior environment to changes in the exterior environment; alternatively we could return to a greater use of daylight and of natural ventilation, at least in smaller buildings.

In the late 1960s and early 1970s there was a wide-spread reaction against modern technology and the Affluent Society, and this produced designs for a number of Autonomous Houses which were to be totally self-sufficient in their use of energy. The earliest of these designs preceded the energy crisis of 1973. These Autonomous Houses had some admirable features, such as the use of thermal stores and other passive methods of utilizing solar energy. Some other devices were of questionable value and the concept of recycling sewage has potential dangers to public health if it were to be used generally in an urban area. The design philosophy of the first Autonomous Houses was based on the concept that the resources of the Planet Earth are finite and that conservation of these resources is essential for survival in the long term. This was derived from forecasts of bodies, such as the Club of Rome, which were, I believe, based on incorrect assumptions. Many of the raw materials claimed to be in short supply are, with proper management, available in more than adequate quantities, provided population growth can be stabilized in the developing countries as it has already been stabilized in the developed countries. For example, timber can be regenerated with proper afforestation and raw materials for concrete and glass are available in virtually unlimited quantities. The disposal of waste paper and old bottles is a separate problem.

Another issue widely discussed ten years ago was the desirability of zero economic growth. Many people, including many architects who participated in the Centenary Congress of the RAIA in Sydney in 1971, were impressed by the evils of a consumer-oriented society. Shortly thereafter the economic crisis produced by the increase in the cost of energy in 1973 demonstrated the far greater evils of zero economic growth. I think we must therefore accept economic growth as an essential part of our society, and with it a growth in our consumption of energy. That does not mean, however, that we must accept an annual growth rate in energy consumption of 5% or an avoidable waste of energy.

Similarly the call of pressure groups for the wider use of solar energy must be considered in relation to the cost of utilizing solar energy. At present the economic crisis is more serious than the energy crisis and any measures which conserve energy while increasing its cost are unlikely to be adopted except by a few idealists, or by people who wish to build a newsworthy house. However, we should encourage some initial advantage for solar devices which could become economical in the foreseeable future. For example, more favourable tariffs for electricity or gas used in conjunction with solar water heaters or some tax concession or subsidy for the initial purchase of solar collectors are worthy of consideration as a temporary measure.

1.4. PRESENTLY USEFUL FORMS OF SOLAR ENERGY

Most of the following lectures are concerned with passive methods of solar energy, which are at the present time more economical than active methods. Passive methods are essentially those applications of solar energy which we have always used in buildings.

Active methods employ a solar collector. Solar collectors and the associated plumbing cost money and the interest charges on this money must be balanced against the solar energy collected. Furthermore, solar collectors, because of their exposure to the weather, deteriorate and need to be renewed from time to time and the replacement cost must also be allowed for in calculating the true price of solar energy.

At the present time solar water heaters are economical in regions where the price of conventional energy is high, such as remote country districts anywhere in Australia and such cities as Darwin; they would be economical in Sydney only in special circumstances or if they were given an open or a concealed subsidy, such as an adjustment of the electricity or gas tariff, or a tax concession on their purchase. It is doubtful whether solar air conditioning is at present economical in any part of Australia. Solar space heating is intermediate between these two.

Because of their present limited usefulness, we shall deal relatively briefly with active methods of solar energy. Many passive methods are, however, immediately economical and we shall therefore discuss these in much greater detail. It is only proper to point out that we used passive solar energy methods long before the term came into use. The four principal techniques are:

1. Allowing sunlight penetration through windows during winter and/or excluding sunlight during summer.
2. Allowing water to evaporate to cool a building in a hot-arid climate, and providing natural ventilation to cool a building in a hot-humid climate.
3. Storing heat or coolness through the use of a thermal store, which could consist of massive walls or floors, or a separate mass of stone or water, frequently kept underground.
4. Insulating the interior from the exterior to prevent undesired heating or cooling by radiation or conduction.

Thermal storage and insulation can often be performed by the same part of the building, as for example by massive walls.

All these methods have been known, at least in principle, since antiquity. Some of Vitruvius's rules would today be considered as passive solar energy techniques. Many vernacular buildings, particularly in hot climates, make use of these principles. On the other hand, not all vernacular construction is thermally correct. For example, mud huts which have high thermal storage and do not encourage natural ventilation, are found in many parts of Africa in hot-humid forest regions, where timber and reeds are readily available.

Sound thermal design principles were also a feature of many early Australian buildings, but the numerical data used in the design were often incorrect. Thus many Australian verandahs of the mid-19th century are wider than thermal comfort requires, and as a result too much daylight was excluded.

The scientific design of buildings for thermal comfort started in the 1920s after the founding of the British Building Research Station. Australia has made a leading contribution since the establishment of the Experimental Building Station and the Division of Building Research CSIRO in the 1940s. We have invited Mr. Ralph Phillips to give one of the lectures and Mr. Walt Drysdale to take the chair at one of the sessions, partly in recognition of their pioneer work in this field, and partly because some of the problems and techniques of passive solar energy have not changed for twenty years, even though the name itself is new. Like M. Jourdain in Molière's *Le Bourgeois Gentilhomme,* we have been talking solar energy for the last twenty years and have never known it. Some Australian architects have used passive methods of solar energy long before 1973, but others have, until recently, ignored them.

We have a number of advantages over people who designed buildings 20 years ago. Climatic data are today available in much more detail and they can be placed in computers so that their effect on the thermal behaviour of a building can be modelled mathematically. We are thus able to predict the physical environment in a building over the entire year from the specified properties of the materials and surfaces and to modify the design if it fails to produce the desired environmental conditions. We have allocated two sessions to computer programs.

Remodelling or retrofitting existing buildings is a matter of great importance if energy conservation measures are to produce a significant effect in the near future, since new buildings at present add only between 2% and 3% annually to the existing housing stock. The problem is one of great complexity; some houses can be retrofitted at a reasonable cost to produce energy savings commensurate to the cost of the alteration, others are best left as they are. This subject is discussed in the last chapter.

The space given to active methods of solar energy in buildings in this book is far less because we believe that they can make only a limited contribution at the present time to the buildings in Sydney and Melbourne where 40% of Australians live.

We have excluded from this book the generation of electricity directly from the sun, because this is a development for the more distant future, except for regions with a low population density. At present it seems likely that metropolitan electric power stations which utilize solar furnaces, photovoltaic conversion, wind generators, wave action or tidal power (Ref. 11) belong to the next century, even though these methods are already useful for specialized applications. Telecom Australia, for example, has built a telecommunications link between Alice Springs and Tennant Creek using photovoltaic cells; but the repeater stations are in remote locations and the power required by each is very small. Wind generators are useful for supplying electricity to a house in the Outback, but so far there are only a few experimental wind-power stations in consistently windy locations in countries such as Denmark.

It is appropriate to consider what might happen in the future. Most of the houses we build now should still be inhabited in the year 2020. Some may still be in existence in the year 2100 if they are well maintained. It is difficult to predict at the present time whether houses will in that distant future draw their power from a central source, as they do at present, or whether they will utilize only solar power from collectors mounted on the roof, so that it would no longer be necessary to provide for the reticulation of electricity and gas. In our present state of knowledge it does not seem likely that houses will rely entirely on their own energy generation, but it is probable that solar water heaters will become economical in Sydney and Melbourne during the life of all the houses now built. It is therefore sensible to give some thought to the possible installation of future solar collectors in considering the design of a roof for a new building.

REFERENCES

1. *Conference on Energy, 1977. Submissions of Working Parties,* National Conference Publication No. 77/6, Canberra 1977.
2. Wooldridge, M. J., 'The Need for Energy Conservation in Buildings', *Symposium on Energy Conservation in Buildings,* Sydney, 8–9 November 1978.
3. White, D. C., 'Energy, The Economy and the Environment', *Technology Review,* **70** (October–November 1971) 18–31.
4. *Recommendations for an Energy Policy for Australia,* Institution of Engineers Australia, Canberra, October 1977, 10.
5. *1977 Handbook of Fundamentals,* ASHRAE (American Society of Heating, Refrigerating and Air-Conditioning Engineers), New York 1977. Section II, General Engineering Data.
6. Fanger, P. O., *Thermal Comfort,* Danish Technical Press, Copenhagen, 1970.
7. Blake, P., *Form Follows Fiasco—Why Modern Architecture Hasn't Worked,* Little, Brown and Company, Boston 1977.
8. Jenks, C., *The Language of Post-Modern Architecture,* Academy Editions, London 1978.
9. Hilbereimer, L., *Mies van der Rohe,* Paul Theobald, Chicago 1956.
10. Cowan, H. J., *Science and Building,* Wiley, New York 1978, Chapter 8, 215–265.
11. Daniels, F., *Direct Use of the Sun's Energy,* Yale University Press, New Haven 1964.

2

What Makes People Accept a Thermal Environment as Comfortable?

'Long and great heats always very much exalt the acrimony of the bilious humours.' (Ref. 1)

R. K. MACPHERSON
School of Public Health and Tropical Medicine, University of Sydney, Australia

If you were confronted with the question, 'What makes people accept a thermal environment as comfortable?', it would not be mere semantic quibbling to reply that it all depends on what is meant by 'comfortable'. Anyone who has used the well known comfort-vote technique for the assessment of the thermal environment will have encountered the man who, though his flushed face is beaded with perspiration, resolutely records his vote as 'comfortable'. If it is queried, he will in all honesty make some such reply as, 'I know it's hot but I'm still comfortable.' The difficulty is further compounded by the use of such well accepted familiar expressions as 'comfortably warm' and 'comfortably cool'. It is not easy to define the exact difference in the thermal state of the man who says, 'It was hot but I was comfortably cool in my new light-weight suit', from that of the man who says, 'It was cold but I was comfortably warm in bed last night'.

Recourse to a dictionary does not immediately resolve the matter. The list of meanings, both current and obsolete, given for 'comfortable' is long. However, I propose, for reasons which I hope to make plain, to adopt the following definition from among those given in the Oxford Dictionary—'free from pain and trouble, at ease'.

In that it implies that comfort exists only in the absence of discomfort, it is in essence a negative, or at best circular, definition. Nevertheless it does lead to a usable definition of a comfortable thermal environment. A thermal environment may be said to be 'comfortable' when the physiological strain resulting from the imposed thermal stress either does not impinge on consciousness, or if any sensation of heat or cold is evoked, this sensation is judged to be not unpleasant.

13

This definition implies that whether or not any given situation is accepted as thermally comfortable depends in part on the environment, and in part on the individual exposed to the environment. It is proposed to discuss the role of each separately, but before doing so it is desirable to give a brief account of current views on the mechanisms concerned in temperature regulation in man.

2.1. TEMPERATURE REGULATION IN MAN

In the hypothalamus at the base of the brain close to the pituitary gland there are two populations of nerve cells which respond respectively to heat and to cold. These central temperature sensors with their associated neurons constitute a control system which functions in a manner familiar to all engineers. A feed-back circuit (in this case the blood supply to the brain) provides information on body temperature. This temperature is then compared with a reference temperature (the set point) and, if a discrepancy exists, a signal is emitted which initiates corrective action. If the temperature monitored is above the set point, heat loss from the body is increased by vasodilatation or, if necessary, by sweating. If the monitored temperature is below the set point, heat is conserved by vasoconstriction or, if this is insufficient, the production of heat is augmented by shivering. The corrective action is accompanied by the appropriate sensations of heat or cold mediated by nerve impulses relayed in the thalamus (the chief relay station for sensory inputs) on the way to the cerebral cortex (see Fig. 1). The characteristics of the centre are such that proportional control, rate control and possibly integral control can be identified. The set point can be adjusted upwards as in fever (and downwards too, as in the case of hibernating mammals) and it cycles over a narrow band every twenty-four hours, thus providing the basis for the circadian rhythm in body temperature.

This arrangement might appear at first to provide not only a satisfactory method of body temperature control, but also a mechanism for the appreciation of thermal discomfort if it is postulated that the degree and nature of the discomfort is determined by the magnitude and the sign of the difference between deep body temperature and the set point.

The system as described, however, has some very obvious short-comings as a control mechanism. For example, in an animal of substantial mass, such as man, the response time would be extremely

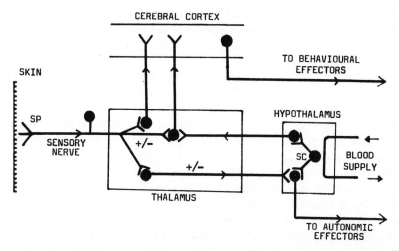

Fig. 1. A simplified schematic diagram of the temperature control system in man. For simplicity, only one modality (heat or cold) is represented. SC, central sensor; SP, peripheral sensor; +/−, excitatory or inhibitory.

slow, but in fact we know that the response time is rapid. On entering a Turkish bath sweating begins long before there could be any significant alteration in deep body temperature. Similarly on coming out of the cold into a warm room, particularly if there is a source of radiant heat such as a fire, the sensation of coldness gives way to a feeling of warmth in a matter of seconds.

It therefore comes as no surprise to learn that, as well as the central sensors described, there are peripheral sensors situated in the skin or superficial subcutaneous tissue (see Fig. 1). These sensors may or may not (probably not) be identical with those nerve endings that sense the temperature of objects in contact with the skin. The nervous impulses arising from these peripheral sensors are conducted by way of the ordinary sensory nerves to the thalamus and thence to the cortex where they are interpreted as sensations of warmth or cold. At the same time they provide an input, either excitatory or inhibitory, to the central control system so that its effective response and the sensations evoked by it are modified, or even overridden, by the peripheral sensory input. This could be done either by altering the sensitivity of the central sensors or by adjusting the set point which determines the response. However, for our present purposes the important thing to note is that the peripheral sensors, by virtue of their cortical connections, make possible the intelligent anticipatory behavioural control of body temperature.

2.2. THE ENVIRONMENTAL DETERMINANTS OF HEAT STRESS

There are four environmental factors—air temperature, humidity, air movement and the mean radiant temperature of the surroundings —which primarily determine the level of heat stress, but their combined effect can be profoundly modified by other factors, the chief of which are his rate of working (metabolic heat production) and the clothing worn by the individual exposed to the environment. Furthermore there is a considerable degree of interaction, the effect of any one factor commonly depending upon the level of the other three factors.

2.2.1. Air Temperature
Air temperature is usually considered to be the fundamental determinant of heat stress. It is, indeed, the factor on which attention usually centres, and understandably so as our appreciation of the environment is in terms of 'heat' and 'cold'. We are often content to describe an environment in terms of dry-bulb temperature alone, as when we say the 'preferred temperature is 23°C'. This usually means not that the interaction with other factors is ignored but rather that the other factors are tacitly assumed to be held constant at some agreed on value. In this case it might be assumed that the relative humidity is 50%, that the air movement is less than 0.3 ms^{-1} and the mean radiant temperature is equal to the air-temperature. For many day-to-day purposes air temperature by itself is an adequate, if by no means precise, indication of the prevailing level of heat stress. The daily forecast maximum temperature is a sufficient basis on which to decide how to dress for the day and the level of thermal comfort to be expected.

Associated with the air temperature there are other factors important for thermal comfort whose exact nature is difficult to define. Two such are 'stuffiness' and 'freshness'. We say, 'It is hot and stuffy in here. Come out into the cool, fresh air.', never 'It is cold and stuffy. Come out into the warm, fresh air.' 'Stuffiness' would appear to be the product of warmth in association with humid stagnant air. 'Freshness' on the other hand results from coolness, relative dryness and perceptible air movement. Another unpleasant thermal sensation is 'dankness', the product of cold, wet, still air. In an indoor context 'close' seems to be synonymous with 'stuffy'. Out-of-doors it is applied to hot humid windless weather, nowadays more often described as 'sultry', especially if the temperature is high. 'Sweltering' is an epithet often used to describe extremely hot windless conditions. Some other expressions related at least in part to thermal comfort, such as 'bracing' and 'relaxing' are difficult to define, if indeed such attributes do exist. This plethora of epithets is in itself an indication of the importance attached to thermal comfort in everyday life.

2.2.2. Humidity

The prevailing humidity is an important determinant of the level of heat stress, but paradoxically it plays only a minor rôle in thermal comfort (Ref. 2). The importance of humidity lies in its effect on the rate of evaporation of sweat in the zone of evaporative heat regulation. However, the zone of thermal comfort is usually considered to be coextensive with the zone of vaso-motor control—the regulation of the body's heat exchange by controlling the blood supply to, and hence the temperature of, the skin. If this view is correct, sweating does not occur in the thermally comfortable. In consequence thermal comfort, as distinct from discomfort, is largely independent of humidity. Whether any degree of sweating is, in fact, compatible with thermal comfort is, however, debatable and this point is discussed in the later section on heat balance.

There are two other sources of evaporative heat loss besides sweating, namely insensible perspiration and respiratory water loss. The outer layers of the skin, the epidermis, are permeable to water vapour, so that water vapour derived from tissue fluid is lost continuously from the skin at a rate depending upon the temperature (and hence the vapour pressure) beneath the skin and the vapour pressure in the air. The amount of water lost by this process of passive diffusion which is known as 'insensible perspiration' is not large. It amounts to only a few grams per hour and consequently its contribution to evaporative heat loss is usually negligible.

Inspired air exchanges heat and moisture with the lining of the upper respiratory tract and in the lungs it is saturated with water vapour at body temperature. On expiration the process is reversed, the mucous membranes of the upper respiratory tract acting as a regenerative heat-exchanger for both sensible and latent heat. However, the exchange is not 100% effective, so that both the temperature and the humidity of the expired air differ from that of the inspired air. Expired air may be either warmer or cooler but is almost always moister than the inspired air. Unlike the heat loss in animals which pant, this respiratory evaporative heat loss in man is but a small fraction of the total heat loss, perhaps 10%, depending primarily on the absolute humidity of the air and the respiratory volume. A combination of very dry air and a high rate of ventilation, as in mountain climbing at high altitudes, can result in significant heat loss and, if accompanied by a restricted water intake, as often happens, it can lead to serious dehydration.

The popular use of the term 'relative humidity' in connection with the level of heat stress is unfortunate. The rate of evaporation of moisture from the surface of the body is determined, not by the relative humidity of the ambient air, but by the difference between the partial pressure of water vapour in the air and the vapour pressure of the sweat on the skin.

The temperature of freely sweating skin is approximately 35°C and the vapour pressure of the sweat consequently 5.6 kPa (see Table 1).* At 0°C the saturated pressure of water vapour is only 0.6 kPa, so that whether the air is completely dry or its relative humidity is 100% will make little difference to the rate of heat loss by evaporation. Table 1 also shows that the vapour pressure of saturated air (R.H. 100%) at 28°C (3.8 kPa) is much the same as that for 50% R.H. at 40°C. It can be expected that, if other factors such as air speed are held constant, evaporation of sweat will proceed at the same rate in these two very different conditions.

There are other effects of humidity which, though not directly relevant to thermal comfort, nevertheless merit consideration because they do determine permissible levels of humidity. Some people are particularly sensitive to drying of the nasal mucosa. For them dry air is uncomfortable quite apart from any thermal sensations evoked.

Hair and the outer layers of the skin are composed of a protein,

TABLE 1
SATURATED WATER VAPOUR PRESSURE
AT SELECTED TEMPERATURES

Temperature (°C)	−40	0	23	28	33	35	37	40
Pressure (kPa)	0·01	0·61	2·81	3·78	5·03	5·62	6·27	7·37

* If the depression of the vapour pressure of sweat by its salt content is neglected its vapour pressure can be taken to be that of water at the same temperature.

keratin, which is particularly sensitive to changes in humidity, softening and swelling when wet and shrinking and hardening when dry. (A common type of hygrometer uses human hair as its sensing element.) It would seem at least possible that these changes are perceived and perhaps modify the basic sensations of thermal comfort. The existence of words such as 'dankness' which have been mentioned earlier suggests that they do. It has even been claimed that there are specific nerve endings in the skin which are sensitive to the degree of dehydration of the epidermis.

2.2.3. Mean radiant Temperature

Heat exchange by radiation, like that by convection, can be either positive or negative, so that the one can either add to or diminish the effect of the other. Hence, when the air temperature out-of-doors is low we seek to achieve thermal comfort by exposing ourselves to the warmth of the sun—the classic example of behavioural temperature regulation.

Perhaps the commoner situation is that in which the effect of the one exacerbates the effect of the other. Most industrial processes involve the use of heat, so that in industry it is usual to find a high air temperature accompanied by a high level of radiant heat. The discomfort of a low air temperature being added to by heat loss by radiation can also be seen in industry. It is apt to occur in cold weather in buildings of flimsy construction, particularly in the early morning if wall temperatures reach low values overnight. It can also be a feature of glass-clad, multi-storey buildings on their shady side in winter. On their sunny side in summer the problem is heat gain from penetrating solar radiation.

The importance of the radiant heat load in thermal comfort is perhaps most dramatically demonstrated by the difference in thermal comfort when one is exposed to the direct rays of the sun and when one is protected from them. It is difficult to convince the laity that, provided there is some air movement, air temperature in the shade of a tree does not differ from that in the sun.

The solar heat load on an individual exposed to the sun is difficult to quantify. The effect of the direct incident radiation depends upon the altitude of the sun and its azimuth with respect to the person concerned. To this must be added the scattered component of the incident radiation, the sunlight reflected from the clouds, and that reflected from the terrain, the last depending upon the albedo of the surface of the terrain. There is also long-wavelength, infra-red radiation from the ground which, in the case of desert sand, may have a temperature as high as 70°C. It is not surprising, therefore, that estimates of the solar heat load in hot deserts vary widely, but it has been calculated that the total radiant heat load of soldiers marching in the desert could well be in excess of 400 W for each man. In such circumstances the question of comfort becomes irrelevant. High levels of solar radiation are not confined to the great deserts of the world. They can, and do, occur also on high mountains above the cloud line. Temperatures in excess of 40°C have been recorded in a closed tent exposed to the sun on the slopes of Mt Everest.

Radiation to the sky is greatest on clear cloudless nights when the air is dry. A night with overcast skies feels warmer out-of-doors, therefore, than a night with the same air temperature but with a clear sky. The clear sky and dry air of deserts is exploited by the custom, common in some Middle East countries, of sleeping in summer on the flat roof of the house, exposed to the sky at night—an example, by the way, of comfort cooling by radiation.

2.2.4. Air Speed

The rate of air movement comes second only to adjustment of the clothing worn as the most used means of improving thermal comfort. To open or close a door or window is the usual reaction to an environment which is either too warm or too cold. The use of fans is almost universal in the warm moist tropics where, except when air-conditioning is used, buildings are designed to provide through-and-through ventilation.

The body's perception of air speed is much affected by the temperature of the air. If it is close to that of the skin, an air movement of 0.5m s^{-1} or more may be imperceptible. If, on the other hand, the air is much below skin temperature, a slowly moving current of air usually described as a 'draught', may provoke unpleasant sensations. Individuals vary greatly in their perception of draughts and their reaction to them. Indeed one psychiatrist has gone so far as to say, 'Show me a person who habitually complains of draughts and I will show you a neurotic personality'.

When the air temperature is below the temperature of the skin, increasing the air speed always increases the rate of heat loss by convection. It will also, if the subject is sweating, facilitate the evaporation of the sweat. In a warm environment both actions ameliorate the level of heat stress. In a cold environment the increasing heat loss by convection increases the level of cold stress and the effect on the rate of evaporation of sweat is irrelevant.

When in a hot environment the air temperature is above skin temperature, increasing the air speed facilitates the evaporation of sweat but it also increases the convective heat gain. The air velocity at which the ameliorating effect of enhanced evaporative cooling is outstripped by the detrimental effect of increased convective heat gain, is determined by the temperature of the air and its absolute humidity and by the metabolic rate and clothing of the person exposed. It is lowest for the resting nude subject in hot, dry air and highest for the clothed subject working hard in warm, humid conditions. Such conditions are clearly incompatible with thermal comfort and the effects described are mentioned only to make the important point that high levels of heat stress such as those that occur in deep mines and hot industries may not be ameliorated and may even be made worse by an increased rate of ventilation.

2.2.5. Heat Balance

Because man is a homeotherm, the well known heat balance equation must be satisfied. That is to say over any significant interval of time

$$M - E + C + R = 0$$

where M is the metabolic rate less any external work done; E is the evaporative heat loss; C is the rate of heat exchange by conduction and convection, which may be either positive or negative; and R is the rate of heat exchange by radiation, which can likewise be either positive or negative. Satisfaction of the equation is also, of course, a necessary condition for thermal comfort but it is apparently not a sufficient condition. Experience seems to show that there are upper limits to the values of the individual terms which are consistent with comfort. Unfortunately, experience is a very inexact science and these limits are at best ill-defined. The most that can be said is that thermal comfort appears to be associated with the passive loss of heat, restricted in amount, down a modest thermal gradient.

For example, we know that the lowest value for M, that which occurs during sleep (for an adult male approximately 65 kcal hr^{-1} or 74 W), is completely compatible with comfort when the air temperature is 28°C, the commonly observed temperature of an occupied bed at night. We also know that a sedentary or light occupation (energy expenditure 100 to 150 W) is compatible with thermal comfort at air temperatures of 20–25°C. At the other extreme, a marathon runner producing more than 1 kW of heat and secreting 1.5 litres hr^{-1} of sweat with a deep body temperature of 40–41°C is certain to be thermally uncomfortable whatever the environmental temperature. In short all that can be said with confidence is that thermal comfort *seems* to be associated with low rates of energy expenditure.

Although M may be voluntarily increased to compensate for excess heat loss due to high negative values of C and R, as when we walk briskly on a cold night to keep warm, such an increase is biologically inefficient as high levels of M result in fatigue and, of course, require an increased food intake. An involuntary increase in M for the same purpose, shivering, is definitely incompatible with comfort.

Permissible values of E are also debatable. Most people would agree, as mentioned earlier, that any sweating is incompatible with thermal comfort, hence the saying 'If sweating, then uncomfortably warm'. This would mean that the permissible value for E is zero if we neglect obligatory evaporative losses due to insensible perspiration and to respiration. Fanger (Ref. 3) however, maintains that modest rates of sweating are not incompatible with thermal comfort, the acceptable rate being determined by the rate of energy expenditure according to the equation

$$E = 0.42A(H/A - 50) \text{ kcal hr}^{-1}$$

where E is the evaporative heat loss compatible with comfort; A is the surface area of the body (for an adult male approximately 1.8 m^2) and H the total heat of metabolism. As the metabolic cost of sitting is approximately 50 kcal m^{-2} hr^{-1} for sedentary persons, E is equal to zero and therefore sweating is not compatible with thermal comfort for persons sitting at rest. For a person walking at 5 km hr^{-1}, H would be 250 kcal hr^{-1}, which is roughly equivalent to a sweat secretion of 100 ml hr^{-1}. This matter clearly merits further investigation.

As C and R may be different in sign a positive value for the one may be offset by an appropriate negative value for the other. For instance in a cold room the low air temperature may be offset by sitting in front of the fire—but only up to a point, high levels of radiant heat can be painful and even damaging to the skin. Moreover as the body is not a perfect integrator, the heating of one side of the body by radiation and the chilling of the other by convection does not necessarily result in thermal comfort. That this phenomenon was once somewhat maliciously referred to as 'the English drawing-room effect' is a reminder of the days when open fires were the sole means of domestic heating. The reverse procedure, the use of radiant cooling in a hot environment, has been investigated (Ref. 4), but found to be technically extremely difficult.

2.3. THE INDIVIDUAL IN THE ENVIRONMENT

Anyone who has investigated the phenomenon of thermal comfort will have been struck by the variation between individuals. Reid (Ref. 5) was embarrassed to find that one member of the House of Commons preferred an air temperature of 52°F while another required 71°F.

Hindmarsh and Macpherson (Ref. 6) in a study of thermal comfort in Sydney were likewise disconcerted to find that, whereas some said they were too warm at 18°C, others protested that they were too cool at 27°C. These were extremes; but even at the preferred temperature (23°C), at which 80% described themselves as comfortable, 10% were too warm and the remaining 10% were too cold.

Are these differences between individuals to be dismissed as idiosyncratic or are there identifiable causes which could explain why one person accepts as comfortable an environment which another rejects as uncomfortable, or accepts as comfortable on one occasion and rejects on another? The exploration of this question forms the basis of the next section.

2.3.1. Physical Characteristics

The most obvious source of differences between individuals lies in their physical characteristics such as age, sex, race and body build. What evidence there is suggests that age makes little difference to the preferred temperature. The view that with increasing age a somewhat higher temperature is preferred is not supported by evidence. Indeed, an investigation in the United Kingdom of the indoor temperature of the houses of old people living alone revealed that it was lower than that of the houses inhabited by younger age groups. This finding could be explained as due to factors only indirectly related to age, such as the inability to afford more effective heating. Another explanation is that the blunting of the senses which often accompanies old age resulted in a lack of temperature discrimination. A further piece of evidence that is perhaps worth mentioning is that a study of the mortality rate in a hospital for the aged and infirm (Ref. 7) showed that it was minimal when the daily maximum temperature was between 21°C and 26°C, which suggests that this range includes the optimum temperature level for the aged.

Women commonly prefer a slightly warmer temperature than men. This does not represent a difference between the sexes but a difference in the insulation value of the clothing worn (Ref. 8). In cross-over experiments in which both men and women wore both male and female clothing assemblies, it was found that when the same clothing was worn there was no difference between the thermal preference.

It would seem reasonable to expect that because of their greater relative surface area the slenderly built and thin would accept as comfortable warmer temperatures than their stouter and fatter counterparts, and the latter in their turn would accept cooler conditions than the former. When sitting at rest or engaged in light activity there appears to be little difference in the preference of the two groups. However when engaged in activities the metabolic cost of which is determined by body weight, the obese are clearly at a disadvantage in a warm or hot environment.

With respect to race, investigators are agreed that when other things, such as acclimatization, clothing and mental attitudes are equal, and the way of life is the same, the same environments are accepted as comfortable by all races. Skin colour at one time was thought to confer an advantage on dark-skinned races in hot climates. It proves in fact to have little significance in determining the acceptable thermal environment. Skin whatever its colour behaves as a black body (absorptance 0.9) with respect to infra-red radiation. In the visible range the absorptance of black skin is perhaps twice that of white skin (0.6 compared with 0.3). Over the whole solar spectrum the white skin absorbs about 60% of the incident radiation and black skin about 80%. When people are clothed these differences make little difference to the heat exchange but pigmentation does prevent damage to the deeper layers of the epidermis from ultraviolet light in the range 0.3–$0.4\,\mu$m. Just conceivably this might permit the wearing of scantier clothing in the sun and thus a higher acceptable environmental temperature.

2.3.2. Clothing
Because the adjustment of the amount and disposition of his clothes provides man with a powerful means of behavioural regulation of his body temperature, clothing is the determinant *par excellence* of the acceptable thermal environment. The invention of clothing, together with fire and shelter, has enabled man, a tropical animal, to inhabit the world from the equator to the poles, and specialised clothing has made it possible for him to walk on the moon.

Unfortunately, as a general rule civilized man cannot adjust his clothing solely on the basis of achieving thermal comfort. Fashion and convention prescribe the clothing to be worn, often with scant regard to thermal needs. Removing the constraints of civilization does make clothing a more effective regulator of thermal comfort. Palmai (Ref. 9) conducted a thermal comfort survey among the members of an expedition to Macquarie Island which is situated about 1600 km south-east of Tasmania, only to find that most of his subjects were comfortable most of the time. The explanation was that if the temperature rose or fell they donned or shed, as the case might be, yet another woollen pullover.

Fashion also serves to fix the general level at which thermal comfort is achieved. Citizens of the United States of America wear lighter clothing indoors in winter than their United Kingdom counterparts and consequently prefer higher indoor temperatures. Bedford in the 1930s found that, for workers in England engaged in light industry, the preferred indoor temperature was 65°F (18.3°C) and for those entirely sedentary a degree or two higher (Ref. 10). A similar investigation conducted today would indicate 73°F (23°C) as the preferred temperature in light industry. The substantial difference is satisfactorily explained in terms of the clothing worn. Fashions have changed. Outer clothing is now lighter in weight and heavy woollen underwear is no longer universally worn.

As a footnote to history, I would add that 100 years after Reid the late Dr Thomas Bedford was consulted on the ventilation of the present House of Commons. His recommendation (based on his earlier investigations just described) was that during an ordinary sitting the temperature should be maintained at 67–68°F. This was adopted and found to be satisfactory.

Clothing is usually thought of as providing protection from cold but in some situations, such as hot deserts, it may serve to protect from solar radiation and convective heat gain from hot dry winds. In hot climates, however, clothing adjustment is of less value in achieving thermal comfort than in cold climates, if for no other reason than there is, besides the more variable limit determined by social conventions, an absolute limit to the amount of clothing which can be removed.

2.3.3. Acclimatization
It is common knowledge that a newcomer to a hot climate is more distressed by it than the established resident, but, as time passes, his

distress diminishes and he is said to have become acclimatized. Acclimatization at first proceeds rapidly (about 80% of the expected change occurs in the first few weeks of exposure) and then more slowly over the ensuing months or perhaps even years. On removal from the hot environment acclimatization is lost as it was acquired—rapidly at first and then more slowly.

Acclimatization to cold also occurs and indeed acclimatization to heat and to cold can coexist (Ref. 11). However, acclimatization to cold is the more difficult to demonstrate, possibly because residents of a temperate climate have already developed a considerable degree of cold acclimatization (Ref. 12).

Much work has been done in an attempt to elucidate the physiological basis of acclimatization but it is still imperfectly understood. The results are readily demonstrable but how they are brought about is still largely a mystery. It is possible, however, to give a formal definition which precisely defines its effect. Acclimatization is a physiological change as the result of which the application of a constant environmental stress produces a diminished physiological strain. This is schematically represented in Fig. 2.

Stress can be measured in physical terms such as air temperature, rate of energy expenditure and so on. Strain can similarly be measured in physiological terms, change in heart rate or change in body temperature or the amount of sweat secreted. However, at low levels of thermal stress, the degree of thermal comfort or rather discomfort

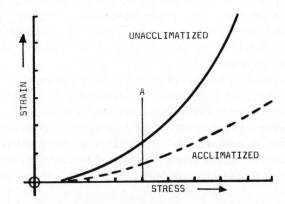

Fig. 2. Schematic representation of the effect of acclimatization. Although the point of thermal neutrality remains unchanged, the imposition of a given level of heat or cold stress produces less physiological strain in the acclimatized.

experienced, if properly assessed, provides the best measure of physiological strain. Consideration of Fig. 2 will show that at a modest level of thermal stress, for example that indicated by the line marked A in the figure, the unacclimatized person may experience perhaps twice the strain experienced by the acclimatized. Or if we use comfort as our measure of strain we may say that a thermal environment which causes real distress to an unacclimatized person may result in only trivial discomfort to the same person after acclimatization. However, as the diagram shows, zero stress as indicated by zero strain is the same for both acclimatized and unacclimatized.

Although acclimatization is essentially a physiological process it has also a considerable behavioural component. Part of becoming acclimatized to heat consists of the discarding of excessive clothing, a reduced food intake, an increased intake of salt and water and the avoidance of heat stress. The acclimatized person walks on the shady side of the street, reduces his rate of energy expenditure by working in a more leisurely way and adjusts his way of life so that his heaviest tasks are performed in the coolest part of the day and he does not go out in the midday sun unnecessarily.

There is also a mental component of acclimatization, namely habituation (Ref.13) which may be defined as a gradual diminution of the response when an appropriate stimulus is repeatedly applied over a long period. It is, in fact, a sort of negative conditioned reflex or negative learning. The discomfort of a hard bed may prevent sleep on the first occasion but after a time the sensations evoked are disregarded and though the bed is as hard as ever one sleeps profoundly. The acclimatized individual likewise may come to disregard a constant degree of discomfort and accept his environment as comfortable.

2.4. MENTAL AND EMOTIONAL FACTORS

The day that a man finds climatically delightful when lying on the beach drowsily listening to the sound of the sea might be considered uncomfortably hot by the same man if he were compelled to stay at home and labour in his garden or go to his office dressed in a collar and tie. The difference in his thermal judgement might not be solely due in the one case to an increased energy expenditure or in the other to the much greater amount of clothing worn. It would also owe much to his mental attitude. He may resent having to stay at home and work when

he might be surfing, or having to face up to the daily harassment of work
and its emotional stresses.

Climatic stress, especially heat stress, and mental and emotional
activity interact. We have all found ourselves with a flushed face, collar
unconsciously unbuttoned and tie loosened when wrestling with a
difficult mathematical problem or composing a 'difficult' letter in an
environment which by all ordinary standards is thermally comfortable.
In the operating theatre whilst his assistant, who carries little responsibility, is surreptitiously shifting his weight from one foot to the other to
keep himself warm the surgeon who is 'in a bit of trouble' will be calling
for a nurse to wipe the sweat from his forehead.

The usual effect of thermal stress is to cause a decrement in the
performance of mental and skilled manual tasks but this is not always
so. It has been shown that small increments in heat stress often result in
an improvement in performance until, a maximum having been
reached, deterioration occurs so that performance can be represented
by an inverted U-shaped curve. This phenomenon, to which the term
'arousal' has been applied, is in accordance with the everyday
experience that stimulation of the sensorium improves alertness and
that absolute comfort inhibits mental activity, especially creative
activity.

Twenty-odd years ago I conducted an enquiry into social and
environmental problems in tropical Australia (Ref. 12) and I came to
the conclusion that many of the social problems were directly related to
the harshness of the climate. In some mining enterprises, for example,
the labour turnover in the wages staff often exceeded 200% per annum.
Men, attracted by high wages, came, stayed a little while and then left,
having found the combination of a harsh climate and a lack of amenities
unacceptable. But there has been a steady improvement with time. In
his latest annual report the Chairman of Mt Isa Mines (Ref. 14)
comments on the increasing stability of the Company's work force. In
1967–1968 the annual employee turnover was 37%; in 1977–1978 it had
dropped to 17%. Ten years ago 64.4% of employees had less than one
year's service with the Company; in 1977–1978 the figure had dropped
to 3.9% and, even more significantly, 12.1% now had over twelve years'
service. These changes the Chairman attributes, correctly I am sure, to a
number of factors such as an increase in home ownership, a desire to
make a career with the Company and the present unfavourable
economic and employment situation. He might well have added an
improvement in amenities.

The climate of Mt Isa, however, has remained unchanged. It is still second only in severity to that in the north-west of Western Australia. Does this mean that climate, that is to say thermal comfort, is unimportant? I think not. The total situation is represented by the interaction of the climate with other emotion-provoking factors. In Australia's arid lands we hate the dust and the flies more because of the heat, and hate the heat more because of the dust and the flies. The truth is that the improvement in amenities, along with all the other things listed, has made the heat of the Mt Isa summer more bearable.

2.5. DURATION OF EXPOSURE

The degree of comfort experienced in a thermal environment may change with time. Any environment which tends to restore thermal equilibrium is usually accepted as comfortable, though later it may be rejected when thermal equilibrium has been attained. If we are cold we are delighted to be warmed, but being no longer cold we find the heat oppressive. Similarly escape from the heat to a cold environment, though at first pleasant, may with time lead to feelings of chilliness.

A rapid change from one environment to another can in some circumstances result in spurious thermal sensations. All natural fibres take up an amount of water depending on the relative humidity of the environment. This uptake of moisture is accompanied by a liberation of heat referred to as the heat of sorption. So that if one moves from a dry to a moist environment, particularly if wearing woollen clothing, there is a spurious sensation of warmth due to the uptake of water by the clothing and if one moves from a moist to a dry environment there is a loss of moisture and consequently heat loss from the clothing.

In the construction of the Effective Temperature Scale, the subjects were required to pass at short intervals from a room saturated with water vapour to a warmer drier room to determine the lines of equal comfort on which the Effective Temperature Scale was based. Failure to recognise the effects of the heat of sorption in these circumstances led the authors of the scale into error in their determination of the effect of humidity on thermal comfort. Although this source of error was later recognised by the authors (Ref. 15), it has proved impracticable to modify the scale which is still in error in this respect.

However, the long-term effects of thermal stress on an acceptable degree of comfort are probably more important than the short term.

Even a minor degree of discomfort long continued may prove intolerable and an environment which has been accepted even for years may finally be rejected and the person concerned will try to escape to a kinder climate, or change his occupation as the case may be.

2.6. CONCLUSION

In answer to the question, 'What makes people accept a thermal environment as comfortable?', I have endeavoured to show that, whilst thermal comfort rests on a firm physical basis, it is ultimately a subjective judgement much influenced by the past experience and the prevailing emotions of the person concerned. By way of conclusion I should like to say a little on the biological significance of thermal comfort.

In the past biologists have tended to regard thermal comfort as a matter of slight importance. Some perhaps might even have regarded it as merely an expression of man's sybaritic nature. All this has been changed by the increasing recognition over the last 20 years or so of the rôle of behaviour in the control of body temperature. Animals were traditionally divided into the homeotherms and the poikilotherms. The homeotherms (the birds and mammals) maintained a constant body temperature and this conferred on them a biological advantage not shared by the poikilotherms whose body temperature was thought to vary with that of the prevailing air temperature. It is now known that many poikilotherms, both vertebrate and invertebrate, can adjust their body temperature with considerable precision by controlling, by means of their behaviour, their heat gain from the environment. Two forms of homeothermy can therefore now be recognised, endothermic in which body heat arises from within and ectothermic in which the body heat is derived from without.

It seems obvious therefore that behavioural temperature regulation preceded physiological temperature regulation (vaso-constriction, shivering, pilo-erection and sweating) in the evolutionary scale. Or, to put it another way, behaviour is the fundamental method of body temperature regulation common to all vertebrates and to at least some invertebrates as well. To it there was added, not substituted for it, in the birds and mammals (the homeotherms or warm-blooded animals) an additional method of temperature regulation previously described as physiological regulation but for which, because there is nothing unphysiological about behavioural regulation, the term 'autonomic' regulation is now generally preferred. The biological significance and respectability of thermal comfort is at once established when it is pointed out that it is the basis of behavioural temperature regulation in man.

It can, of course, be argued that there is no way in which it can be shown that it is comfort that initiates a behavioural response in animals other than man. I admit there are difficulties in determining whether a lizard is or is not consciously aware that he is thermally comfortable or uncomfortable, but I am convinced that in some animals at least a conscious perception of thermal comfort exists. I am sure that anyone who has attempted to drive a flock of sheep from the comparative comfort of the shade of a tree into the heat of the sun on a hot summer day will agree with me. A more homely example is perhaps the obvious contentment of a cat drowsily purring on the hearth rug or, if it is a very pampered cat, its equally obvious pleasure when, on a cold winter's night, it is put to bed with a hot-water bottle.

REFERENCES

1. Huxham, J., 'On the extraordinary heat of the weather in July 1757 and its effects', *Philosophical Transactions of the Royal Society,* **50,** 523–529, 1758.
2. Koch, W., Jennings, B. H. and Humphreys, C. M., 'Is humidity important in the temperature comfort range?', *ASHRAE Journal,* **2,** 4, 63–68, 1960.
3. Fanger, P. O., *Thermal Comfort,* Danish Technical Press, Copenhagen, 1970.
4. Kaletzky, Esther, Macpherson R. K. and Morse, R. N., 'The effect of low temperature cooling on thermal comfort in a hot moist environment,' *Electrical and Mechanical Transactions of the Institution of Engineers, Australia,* **E.M.5,** 60–65, 1960.
5. Reid, D. B., *Illustrations of the Theory and Practice of Ventilation with Remarks on Warming, Exclusive Lighting, and the Communication of Sound,* Longman, Brown, Green and Longmans, London, 1844.
6. Hindmarsh, Margaret E., and Macpherson, R. K., 'Thermal comfort in Australia,' *Australian Journal of Science,* **23,** 335–339, 1962.
7. Macpherson, R. K., Ofner, F. and Welch, J. A., 'The effect of the prevailing air temperature on mortality', *British Journal of Preventive and Social Medicine,* **21,** 17–21, 1967.
8. Yaglou, C. P. and Messer, Anne, 'The importance of clothing in air conditioning,' *Journal of the American Medical Association,* **117,** 1261–1262, 1941.
9. Palmai, G., 'Thermal comfort and acclimatization to cold in a subantarctic environment,' *Medical Journal of Australia,* **1,** 9–12, 1962.
10. Chrenko, F. A. (Ed.), *Bedford's Basic Principles of Ventilation and Heating,* Third Edition, H. K. Lewis, London, 1974.
11. Davis, T. R. A., 'Effect of heat acclimatization in man,' *Journal of Applied Physiology,* **17,** 751–753, 1962.

12. Macpherson, R. K., *Environmental Problems in Tropical Australia*, Commonwealth Government Printer, Canberra, 1956.
13. Glaser, E. M., *The Physiological Basis of Habituation*, Oxford University Press, London, 1966.
14. Foots, J. W., *M. I. M. Holdings, Annual Report*, 1978.
15. Yaglou, C. P., 'Indices of Comfort', in L. H. Newburgh (Ed.), *Physiology of Heat Regulation and the Science of Clothing*, W. B. Saunders, Philadelphia, 1949.
16. Glaser, E. M. and Shephard, R. J., 'Simultaneous experimental acclimatization to heat and cold in man,' *Journal of Physiology*, **169**, 592–602, 1977.

3

The Design of Sun Shading Devices

A. MONEM SALEH
Department of Architectural Science, University of Sydney, Australia

3.1. WHEN IS SHADING NEEDED?

The function of external shading devices is to intercept the sun rays before reaching the building envelope during hot weather (Fig. 1). No protection is needed during cold weather; in fact, solar radiation should be allowed to warm the building up in cold periods. The first step in the

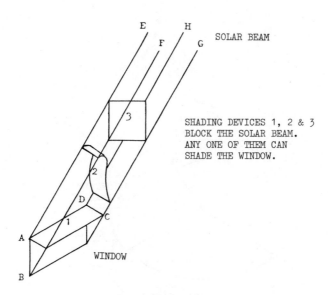

SHADING DEVICES 1, 2 & 3 BLOCK THE SOLAR BEAM. ANY ONE OF THEM CAN SHADE THE WINDOW.

Fig. 1. The solar beam.

design of shading devices is to define the period during which they should be in operation.

3.1.1. The Overheated Period of the Year

The summer season in Australasia is defined (Ref. 1) as the period between November 28 and February 26. This roughly is the time when complete shading is needed. However, the study of the local climate of the area under consideration should determine the "overheated period" for that area more precisely. This is the period during which the outdoor dry-bulb temperature reaches or exceeds a specified value. It is assumed that this is also the period during which the internal temperature of an unshaded building would exceed the comfortable level. Olgyay and Olgyay (Ref. 2) recommend 70°F (21°C) to be the limiting temperature for the temperate regions. For the present paper this temperature will be assumed to be applicable to the Australian conditions.

3.1.2. Temperature Records for Some Australian Cities

The record of the outdoor dry bulb mean hourly temperatures for each month of some Australian cities (Ref. 3) has been compiled. Figs. 3a–g

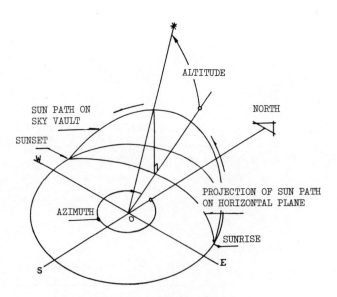

Fig. 2. The position of the sun.

BRISBANE, LATITUDE 27·5 SOUTH

HR···MONTH	JUN	JUL	AUG	SEP	OCT	NOV	DEC	JAN	FEB	MAR	APR	MAY
01	13·0	11·8	13·1	14·7	18·1	19·9	21·7	22·6	22·2	21·2	18·1	15·8
02	12·6	11·3	12·5	14·1	17·7	19·5	21·4	22·3	22·2	20·7	17·7	15·5
03	12·2	10·8	12·1	13·6	17·2	19·2	21·0	22·1	21·4	20·4	17·1	15·1
04	11·9	10·4	11·6	13·1	16·8	18·9	20·7	21·7	21·2	20·1	17·0	14·7
05	11·6	10·1	11·2	12·7	16·4	18·6	20·4	21·6	20·9	19·8	16·8	14·4
06	11·4	9·8	10·8	12·3	16·4	18·9	20·7	21·6	20·8	19·7	16·6	14·1
07	11·2	9·7	10·8	12·9	17·7	20·3	22·0	22·4	21·4	20·2	16·8	14·1
08	12·7	10·9	12·7	15·6	20·1	22·1	23·9	24·1	23·1	21·7	18·4	15·6
09	14·7	13·5	15·6	18·7	22·3	23·9	25·7	25·8	25·1	23·2	20·9	18·0
10	16·2	15·4	17·6	20·4	23·6	25·1	26·5	26·9	26·2	24·6	22·3	19·4
11	17·7	17·1	19·1	21·7	24·6	25·8	27·3	27·7	26·9	25·4	23·2	20·7
12	18·7	18·2	20·1	22·4	25·1	26·1	27·7	28·2	27·4	26·2	23·9	21·5
13	19·4	18·9	20·7	22·8	25·1	26·2	27·9	28·3	27·6	26·5	24·4	22·2
14	20·0	19·3	20·9	22·7	24·7	25·9	27·7	28·2	27·7	26·6	24·6	22·4
15	19·7	19·0	20·6	22·2	24·1	25·6	27·3	27·7	27·7	26·2	24·4	22·1
16	19·1	18·4	19·9	21·5	23·5	25·0	26·6	27·3	26·8	25·7	23·8	21·4
17	18·3	17·7	19·1	20·6	22·7	24·2	25·9	26·6	26·2	25·2	22·8	20·7
18	17·2	16·5	17·9	19·4	21·8	23·4	25·1	25·8	25·3	24·3	22·1	19·8
19	16·4	15·6	17·0	18·6	21·0	22·7	24·4	25·1	24·6	23·5	21·2	19·1
20	15·7	14·9	16·2	17·8	20·5	21·8	23·7	24·5	24·1	23·1	20·6	18·4
21	15·1	14·2	15·5	17·2	19·9	21·5	23·2	23·9	23·7	22·6	19·9	17·8
22	14·5	13·6	15·1	16·7	19·5	21·1	22·8	23·6	23·3	22·3	19·4	17·3
23	13·9	13·0	14·3	16·1	19·1	20·8	22·6	23·3	22·9	21·9	18·9	16·8
24	13·3	12·3	13·7	15·4	18·6	20·3	22·1	23·1	22·6	21·6	18·4	16·3

Fig. 3a. Mean monthly temperatures.

PERTH, LATITUDE 32·0 SOUTH

HR··MONTH	JUN	JUL	AUG	SEP	OCT	NOV	DEC	JAN	FEB	MAR	APR	MAY
01	11·9	10·8	11·9	12·8	14·1	16·7	18·6	19·5	20·4	19·2	16·5	13·7
02	11·4	10·5	11·6	12·4	13·7	16·4	18·2	19·0	19·8	18·7	16·1	13·5
03	11·2	10·3	11·4	12·2	13·3	16·0	17·7	18·5	19·3	18·2	15·6	13·3
04	11·0	10·1	11·3	11·9	13·1	15·6	17·3	18·2	18·8	17·8	15·3	13·1
05	10·7	9·9	11·1	11·6	12·8	15·3	16·9	17·7	18·3	16·9	15·0	12·8
06	10·8	9·4	10·7	11·9	13·3	16·2	17·9	18·1	17·2	17·1	14·7	12·6
07	10·8	9·4	10·4	12·3	14·7	17·6	19·4	19·4	19·6	17·8	15·1	12·6
08	11·6	10·3	11·9	14·0	16·3	19·3	21·0	21·1	21·4	19·5	16·8	13·7
09	13·1	12·1	13·6	15·8	17·8	21·0	22·6	22·7	23·4	21·6	18·9	15·4
10	14·6	13·5	15·0	17·2	19·0	22·2	23·8	24·3	25·5	23·4	20·9	16·9
11	15·7	14·8	15·9	18·1	19·8	23·2	25·0	25·5	26·9	25·0	22·2	18·1
12	16·6	15·7	16·6	18·9	20·4	23·9	25·7	26·4	27·8	26·1	23·1	18·9
13	17·1	16·1	16·9	19·3	20·7	24·3	25·9	26·9	28·5	26·7	23·7	19·3
14	17·0	16·3	17·0	19·4	20·6	24·1	25·8	27·1	28·6	26·9	24·0	19·5
15	16·8	16·3	16·9	19·2	20·2	23·7	25·5	26·8	28·2	26·4	23·7	19·4
16	16·6	15·8	16·4	18·4	19·6	23·1	24·9	26·0	27·4	25·8	23·1	18·8
17	15·6	14·9	15·6	17·5	18·6	22·2	24·4	25·5	26·6	24·7	21·8	17·7
18	14·5	14·1	14·9	15·9	17·3	20·9	22·8	24·4	25·3	23·4	20·2	16·5
19	14·0	13·1	13·9	15·3	16·4	19·5	21·3	22·8	23·5	21·9	19·4	16·0
20	13·4	12·7	13·4	14·8	16·0	18·9	20·5	21·9	22·7	21·4	18·8	15·5
21	13·0	12·3	13·1	14·3	15·6	18·4	20·2	21·2	22·2	20·9	18·2	15·0
22	12·7	11·9	12·7	13·9	14·7	18·3	19·8	20·9	21·7	20·4	17·7	14·6
23	12·2	11·4	12·4	13·6	14·8	17·8	19·4	20·6	21·2	20·0	17·3	14·3
24	11·6	11·1	12·2	13·3	14·4	17·3	19·1	20·1	20·8	19·6	16·9	14·0

Fig. 3b. Mean monthly temperatures.

SYDNEY, LATITUDE 33·9 SOUTH

HR··MONTH	JUN	JUL	AUG	SEP	OCT	NOV	DEC	JAN	FEB	MAR	APR	MAY
01	11·1	10·0	11·2	12·9	15·0	17·1	18·7	20·3	20·1	19·1	16·2	13·6
02	10·7	9·4	10·6	12·5	14·6	16·8	18·4	19·8	19·8	18·9	15·8	13·4
03	10·4	9·2	10·2	12·1	14·3	16·6	18·1	19·6	19·4	18·7	15·6	13·1
04	10·2	8·8	9·9	11·7	14·0	16·2	17·8	19·4	19·2	18·3	15·1	12·6
05	10·0	8·6	9·7	11·4	13·7	16·1	17·7	19·2	19·1	18·2	14·9	12·3
06	9·8	8·4	9·4	11·2	13·8	16·5	18·2	19·5	19·0	17·9	14·7	12·1
07	9·7	8·3	9·4	11·6	14·8	17·8	19·6	20·7	19·8	18·4	14·9	12·1
08	10·2	9·1	10·6	13·1	16·7	19·3	21·0	21·9	21·2	19·6	16·2	12·7
09	11·6	10·5	12·4	15·3	18·2	20·6	22·2	23·1	22·7	21·2	17·6	14·4
10	12·8	11·9	14·1	17·2	19·2	21·3	22·8	23·8	23·5	22·4	18·8	15·2
11	14·1	13·5	15·4	18·4	19·9	21·8	23·3	24·2	24·1	22·9	20·3	17·4
12	15·6	15·4	16·2	18·7	20·2	22·2	23·4	24·4	24·5	23·4	20·7	18·3
13	16·1	15·4	16·7	18·7	20·2	22·2	23·5	24·3	24·6	23·4	21·2	18·7
14	16·3	15·6	16·8	18·6	20·2	22·0	23·3	24·3	24·5	23·4	21·1	18·7
15	16·2	15·6	16·6	18·6	19·9	21·6	22·9	24·1	24·2	23·1	20·6	18·6
16	15·4	15·1	15·9	17·5	19·2	21·6	22·6	23·7	23·6	22·5	20·0	17·9
17	14·8	14·1	15·2	16·9	18·6	20·4	22·1	23·1	23·1	21·9	19·5	17·2
18	14·2	13·5	14·5	16·2	17·9	19·7	21·6	22·6	22·3	21·4	18·9	16·6
19	13·7	12·8	13·7	15·8	17·3	19·1	20·9	21·9	21·9	20·9	18·5	16·2
20	13·2	12·3	13·4	15·4	17·1	18·4	20·3	21·5	21·6	20·8	18·2	15·8
21	12·8	11·8	12·9	15·0	16·8	18·3	20·2	21·2	21·3	20·6	17·8	15·4
22	12·3	11·1	12·4	14·6	16·5	18·1	19·9	20·9	21·1	20·3	17·5	14·9
23	11·8	10·6	11·8	13·9	16·1	17·7	19·6	20·7	20·7	19·9	16·9	14·3
24	11·4	10·2	11·4	13·5	15·6	17·4	19·2	20·4	20·3	19·6	16·5	13·9

Fig. 3c. Mean monthly temperatures.

ADELAIDE, LATITUDE 34·9 SOUTH

HR···MONTH	JUN	JUL	AUG	SEP	OCT	NOV	DEC	JAN	FEB	MAR	APR	MAY
01	9·7	8·9	9·4	10·8	12·7	14·7	17·1	17·7	18·9	16·7	14·3	12·0
02	9·6	8·7	9·2	10·5	12·4	14·4	16·7	17·3	18·6	16·3	14·1	11·8
03	9·4	8·6	9·1	10·3	12·2	14·1	16·4	16·9	18·2	16·0	13·8	11·6
04	9·2	8·4	8·9	10·1	12·0	13·8	16·1	16·7	17·9	15·7	13·6	11·4
05	9·1	8·3	8·8	9·9	11·8	13·7	15·9	16·4	17·6	15·5	13·4	11·3
06	8·9	8·2	8·6	9·9	12·0	14·4	16·9	16·9	17·5	15·4	13·2	11·2
07	8·9	8·1	8·7	10·6	13·8	16·7	19·2	19·2	19·1	16·2	13·4	11·2
08	9·5	8·7	9·9	12·4	15·8	18·6	21·1	21·3	21·8	18·7	15·5	12·2
09	11·3	10·6	12·2	14·7	17·8	20·7	23·1	23·5	24·3	21·6	18·1	14·5
10	12·8	11·8	13·4	15·9	18·9	21·7	24·3	24·7	25·7	22·9	19·6	15·9
11	13·9	13·0	14·6	16·8	19·7	22·4	25·3	25·7	26·8	24·1	20·6	16·9
12	14·6	13·8	15·2	17·4	20·3	23·0	25·8	26·3	27·6	24·7	21·2	17·6
13	15·1	14·3	15·6	17·7	20·7	23·3	26·2	26·9	28·1	25·2	21·6	17·9
14	15·1	14·4	15·7	17·7	20·8	23·5	26·4	27·2	28·3	25·1	21·3	18·0
15	14·7	14·1	15·3	17·3	20·4	23·1	26·2	26·8	28·1	24·9	20·7	17·5
16	14·0	13·5	14·8	16·8	19·8	22·7	25·6	26·4	27·6	24·5	19·5	16·8
17	12·7	12·2	13·7	15·8	18·8	21·7	24·8	25·5	26·7	23·6	17·7	15·4
18	11·9	11·2	12·2	14·1	17·2	20·3	23·4	24·3	25·3	21·7	16·7	14·4
19	11·3	10·6	11·4	13·0	15·6	18·3	21·3	22·2	22·9	19·9	16·1	13·7
20	10·9	10·2	10·9	12·4	14·8	17·4	19·7	20·5	21·5	18·9	15·6	13·3
21	10·6	9·8	10·5	11·8	14·2	16·4	18·8	19·5	20·6	18·2	15·2	12·8
22	10·3	9·6	10·2	11·6	13·8	16·0	18·3	19·0	20·1	17·8	14·8	12·6
23	10·1	9·3	9·9	11·2	13·4	15·6	17·8	18·5	19·7	17·4	14·4	12·4
24	9·9	9·1	9·7	11·0	13·1	15·2	17·4	18·2	19·3	17·0	14·1	12·1

Fig. 3d. Mean monthly temperatures.

MELBOURNE, LATITUDE 37·8 SOUTH

HR···MONTH	JUN	JUL	AUG	SEP	OCT	NOV	DEC	JAN	FEB	MAR	APR	MAY
01	8·2	7·7	8·4	9·8	11·3	12·7	14·8	15·7	16·4	15·3	12·4	10·0
02	8·1	7·4	8·2	9·4	10·9	12·4	14·4	15·3	16·0	14·9	12·2	9·7
03	7·8	7·2	7·9	9·2	10·6	12·1	14·1	14·9	15·7	14·5	11·8	9·5
04	7·7	7·1	7·8	8·9	10·3	11·9	13·8	14·7	15·4	14·2	11·6	9·3
05	7·6	6·9	7·6	8·7	10·1	11·8	13·6	14·5	15·2	14·0	11·4	9·2
06	7·4	6·8	7·5	8·6	10·3	12·4	14·4	14·8	15·2	13·8	11·3	9·1
07	7·4	6·7	7·6	9·1	11·7	14·0	15·9	16·4	16·3	14·4	11·5	9·1
08	7·7	7·1	8·3	10·6	13·6	15·5	17·5	17·9	18·1	16·1	12·6	9·7
09	8·9	8·4	10·0	12·7	15·4	17·0	19·0	19·7	20·1	18·4	14·6	11·2
10	10·2	9·9	11·3	13·7	16·3	17·8	19·8	20·8	21·3	19·7	15·8	13·0
11	11·5	11·2	12·5	14·7	17·3	18·7	20·8	21·8	22·5	20·9	17·1	14·3
12	12·4	12·1	13·2	15·4	18·1	19·4	21·5	22·7	23·3	21·7	17·9	15·3
13	12·9	12·7	13·7	15·8	18·5	19·8	22·0	23·3	23·8	22·3	18·5	15·9
14	13·1	12·8	13·9	16·1	18·7	20·0	22·2	23·4	24·1	22·6	18·8	16·1
15	12·9	12·6	13·9	15·9	18·4	19·8	22·2	23·4	24·1	22·6	18·7	15·9
16	12·4	12·2	13·5	15·6	18·1	19·4	21·8	23·1	23·8	22·3	18·2	15·4
17	11·7	11·3	12·7	14·8	17·4	18·7	21·2	22·4	23·1	21·6	17·4	14·5
18	10·9	10·6	11·8	13·8	16·3	17·7	20·3	21·6	22·2	20·5	16·3	13·6
19	10·4	10·0	11·1	13·0	15·2	16·6	19·1	20·3	20·8	19·2	15·5	12·9
20	9·9	9·6	10·6	12·3	14·4	15·7	18·1	19·1	19·8	18·3	14·8	12·3
21	9·5	9·2	10·1	11·8	13·7	15·0	17·2	18·2	18·9	17·5	14·2	11·8
22	9·1	8·7	9·6	11·2	12·9	14·4	16·5	17·4	18·2	16·8	13·7	11·3
23	8·7	8·3	9·2	10·7	12·3	13·8	15·9	16·8	17·4	16·2	13·2	10·8
24	8·4	7·9	8·8	10·3	11·8	13·2	15·3	16·2	16·9	15·7	12·7	10·3

Fig. 3e. Mean monthly temperatures.

DARWIN, LATITUDE 12·43 SOUTH

HR···MONTH	JUN	JUL	AUG	SEP	OCT	NOV	DEC	JAN	FEB	MAR	APR	MAY
01	22·1	21·5	22·8	26·0	27·0	27·0	26·8	26·3	26·5	26·1	26·0	24·2
02	21·8	21·4	22·4	25·4	26·3	27·0	27·1	26·4	27·5	26·3	25·5	23·9
03	21·6	20·9	22·1	24·5	26·4	26·9	26·9	26·5	26·4	26·0	25·5	23·6
04	21·2	20·7	21·8	25·3	26·1	26·1	26·2	25·9	26·1	25·5	25·2	23·3
05	20·9	20·4	21·5	24·8	25·8	26·0	26·2	25·9	26·1	25·6	24·9	23·0
06	20·6	20·0	21·2	23·5	25·5	26·2	26·3	26·1	26·0	25·5	24·6	22·7
07	21·0	22·4	21·7	24·3	25·8	26·1	26·3	26·0	26·1	25·2	25·1	23·2
08	21·3	20·9	22·2	25·6	27·7	28·0	27·7	26·5	27·5	26·7	25·6	23·7
09	23·0	22·4	24·2	26·6	28·5	29·0	28·6	27·9	27·5	27·4	27·2	25·2
10	24·5	24·2	25·7	28·9	29·6	29·5	28·8	28·6	28·2	27·7	28·3	26·7
11	26·0	26·0	27·2	29·8	30·3	30·2	29·6	29·4	29·0	29·0	29·4	28·2
12	28·1	27·8	29·0	30·4	31·1	31·4	30·7	29·8	29·4	30·0	30·9	29·8
13	28·5	28·3	29·3	32·3	31·4	31·2	30·3	30·1	29·5	29·4	31·1	30·2
14	29·0	28·8	29·6	32·0	32·3	31·6	31·8	30·8	31·4	28·7	31·2	30·6
15	29·7	29·5	30·1	31·1	31·8	31·8	31·1	30·1	29·8	30·3	31·7	31·0
16	29·2	28·7	29·5	32·2	31·5	30·5	30·2	29·9	28·9	29·3	31·4	30·6
17	28·7	28·2	28·8	31·0	30·6	30·5	29·9	29·8	28·6	29·3	30·6	30·1
18	27·5	27·4	28·7	29·4	29·8	30·3	29·6	28·9	29·1	30·1	30·4	30·3
19	26·3	26·2	27·3	29·4	29·1	28·9	28·5	28·2	27·8	28·1	29·3	28·8
20	25·2	24·9	25·9	28·2	28·7	28·8	28·8	27·6	28·1	25·0	28·2	27·3
21	24·1	23·6	24·8	26·7	28·2	28·4	28·1	27·7	27·3	27·1	27·4	26·0
22	23·5	22·9	24·3	26·4	27·9	28·2	27·7	27·4	27·3	26·9	27·1	25·5
23	23·0	22·3	23·7	26·0	27·6	28·1	27·5	27·1	27·1	26·2	26·7	25·0
24	22·4	21·6	23·2	25·7	27·3	27·9	27·5	27·0	26·8	26·4	26·4	24·5

Fig. 3f. Mean monthly temperatures.

ALICE SPRINGS, LATITUDE 23.8 SOUTH

HR···MONTH	JUN	JUL	AUG	SEP	OCT	NOV	DEC	JAN	FEB	MAR	APR	MAY
01·········	8·3	7·9	10·3	14·0	19·8	20·6	24·0	25·5	24·4	22·5	14·0	11·9
02·········	8·0	7·6	9·8	13·5	19·5	21·9	24·3	27·0	24·4	22·5	15·0	11·2
03·········	8·2	7·3	9·1	12·9	17·8	20·3	22·7	24·2	23·9	20·4	16·0	11·2
04·········	7·4	6·6	8·4	15·5	17·7	18·6	21·7	23·1	22·4	20·2	15·1	10·6
05·········	6·5	5·9	7·7	14·1	16·2	18·5	21·4	22·1	21·4	19·3	14·2	9·9
06·········	6·9	5·8	7·6	11·1	16·0	18·7	20·8	22·3	21·9	18·6	14·1	9·7
07·········	7·3	6·4	8·6	15·3	17·9	19·6	22·9	23·8	21·8	19·3	15·2	10·6
08·········	7·7	6·9	9·6	16·8	24·8	24·3	28·4	28·2	24·3	22·8	16·3	11·5
09·········	10·3	9·5	12·4	17·4	22·7	25·6	27·5	28·2	26·9	23·8	19·5	13·6
10·········	12·4	11·9	14·7	25·6	24·8	26·1	29·3	30·3	27·6	27·1	21·1	15·9
11·········	14·5	14·4	17·0	26·3	25·7	27·7	30·7	31·1	28·9	28·4	22·7	18·2
12·········	16·9	16·2	18·6	22·7	27·3	29·9	31·6	32·5	31·4	28·9	25·3	19·7
13·········	17·5	17·2	19·6	29·2	28·5	29·4	32·5	33·8	31·1	31·1	25·7	20·6
14·········	18·2	18·1	20·7	29·1	35·5	32·5	36·1	35·3	32·4	34·5	26·1	21·5
15·········	19·3	18·7	21·1	25·1	29·5	32·0	33·6	34·6	33·6	31·2	27·6	21·9
16·········	18·7	18·5	21·1	25·3	30·0	30·7	34·0	35·2	32·6	32·6	27·0	21·7
17·········	18·2	18·4	21·0	25·5	29·2	31·0	33·6	34·8	32·2	32·1	26·3	21·5
18·········	17·4	17·3	20·1	24·2	28·4	31·0	33·0	34·1	33·1	30·5	26·4	20·3
19·········	15·6	15·5	18·4	22·6	27·1	28·2	31·7	33·4	30·6	30·3	24·6	18·7
20·········	13·8	13·6	16·7	21·0	30·8	27·6	32·3	32·0	30·3	31·8	22·7	17·1
21·········	12·6	12·1	14·7	18·8	23·5	26·1	28·5	30·0	29·2	25·9	21·3	15·7
22·········	11·3	10·8	13·4	17·4	22·8	22·8	27·1	28·2	28·0	24·5	18·5	14·6
23·········	9·9	9·6	12·1	15·9	21·1	22·6	25·7	26·4	26·8	23·0	15·8	13·6
24·········	8·6	8·3	10·8	14·5	19·3	21·9	24·3	24·6	25·6	21·6	13·0	12·5

Fig. 3g. Mean monthly temperatures.

Above temperatures are based upon the computer print-out obtained from Department of Science and the Environment, Bureau of Meteorology, Regional office N.T. (private correspondence dated 6/2/79).

Note: Many temperatures are interpolated by the author.

BRISBANE, LATITUDE 27·5 SOUTH

HR···MONTH	JUN	JUL	AUG	SEP	OCT	NOV	DEC	JAN	FEB	MAR	APR	MAY
01	—	—	—	—	—	—	21·7	22·6	22·2	21·2	—	—
02	—	—	—	—	—	—	21·4	22·3	22·2	—	—	—
03	—	—	—	—	—	—	21·0	22·1	21·4	—	—	—
04	—	—	—	—	—	—	—	21·7	21·2	—	—	—
05	—	—	—	—	—	—	—	21·6	—	—	—	—
06	—	—	—	—	—	—	—	21·6	—	—	—	—
07	—	—	—	—	—	22·1	22·0	22·4	21·4	—	—	—
08	—	—	—	—	22·3	23·9	23·9	24·1	23·1	21·7	—	—
09	—	—	—	—	23·6	25·1	25·7	25·8	25·1	23·2	—	—
10	—	—	—	21·7	24·6	25·8	26·5	26·9	26·2	24·6	22·3	—
11	—	—	—	22·4	25·1	26·1	27·3	27·7	26·9	25·4	23·2	21·5
12	—	—	—	22·8	25·1	26·2	27·7	28·2	27·4	26·2	23·9	22·2
13	—	—	—	22·7	24·7	25·9	27·9	28·3	27·6	26·5	24·4	22·4
14	—	—	—	22·2	24·1	25·6	27·7	28·2	27·7	26·6	24·6	21·7
15	—	—	—	21·5	23·5	25·0	27·3	27·7	27·7	26·2	24·4	21·4
16	—	—	—	—	22·7	24·2	26·6	27·3	26·8	25·7	23·8	—
17	—	—	—	—	21·8	23·4	25·9	26·6	26·2	25·2	22·8	—
18	—	—	—	—	21·0	22·7	25·1	25·8	25·3	24·3	22·1	—
19	—	—	—	—	—	21·8	24·4	25·1	24·6	23·5	21·2	—
20	—	—	—	—	—	21·5	23·7	24·5	24·1	23·1	—	—
21	—	—	—	—	—	21·1	23·2	23·9	23·7	22·6	—	—
22	—	—	—	—	—	—	22·8	23·6	23·3	22·3	—	—
23	—	—	—	—	—	—	22·6	23·3	22·9	21·9	—	—
24	—	—	—	—	—	—	22·1	23·1	22·6	21·6	—	—

Fig. 4a. Mean monthly temperatures. Temps. below 21°C ignored.

PERTH, LATITUDE 32·0 SOUTH

HR··MONTH	JUN	JUL	AUG	SEP	OCT	NOV	DEC	JAN	FEB	MAR	APR	MAY
01	–	–	–	–	–	–	–	–	–	–	–	–
02	–	–	–	–	–	–	–	–	–	–	–	–
03	–	–	–	–	–	–	–	–	–	–	–	–
04	–	–	–	–	–	–	–	–	–	–	–	–
05	–	–	–	–	–	–	–	–	–	–	–	–
06	–	–	–	–	–	–	–	–	–	–	–	–
07	–	–	–	–	–	–	–	–	–	–	–	–
08	–	–	–	–	–	–	21·0	21·1	21·4	–	–	–
09	–	–	–	–	–	–	22·6	22·7	23·4	21·6	–	–
10	–	–	–	–	–	21·0	23·8	24·3	25·5	23·4	22·2	–
11	–	–	–	–	–	22·2	25·0	25·5	26·9	25·0	23·1	–
12	–	–	–	–	–	23·2	25·7	26·4	27·8	26·1	23·7	–
13	–	–	–	–	–	23·9	25·9	26·9	28·5	26·7	24·0	–
14	–	–	–	–	–	24·3	25·8	27·1	28·6	26·9	23·7	–
15	–	–	–	–	–	24·1	25·5	26·8	28·2	26·4	23·1	–
16	–	–	–	–	–	23·7	24·9	26·0	27·4	25·8	21·8	–
17	–	–	–	–	–	23·1	24·1	25·5	26·6	24·7	–	–
18	–	–	–	–	–	22·2	22·8	24·4	25·3	23·4	–	–
19	–	–	–	–	–	–	21·3	22·8	23·5	21·9	–	–
20	–	–	–	–	–	–	–	21·9	22·7	21·4	–	–
21	–	–	–	–	–	–	–	21·2	22·2	–	–	–
22	–	–	–	–	–	–	–	–	21·7	–	–	–
23	–	–	–	–	–	–	–	–	21·2	–	–	–
24	–	–	–	–	–	–	–	–	–	–	–	–

Fig. 4b. Mean monthly temperatures. Temps. below 21°C ignored.

SYDNEY, LATITUDE 33·9 SOUTH

HR	JUN	JUL	AUG	SEP	OCT	NOV	DEC	JAN	FEB	MAR	APR	MAY
01												
02												
03												
04												
05												
06												
07								21·9	21·2			
08							21·0	23·1	22·7	21·2		
09							22·2	23·8	23·5	22·4		
10						21·3	22·8	24·2	24·1	22·9		
11						21·8	23·3	24·4	24·5	23·4		
12						22·2	23·4	24·3	24·6	23·4	21·2	
13						22·2	23·5	24·3	24·5	23·4	21·1	
14						22·0	23·3	24·1	24·2	23·1		
15						21·6	22·9	23·7	23·6	22·5		
16						21·6	22·6	23·1	23·1	21·9		
17							22·1	22·6	22·3	21·4		
18							21·6	21·9	21·9			
19								21·5	21·6			
20								21·2	21·3			
21									21·1			
22												
23												
24												

Fig. 4c. Mean monthly temperatures. Temps. below 21°C ignored.

ADELAIDE, LATITUDE 34·9 SOUTH

HR··MONTH	JUN	JUL	AUG	SEP	OCT	NOV	DEC	JAN	FEB	MAR	APR	MAY
01												
02												
03												
04												
05												
06												
07												
08							21·1	21·3	21·8			
09							23·1	23·5	24·3	21·6		
10						21·7	24·3	24·7	25·7	22·9		
11						22·4	25·3	25·7	26·8	24·1	21·2	
12						23·0	25·8	26·3	27·6	24·7	21·6	
13						23·3	26·2	26·9	28·1	25·2	21·7	
14						23·6	26·4	27·2	28·3	25·1	21·3	
15						23·1	26·2	26·8	28·1	24·9		
16						22·7	25·6	26·4	27·6	24·5		
17						21·7	24·8	25·5	26·7	23·6		
18							23·4	24·3	25·3	21·7		
19							21·3	22·2	22·9			
20									21·5			
21												
22												
23												
24												

Fig. 4d. Mean monthly temperatures. Temps. below 21°C ignored.

MELBOURNE, LATITUDE 37·8 SOUTH

HR···MONTH	JUN	JUL	AUG	SEP	OCT	NOV	DEC	JAN	FEB	MAR	APR	MAY
01												
02												
03												
04												
05												
06												
07												
08												
09									21·3			
10								—	22·5			
11							21·5	21·8	23·3	21·7		
12							22·0	22·7	23·8	22·3		
13							22·2	23·3	24·1	22·6		
14							22·2	23·4	24·1	22·6		
15							21·8	23·1	23·8	22·3		
16							21·2	22·4	23·1	21·6		
17							—	21·6	22·2	—		
18												
19												
20												
21												
22												
23												
24												

Fig. 4e. Mean monthly temperatures. Temps. below 21°C ignored.

DARWIN, LATITUDE 12·43 SOUTH

HR··MONTH	JUN	JUL	AUG	SEP	OCT	NOV	DEC	JAN	FEB	MAR	APR	MAY
01	22·1	21·5	22·8	26·0	27·0	27·0	26·8	26·3	26·5	26·1	26·0	24·2
02	21·8	21·4	22·4	25·4	26·3	27·0	27·1	26·4	27·5	26·3	25·5	23·9
03	21·6	—	22·1	24·5	26·4	26·9	26·9	26·5	26·4	26·0	25·5	23·6
04	21·2	—	21·8	25·3	26·1	26·1	26·2	25·9	26·1	25·5	25·2	23·3
05	—	—	21·5	24·8	25·8	26·0	26·2	25·9	26·1	25·6	24·9	23·0
06	—	22·4	21·2	23·5	25·5	26·2	26·3	26·1	26·0	25·5	24·6	22·7
07	21·0	—	21·7	24·3	25·8	26·1	26·3	26·0	26·1	25·0	25·1	23·2
08	21·3	22·4	22·2	25·6	27·7	28·0	27·7	26·5	27·5	26·7	25·6	23·7
09	23·0	22·4	24·2	26·6	28·5	29·0	28·6	27·9	27·5	27·4	27·2	25·2
10	24·5	24·2	25·7	28·9	29·6	29·5	28·8	28·6	28·2	27·7	28·3	26·7
11	26·0	26·0	27·2	29·8	30·3	30·2	29·6	29·4	29·0	29·0	29·4	28·2
12	28·1	27·8	29·0	30·4	31·1	31·4	30·7	29·8	29·4	30·0	30·9	29·8
13	28·5	28·3	29·3	32·3	31·4	31·2	30·3	30·1	29·5	29·4	31·1	30·2
14	29·0	28·8	29·6	32·0	32·3	31·6	31·8	30·8	31·4	28·7	31·2	30·6
15	29·7	29·5	30·1	31·1	31·8	31·8	31·1	30·1	29·8	30·3	31·7	31·0
16	29·2	28·7	29·5	32·2	31·5	30·5	30·2	29·9	28·9	29·3	31·4	30·6
17	28·7	28·2	28·8	31·0	30·6	30·5	29·9	29·8	28·6	29·3	30·6	30·1
18	27·5	27·4	28·7	29·4	29·8	30·3	29·6	28·9	29·1	30·1	30·4	30·3
19	26·3	26·2	27·3	29·4	29·1	28·9	28·5	28·2	27·8	28·1	29·3	28·8
20	25·2	24·9	25·9	28·2	28·7	28·8	28·8	27·6	28·1	25·0	28·2	27·3
21	24·1	23·6	24·8	26·7	28·2	28·4	28·1	27·7	27·3	27·1	27·4	26·0
22	23·5	22·9	24·3	26·4	27·9	28·2	27·7	27·4	27·3	26·9	27·1	25·5
23	23·0	22·3	23·7	26·0	27·6	28·1	27·5	27·1	27·1	26·2	26·7	25·0
24	22·4	21·6	23·2	25·7	27·3	27·9	27·5	27·0	26·8	26·4	26·4	24·5

Fig. 4f. Mean monthly temperatures. Temps. below 21°C ignored.

ALICE SPRINGS, LATITUDE 23·8 SOUTH

HR···MONTH	JUN	JUL	AUG	SEP	OCT	NOV	DEC	JAN	FEB	MAR	APR	MAY
01············	—	—	—	—	—	—	24·0	25·5	24·4	22·5	—	—
02············	—	—	—	—	—	21·9	24·3	27·0	24·4	22·5	—	—
03············	—	—	—	—	—	—	22·7	24·2	23·9	—	—	—
04············	—	—	—	—	—	—	21·7	23·1	22·4	—	—	—
05············	—	—	—	—	—	—	21·4	22·1	21·4	—	—	—
06············	—	—	—	—	—	—	—	22·3	21·9	—	—	—
07············	—	—	—	—	—	—	22·9	23·8	21·8	—	—	—
08············	—	—	—	—	24·8	24·3	28·4	28·2	24·3	22·8	—	—
09············	—	—	—	—	22·7	25·6	27·5	28·2	26·9	23·8	—	—
10············	—	—	—	25·6	24·8	26·1	29·3	30·3	27·6	27·1	21·0	—
11············	—	—	—	26·3	25·7	27·7	30·7	31·1	28·9	28·4	22·7	—
12············	—	—	—	22·7	27·3	29·9	31·6	32·5	31·4	28·9	25·3	—
13············	—	—	—	29·2	28·5	29·4	32·5	33·8	31·1	31·1	25·7	—
14············	—	—	21·1	29·1	35·5	32·5	36·1	35·3	32·4	34·5	26·1	21·5
15············	—	—	21·1	25·1	29·5	32·0	33·6	34·6	33·6	31·2	27·6	21·9
16············	—	—	21·0	25·3	30·0	30·7	34·0	35·2	32·6	32·6	27·0	21·7
17············	—	—	—	25·5	29·2	31·0	33·6	34·8	32·2	32·1	26·3	21·5
18············	—	—	—	24·2	28·4	31·0	33·0	34·1	33·1	30·5	26·4	—
19············	—	—	—	22·6	27·1	28·2	31·7	33·4	30·6	30·3	24·6	—
20············	—	—	—	21·0	30·8	27·6	32·3	32·0	30·3	31·8	22·7	—
21············	—	—	—	—	23·5	26·1	28·5	30·0	29·2	25·9	21·3	—
22············	—	—	—	—	22·8	22·8	27·1	28·2	28·0	24·5	—	—
23············	—	—	—	—	21·1	22·6	25·7	26·4	26·8	23·0	—	—
24············	—	—	—	—	—	21·9	24·3	24·6	25·6	21·6	—	—

Fig. 4g. Mean monthly temperatures. Temps. below 21°C ignored.

Above temperatures are based upon the computer print-out obtained from Department of Science and the Environment, Bureau of Meteorology, Regional office N.T. (private correspondence dated 6/2/79).

Note: Many temperatures are interpolated by the author.

show the tables of those temperatures converted to the Celsius scale. Figs. 4a–g are the same tables, but with the temperatures below 21°C ignored. These tables give a visual picture of the periods when buildings need shading in the respective cities. One can see how the shading period contracts as one goes towards the southern latitudes.

Looking at Fig. 4 for Perth for example, it can be seen that shading devices should be designed to give protection from 09.00 hrs to 17.00 hrs during November, from 08.00 hrs to 19.00 hrs (around sunset) in December, and from 11.00 hrs to 17.00 hrs in April. The table also shows that shading is not required in May, June, July, August, September and October. (Note that the shading period is not symmetrical around the month of December; this is discussed below in 3.3.5.)

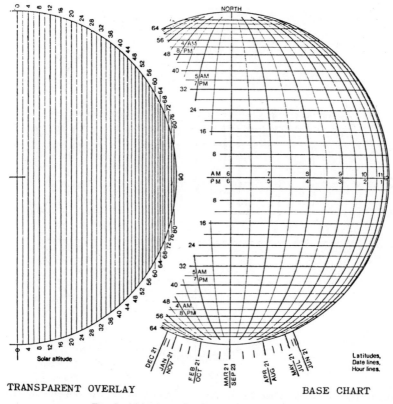

Fig. 5. Altitude angle charts for any latitude.

One should consult the the records of the Bureau of Meteorology for the temperatures of the area under consideration as a first step towards the design of sun shading devices. Where no records are available for the area from the Bureau of Meteorology, these are sometimes obtainable from Universities and research establishments like the CSIRO.

3.2. THE POSITION OF THE SUN

The second step in the process of design of sun shading devices is to define the position of the sun during the overheated period. The

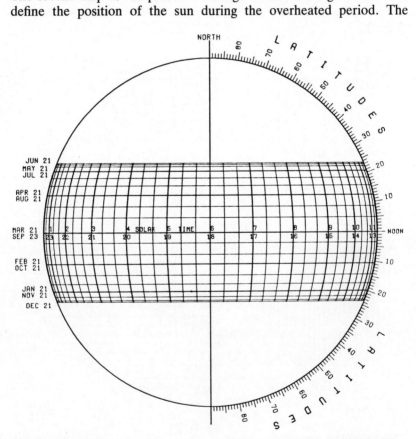

Fig. 6. Azimuth angle. Chart No. 6. This base chart is to be used with Overlay Chart No. 7.

position of the sun at any given time, is defined by its altitude (the angle the solar rays make to the horizontal plane passing through the location) and its azimuth (the angle the horizontal projection of the solar rays make to the north direction at the location) (Fig. 2). The azimuth is sometimes measured from the south direction in the northern hemisphere. The position of the sun can be determined graphically, or by mathematics, or by a combination of both methods.

3.2.1. The Graphical Determination of the Position of the Sun

An example of the graphical method are the two sets of charts, prepared by the author, which can be used to determine the position of the sun for any location. No mathematics was used in their development.

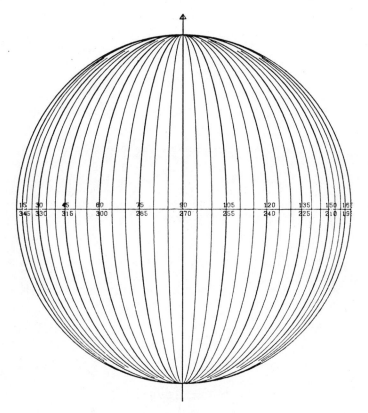

Fig. 7. Azimuth angle. Chart No. 7. This overlay chart is to be used with base chart No. 6.

For the determination of the altitude, one uses the base chart and the transparent overlay shown in Fig. 5. The overlay is put concentrically on the base chart and is rotated till its diameter points to the desired date. One then follows the relevant latitude line where it intersects the desired hour line and reads the altitude of the sun on the overlay. This set of charts also determines the times of sunrise and sunset.

For the determination of the azimuth one uses Figs. 6 and 7 (plotted by computer). The transparent overlay is put concentrically over the base chart and is adjusted so that the arrow points to the correct latitude on the base chart. One then selects the date line and follows it till the required hour line is reached and the azimuth is read on the overlay (Fig. 8).

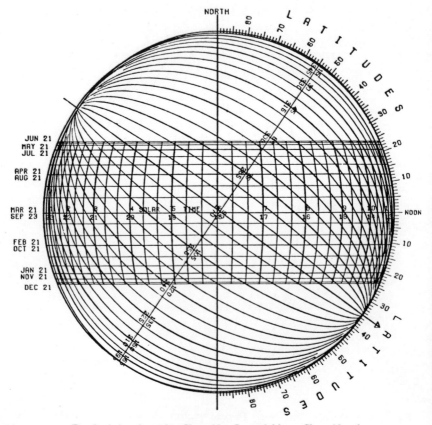

Fig. 8. Azimuth angle. Chart No. 7 overlaid on Chart No. 6.

In the above sets of charts, time is solar time and not clock time, as explained below in 3.2.2.

3.2.2. The Mathematical Determination of the Position of the Sun

Two equations are needed, one for the altitude and one for the azimuth (Ref. 5).

The altitude is given by:

$$\sin(\text{altitude}) = \cos(\text{latitude}) \times \cos(\text{declination}) \times \cos(\text{hour angle})$$
$$+ \sin(\text{latitude}) \times \sin(\text{declination}) \qquad (1)$$

The azimuth is given by:

$$\sin(\text{azimuth}) = \cos(\text{declination}) \times \sin(\text{hour angle})/\cos(\text{altitude}) \qquad (2)$$

Equation (2) gives the sine of the azimuth angle. One should remember that an angle and its supplementary have the same sine, and also that the resulting angle in equation(2) is measured from the south.

From the above equations, it can be seen that the position of the sun depends upon several factors, as follows.

The latitude. All locations on the same latitude have identical solar positions at the same date and the same "solar" time (see *solar time* below) For equation (1) the latitude is entered with a negative sign for south latitudes.

The declination. The angle which the earth-sun axis makes with the plane of the earth's equator. It is negative when the axis lies on the south face of that plane. The declination depends upon the date. Referring back to the sets of charts for the altitude (Fig. 5), the overlay is rotated over the base chart according to the date. The angle of rotation is equal to the angle of declination of the date in question. The declination can be looked up in References, 1, 4, 5, & 6. Spencer (Ref. 7) gives a mathematical curve-fit equation for the determination of the declination as a function of the date, which is convenient for computer programming.

The hour angle. This equals 15° × number of hours from "solar" noon (see *solar time* below) since the earth, on average, completes one revolution of 360° in 24 hours or 15° per hour. This can be related to the hour lines shown on the overlay for the altitude set of charts (Fig. 5), and for the azimuth set (Fig. 7). These hour lines are actually hour circles equally distributed over the surface of the sphere representing the earth, and 15° apart for each hour difference in time.

Solar time. "Solar time" is different from the "clock time" that our watches indicate. "Solar" noon is the instant when the sun is actually crossing the meridian of the place. The conversion from solar to clock time and *vice versa* depends upon the "equation of time" which takes account of the non-uniformity of the orbital velocity of the earth, and upon the difference between the longitude of the place and the "reference" longitude of the time zone (the time meridian) which the location under consideration follows. The equation of time can account for a difference between the solar and standard time of ± 15 minutes. The difference between the local longitude time is ± 4 minutes per degree (Refs. 1, 2 & 5).

3.3. DESIGN AIDS FOR SHADING DEVICES

When the period during which direct sun rays are to be excluded from a certain area of the building envelope is known (see 3.1.1), the position of the sun at different intervals during this period can be determined and the shading device to intercept the solar rays before reaching the area can be designed. It would be time consuming to work out the position of the sun by mathematics. Some architectural references give tables of the sun position; for example *Time Saver Standards* (Ref. 6) gives the solar angles at 2-hour intervals for some northern latitudes. A universal sun chart is given by the *Architectural Graphic Standards*, (Ref. 8), which is good for any latitude, but it involves repetitive measuring operations.

One should look for design tools which simplify the process of defining of the sun's position and the subsequent geometrical shape and dimensions of the shading device. These design tools fall into four categories:

    a—solar charts
    b—shadow charts
    c—computer programs
    d—sun machines (for models)

3.3.1. Solar Charts

Solar charts are sometimes referred to as "sun path diagrams" because they represent the path of the sun across the sky on several chosen days of the year. A sky vault is assumed on which the sun moves and the path of the sun is projected on a horizontal plane passing through the location under consideration. Each sun path diagram is only good for the latitude for which it was done and sun path diagrams are produced as a series of diagrams for a series of latitudes covering a country or a geographical area.

Apart from the charts referred to in 3.2.1 above, some examples of solar charts are as follows.

Sunshine and Shade in Australia by R. O. Phillips (Experimental Building Station) (Ref. 1).

This publication gives a series of eight charts for latitudes ranging from 42.5° south to 5° south, which covers Australia, New Zealand and Papua New Guinea. Fig. 9 shows the chart for latitude 35° south. One

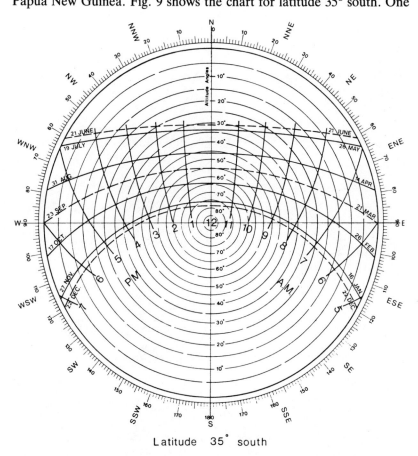

Latitude 35° south

Fig. 9. Solar chart for latitude 35°S (After R. O. Phillips).

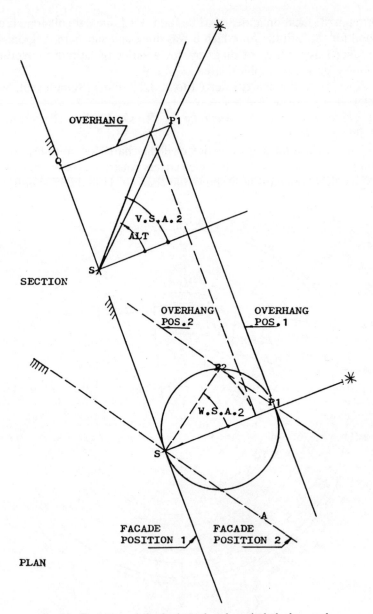

Fig. 10. Geometry of the horizontal and vertical shadow angle.

set of curved lines represent the sun's path for the dates shown on each one of them (date lines). The other set of curves represent the time of day written at their lower ends (hour lines). The point of intersection of a date line and an hour line define a certain instant of time for which the altitude of the sun is read on the concentric circles, and the solar azimuth is represented by the line joining the point and the centre of the diagram, and can be read on the protractor edging the diagram.

The shadow angles. Fig. 10 shows a solar ray Pl-S striking a facade, position 1 in plan and section. The shadow of point Pl lies on S. Q-P1 in section, (S-P1 in plan) is the required projection of a horizontal overhang to cast a shadow of a 'throw' of depth Q-S. The orientation of the facade in 'position 1' was chosen to coincide with the azimuth of the sun. The 'wall solar azimuth' (W.S.A.) is in this case equal to zero degrees. The wall solar azimuth is also known as the 'horizontal shadow angle'. Note that in this case when W.S.A. = 0 the altitude of the sun "ALT" shows in its true value on the section.

If one assumes that the facade is rotated to "position 2" in plan, the projection of the overhang can be reduced to length S-P2 in plan, since point P1 will still cast its shadow on point S regardless of the new orientation of the facade. The new wall solar azimuth (the horizontal shadow angle) is indicated as "W.S.A.2." in plan. The angle indicated as V.S.A.2 on the section is the "vertical shadow angle"; it is the measure of the necessary projection of the overhang to give the same vertical shadow throw Q-S In US publications, the vertical shadow angle is usually referred to as the "profile angle".

For a certain altitude and azimuth angle of the sun and a given facade orientation, a certain wall solar azimuth (horizontal shadow angle) can be determined. A graphical construction similar to the one illustrated in Fig. 10 should give the correct projection of the horizontal overhang which would protect an opening of a height Q-S. It is not enough to construct the overhang shown in plan as "overhang Pos. 2"; one has to be sure that the edge of the overhang reaches point P1 in plan so as to shade point S.

Rather than go through all the graphical construction, the profile angle (vertical shadow angle) can be found from the equation:-

$$V.S.A. = \text{arc tan } (\tan(\text{altitude})/\cos(W.S.A.)) \qquad (3)$$

This equation is put in graphical form in Fig. 11 (which is a computer plot).

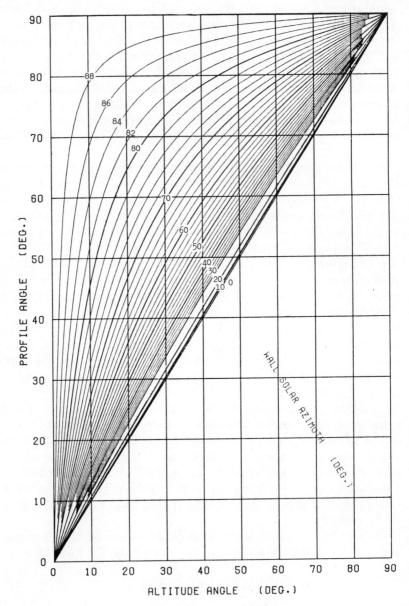

Fig. 11. Profile angle (vertical shadow angle).

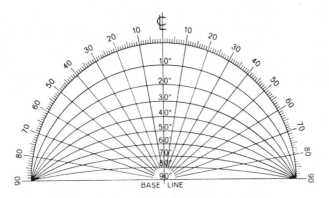

Fig. 12. Shadow-angle protractor.

The shadow-angle protractor. The publication includes a transparent shadow-angle protractor (Fig. 12) which can be used as an overlay to the solar charts. When adjusted to the orientation of the facade, it reads the vertical and horizontal shadow angles.

Control of Sunlight Penetration by The Department of Labour And Immigration (Ref. 9).

This publication is similar to *"Sunshine and Shade in Australia"*, (see above), except that the "sun position diagrams" are worked out for clock time rather than for solar time (see 3.2.2. above). These diagrams are good only for the cities for which they are constructed and not for whole latitudes as the previous ones. The cities

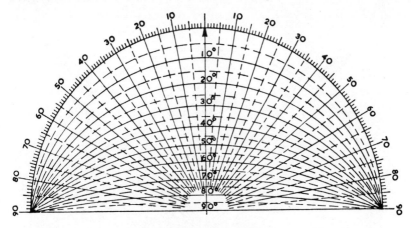

Fig. 13. Shadow-angle protractor.

are Adelaide, Brisbane, Darwin, Hobart, Melbourne, Perth, Sydney, and Townsville. The diagrams can be used for other locations on or near the same latitude, if one allows 4 minutes for each degree of longitude (see 3.2.2. above), provided the city and the location fall within the same time zone. Because the equation of time referred to in 3.2.2. is not symmetrical with respect to any date, a set of two diagrams is needed for each city, one for the period of December 22 to June 21 and the other for the period from June 21 to December 22.

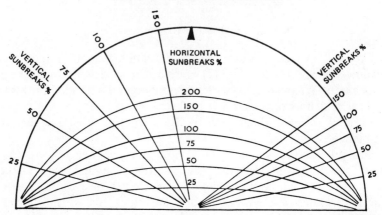

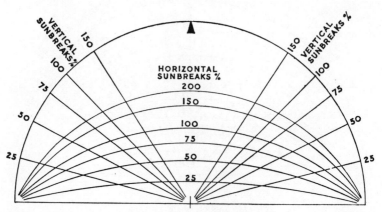

Fig. 14. Sunbreak protractors (Australian Department of Labor and Immigration).

The shadow angle protractor and the shading masks. Included in the publication is a transparent shadow angle protractor (Fig. 13), similar to the one developed by the Experimental Building Station (Fig. 12). It also includes two "sunbreak protractors" (Fig. 14). These form "shading mask" protractors. Shading masks define the areas of a sun path diagram from where no direct sun ray can reach the protected point of the facade (the centre of the projection of the chart). The idea is to project the

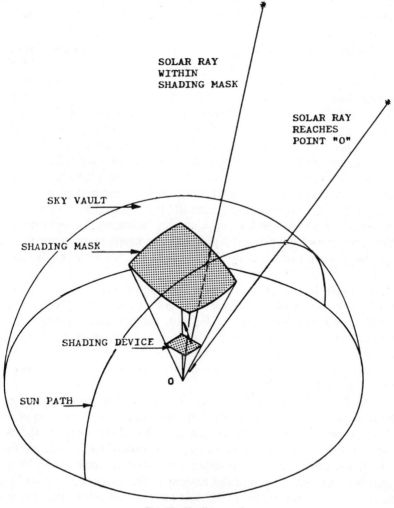

Fig. 15. Shading masks.

shading device on the assumed sky vault by passing rays from the centre
of projection (point O in Fig. 15) along the edges of the shading device.
The shading mask thus obtained is subsequently projected on the
horizontal plane passing through the centre by the same process by
which the sunpaths are obtained (refer to 3.3.1).

Fig. 15 shows in three dimensions how a shading device is projected
on the assumed sky vault. Solar rays falling within the shading mask
cannot reach point O and they will be intercepted by the shading device.
If the shading mask is projected on the same horizontal plane as the
sunpath, one can determine the dates and times when point O will be
shaded.

Shading mask examples. Drawing a shading mask is a straightforward
process if one uses the shadow angle protractor compatible with the
solar chart in use. The shadow angle protractor (Fig. 13) has a series of
curves and a series of radial lines. The first group represents the
projections of the lines of intersection of a plane passing through the
base line (indicated on Fig. 12); the sky dome, as the plane is rotated
around the base line, making different angles to the horizontal plane
passing through the centre of projection. The actual shape of these lines
on the protractor depends upon the method of projection (orthographic, stereographic or equidistant), but the method of projection
should be the same for the sunpath lines and the shadow angle
protractor. Each curved line has a number indicating the inclination to
the horizontal of the plane it represents. For example, referring to Fig.
10, the plane represented by the line S-P1 has the value of the angle
"ALT".

The radial lines represent the intersection of vertical planes passing
through the centre of the diagram (the point to be shaded) with the sky
vault. Again referring back to Fig. 10, for the facade position 2, a
vertical plane passing through S and P1 has an angle equal to the
horizontal shadow angle (W.S.A.2).

Figure 16 shows how a shading mask is constructed for a balcony on
top of a glass door D.

Case 1 is a balcony slab without side walls. The front edge of the
balcony subtends an angle to the horizontal of 49° at the bottom of the
door (see section, Fig. 16). The shading mask to this edge of the slab is a
curve a little above the 50° curve of the shadow angle protractor (Fig.
13). If the edge continues to infinity, the shading mask would be the
area between the curve and the base line. The two other edges of the
balcony subtending angles of 55° and 84° (see elevation, Fig. 16) will

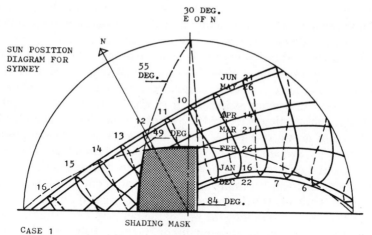

CASE 1
SHADING MASK FOR BALCONY WITHOUT SIDE WALLS

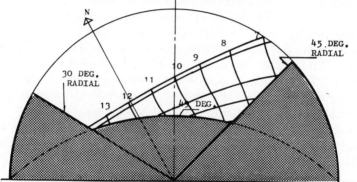

CASE 2
SHADING MASK FOR BALCONY WITH SIDE WALLS

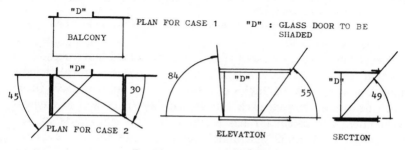

Fig. 16. Shading mask examples.

have two curves marked 55 and 84 on the top diagram of Fig. 16. Note that the shadow angle protractor has to have its base line rotated to the direction parallel to the edge in question. The dotted area between the three curves is the shading mask of the balcony with respect to that particular glass door. It should be noted that this dotted area is the shading mask for the balcony with respect to the door "D", no matter where this construction is located or to which direction it is oriented.

If this construction is located in Sydney and the door is made to face 30° east of north, one places the shading mask on the "sun position diagram" for Sydney, say, the one for the period from December 22 to June 21, as shown by the top diagram of Fig. 16. The diagram shows that the glass door will be completely shaded for about one hour around noon on April 14. It will again be completely shaded on the same day from 15.20 hrs till sunset by the wall of the building, which masks half of the sky vault. Following the sunpaths of March 21, February 26, January 16 and December 22 one can determine the times of complete shading for those dates. One can do the same thing for the period from June to December by using the conjugate chart for that period, which is an identical chart, except for the hour lines shown as dashed curves for case 1 (Fig. 16). Outside the hours of complete shading one can use graphical construction to draw the shadow of the balcony on the glass door and its wall, since the altitude and azimuth of the sun, and also the shadow angles can be determined from the shadow angle protractor.

Case 2 is the same as case 1, but two side walls are added subtending angles of 45° and 30° at the edges of the door as seen on plan (Fig. 16). The shading mask is composed of the 49° curved line of the front edge of the balcony, and the vertical edges of the walls are represented by the 45° and 30° radial lines. For case 2 the shading mask is more spread out, and consequently the length of the shaded periods is greatly increased, as compared with case 1.

The "Sun Angle Calculator" produced by Libbey-Owens-Ford company of the USA (Ref. 10).

This example from overseas (Fig. 17), is presented here, because in addition to the altitude, azimuth and profile angles (vertical shadow angles), it also gives the angles of incidence on vertical surfaces (from which heat gain through glass can be calculated), as well as daylight availability. The calculator has a series of eight sun charts for the latitudes from 24° to 52° north at 4° intervals. This covers the United States and part of Canada. This calculator could be used for Southern latitudes if the dates and compass points are switched around.

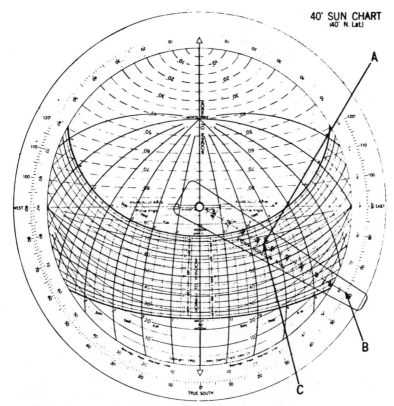

Fig. 17. The Sun Angle Calculator, Libbey-Owens-Ford, USA.

Sunlight penetration. The solar charts in the two previously mentioned publications and the Sun Angle Calculator can be used to determine the times when direct sunlight will strike a window or glass wall. Graphical construction can then give the shape and dimensions of the sunlight areas in a room. Fig. 18 taken from Reference 9 illustrates this.

3.3.2. Shadow Charts
Shadow charts plot the position of the shadow of a point in space cast on a plane surface. They differ from solar charts which plot the position of the sun and define it in terms of the altitude and azimuth. Shadow charts must have a scale marked on them. Two examples are described below.
Sunlight Indicators, New South Wales Planning and Environment Commission (Ref. 11)

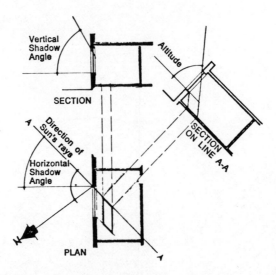

Fig. 18. Plan and section of a room with sunlight entering a window (from *Control of Sunlight Penetration*).

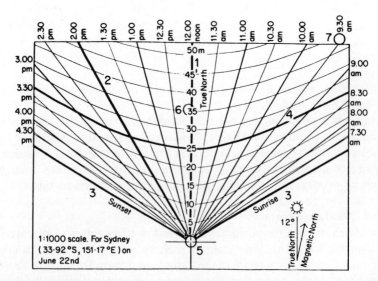

Fig. 19. The June 22 sunlight indicator (After NSW PEC). 1 Vertical axis, true north line. 2 Radial time line. 3 Sunrise and Sunset time lines. 4 Curved lines tracing 5 metre height intervals. 5 Origin. 6 Height intervals. 7 Hour and half hour time intervals.

The primary purpose of the sunlight indicators is "to show the number of hours a point.... will be lighted by the sun", and also define the shadows of buildings on the surroundings. The Indicators are for the latitude of Sydney, for each of the following dates: December 22, June 22, and March 22 together with September 22. Each indicator (Fig. 19), has two sets of radial lines indicating the time of day; the curved lines represent the path on a horizontal plane of the shadow of a point above the origin at heights starting from 5 metres, and increasing by intervals of 5 metres. Figs. 20 and 21, taken from the above publication, show how the shadow of a building can be determined and how sunlight hours can be calculated.

The Kuwait Sunshade Calculator, by the author.

This calculator was designed to read the length of the horizontal and vertical shading devices simultaneously without shadow angles. It is composed of a base chart, a transparent overlay and a cursor, (Fig. 22). It is good for latitude 29.3° degrees north. However, our interest here is only with the base chart (Fig. 23), and the possible application of similar charts for the latitudes of Australia. The curved lines represent the path of a point on a horizontal plane located above the "centre point" of the diagram, at a height equal to the "unit length" shown on the chart; that point always casts its shadow on the centre point. The radial lines are the hour lines. For example, the intersection of the hour line of 09.00 hrs and the date line of November 1 gives the location of the point in the horizontal plane which casts its shadow on the centre point on that date and time, the "casting point".

Let us imagine that the centre point is the lower corner of a window, whose height is equal to the "unit length". If that point is to be shaded, the casting point should be a point on a shading device protecting the window. By moving the centre point along the bottom edge of the window, the casting point moves along a line parallel to the window edge. An edge of a shading device is thus drawn up which casts its shadow as a straight line falling on the bottom edge of the window. This shadow chart enables the designer to draw the shading device directly without bothering about the altitude of the sun, its azimuth, the vertical or the horizontal shadow angles. The following examples demonstrate the use of the shadow chart.

Example 1. Refer to Fig. 24 and design a horizontal shading device to completely shade the given window during the period from April 11 to September 1, from sunrise till 16.00 hrs solar time (4 p.m.). Latitude 29.3° north.

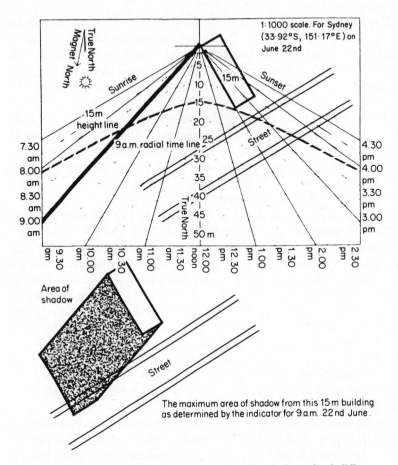

Fig. 20. The PEC sunlight indicators, finding the shadow of a building.

Solution.

(1) The window is drawn, in plan and elevation, on a sheet of tracing paper. Work out the scale such that the height of the window is represented by the "unit length" on the shadow chart.

(2) Through the extreme points A and B of the window draw the north direction (True, not magnetic north).

(3) Place the tracing on the shadow chart. Point A is to coincide with the centre point and the north directions on both the tracing and the chart are also to coincide.

Plan showing two residential blocks of 12m height

No other significant obstructions

Street

12 m

Window sill
height 2 m

True North

12 m

Scale 1 : 1000

The above plan with the indicator superimposed

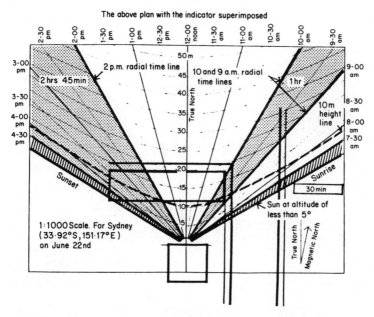

Fig. 21. The PEC sunlight indicators, calculating sunlight hours.

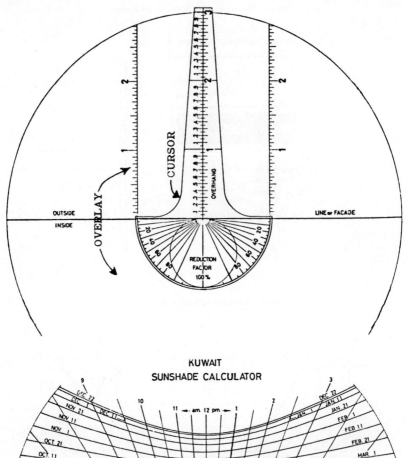

Fig. 22. Transportation overlay and cursor, latitude 29° N, sunshade calculator.

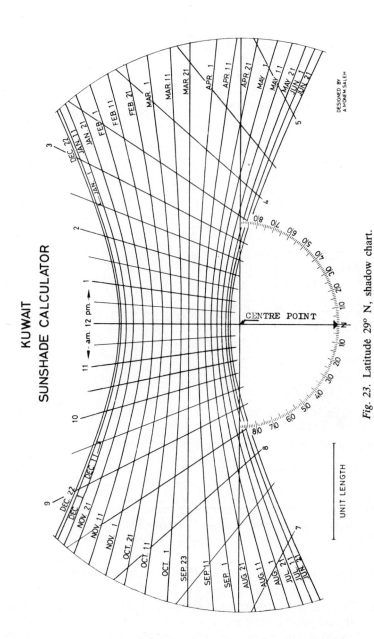

Fig. 23. Latitude 29° N, shadow chart.

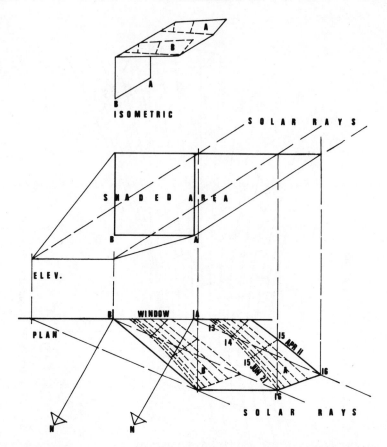

Fig. 24. Latitude 29° N, situation on April 11 and September 1, 16.00 hrs, horizontal
shading device.

(4) Trace all the casting lines (the curved date lines) for the dates
     from April 11 (September 1) through to June 21 and the time
     lines till 16.00 hrs. Ignore those parts of the lines which lie inside
     the building.

(5) Move the tracing so that point B coincides with the centre point
     and repeat steps (3) and (4) above.

(6) Join points representing 16.00 hrs, June 21 for both points A and
     B and join the last point to point B. The extreme lines of the
     construction steps (4), (5) and (6) (the envelope of the

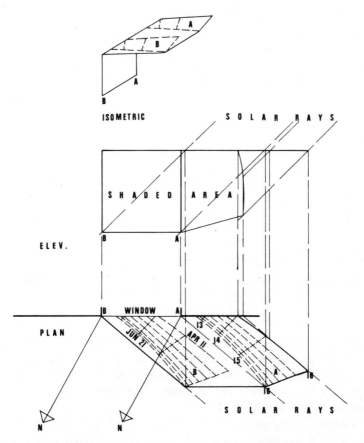

Fig. 25. Latitude 29°N, situation on June 21, 16.00 hrs, horizontal shading device.

construction) give the plan of the required shading device to the scale worked out in step (1).

Fig. 24 shows the shadow cast by the shading device at 16.00 hrs on April 11 and September 1 and Fig. 25 shows the shadow at 16.00 hrs on June 21. Most of the lines shown on both Figs. 24 and 25 are not essential for the drawing of the shading device; they are shown here to clarify the process. What the designer actually needs to draw is shown in Fig. 26.

The solution given by this method is the minimum design for the sunshade. Aesthetics and other practical considerations decide the final

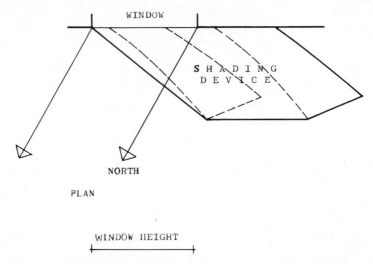

Fig. 26. Latitude 29°N, horizontal shading device to fully shade the window between April 11 and September 1 from sunrise till 16.00 hrs.

design. The shadow at any date and time can easily be drawn by joining the point representing that date and time to the relevant point A or B in plan. This gives the horizontal projection of the solar rays at that time. Projection in elevation is done similarly. The familiar method of casting shadows then follows.

Example 2. Design a shading device of horizontal and vertical elements, for the same situation as in example 1. Protection time is to be extended to 16.30 hrs.

Solution. Refer to Figs. 27 and 28. The same steps are followed as for example 1. It is logical to select point A as the location of the vertical element of the sunbreak. It is stopped in plan by line 16.30—B. A vertical section is needed to show where the outer edge of the vertical break is to change direction. That vertical element of the sun break replaces and does the job of a large part of the horizontal sunbreak.

Example 3. Design a horizontal shading device to shade a circular glass wall during the period of April 11 to September 1, between the hours of 09.00 hrs to 16.30 hrs solar time, latitude 29.3° north.

Solution. Refer to Fig. 29. Locate points 1, 2, 3, 4, 5 and 6 preferably at regular intervals, along the line of the glass wall. For each point repeat the steps followed in example 1. The envelope of the casting path lines, together with the lines joining the end points and the end points of the glass wall, gives the plan of the shading device. 3.3.4 below refers to a check done by the use of "sun machine" on the design of this shading device. The shading device becomes very large towards the west. One can point to several actual examples of circular buildings with horizontal shading devices of uniform projection all around. Such uniform shading devices do not offer uniform protection for all windows around circular or curved facades.

The shadow chart as a shading mask. It can be seen by examining Figs. 24 to 29 that the outline of the horizontal shading device is also the outline of the shading mask for that shading device. The dates and times outside the outline are those when sunlight will strike the "protected" area of the facade in question.

The shadow template. Shadow charts produced on plastic sheets with the date lines slotted at convenient intervals can be used as templates to plot directly the theoretical minimum plans of horizontal shading devices.

3.3.3. Computer Programs

Several computer programs can be used for the design of sunshading devices, including the following programs in the Department of Architectural Science of the University of Sydney.

The sun's position. Several programs giving the sun position in tabular form for any latitude are available.

Sunlight penetration. Program 'RUNSUN'. Input data: Room dimensions (rectangular), orientation, window(s) location and dimensions, eaves projection, date and time (starting hour, finishing hour and time interval). Output: displayed on the screen of the 'Tektronix' terminal and hard copies produced.

The output is in the form of a plot of the plan of the room and the four elevations of the walls with window(s) drawn up and succession of the sunlit areas on the floor and the walls corresponding to the times chosen are plotted. An example of the plot is shown in Fig. 30. The hard copy can be cut and folded into a three-dimensional representation.

Windows and Sunlight Penetration (ref. 12) discusses various aspects of sunlight penetration and its determination and should be of interest to architects.

Shadows of buildings. Program 'RUNSHAD'. Input data: scale of grid, number of corners of the building, after which the cursor is displayed on the screen of the "Tektronix" terminal. This is used by the

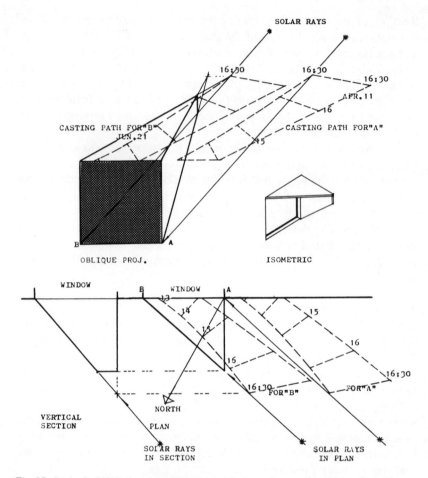

Fig. 27. Latitude 29°N, situation on June 21, 16.30 hrs. Horizontal and vertical shading devices.

user to locate the building corners on the grid. Then the user supplies data concerning the date, the first hour and the last hour and the time step.

The shadow of the building is then plotted, according to its height, at the first hour; the time is increased and the shadow at the new time is plotted, and so on, until the shadow at the last hour is plotted. Fig. 31 illustrates an example of a shadow plot.

The programs referred to in 3.3.3. are available for general use.

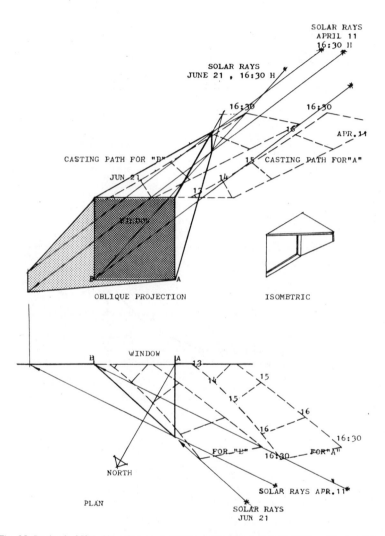

Fig. 28. Latitude 29°N. Situation on April 11 and September 1, 16.30 hrs., Horizontal and vertical shading devices.

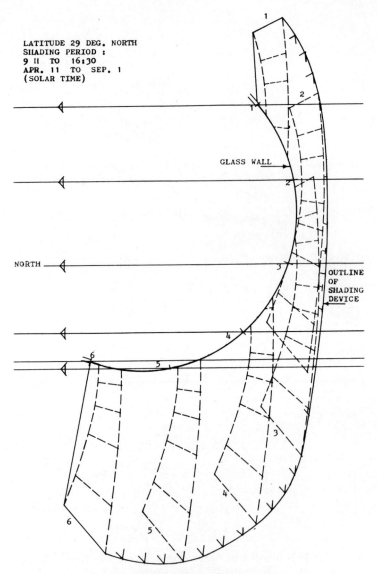

LATITUDE 29 DEG. NORTH
SHADING PERIOD :
9 11 TO 16:30
APR. 11 TO SEP. 1
(SOLAR TIME)

GLASS WALL

NORTH

OUTLINE
OF
SHADING
DEVICE

Fig. 29. Plan of a horizontal shading device for a curved glass wall.

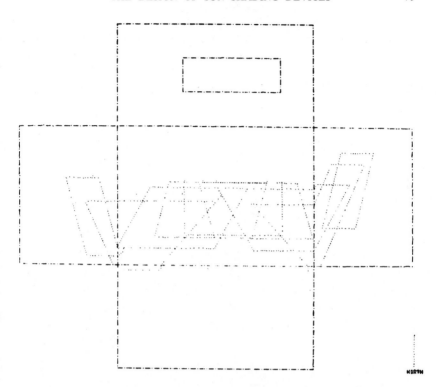

Fig. 30. Sunlight penetration, computer plot, program 'RUNSUN', (Department of Architectural Science, University of Sydney).

3.3.4. Sun Machines

Shadows and sunlight penetration on models can be observed directly. The location of proposed buildings on the site can be adjusted and the effect of the adjustment readily assessed. Photographic records can be made if needed.

In any sun machine there is a platform on which the model is placed and there is a light source simulating the sun. The variables are the latitude of the location of the building, the date and the time. Different machines handle these variables differently.

For example, in the heliodon of Princeton University (Ref. 2), the platform holding the model is tilted for the latitude adjustment and rotated for the time adjustment; the light source is moved up and down

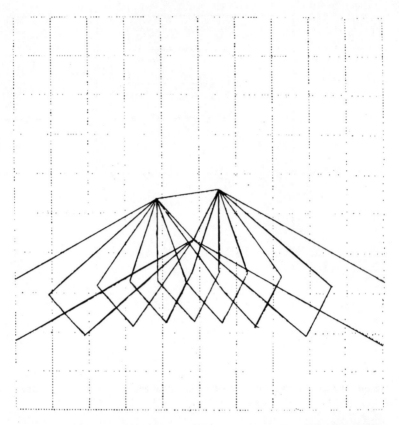

Fig. 31. Shadow of a triangular building, computer plot, Program 'RUNSHAD', (Department of Architectural Science, University of Sydney).

on a vertical guide for the date (declination) adjustment. This heliodon was modelled on the heliodon of the Building Research Station in England.

In the solarscope of the Experimental Building Station at Sydney (Ref. 14), Fig 32, the model always remains horizontal, whereas the sun which is simulated by a light shining on a mirror, rotated about the model. By reflecting the light from the mirror the ray divergence is minimised.

The heliodon of the Department of Architectural Science, University of Sydney, has a fixed light and a platform which rotates along a horizontal axis. The model which can be 1 metre square and 0.3 to 0.4

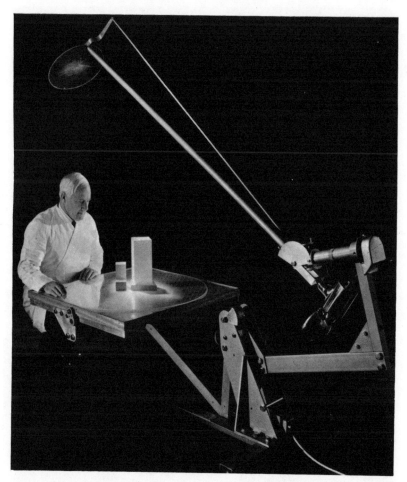

Fig. 32. The solarscope of the Experimental Building Station.

metre high, is bolted to the platform and rotated to the correct wall solar azimuth (see 3.3.1). The solar tables are consulted and the platform is tilted to the correct solar altitude.

Figs. 33, 34 and 35 show some examples studied by the use of the heliodon. Fig. 33 shows the shadow cast by an existing building on a proposed one. Fig. 34 shows a proposed tall building casting its shadow on nearby buildings. It was possible to adjust the position of the new building on the model to interfere as little as possible with the other

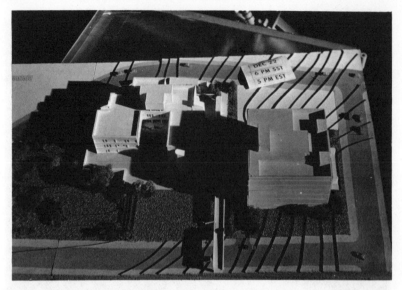

Fig. 33. Shadow study: existing building casting its shadow on a proposed building, using the heliodon of the Department of Architectural Science, University of Sydney.

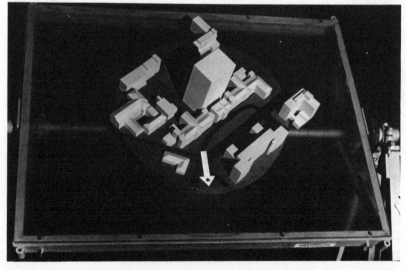

Fig. 34. Shadow study: position of proposed tall building adjusted to interfere as little as possible with existing buildings, using the heliodon of the Department of Architectural Science, University of Sydney.

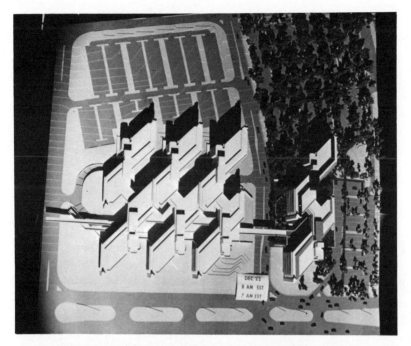

Fig. 35. Shadow study: self shading of a proposed building complex, using the heliodon of the Department of Architectural Science, University of Sydney.

buildings. Fig. 35 illustrates a study of the self-shading effect of a building complex.

"Sun machines" are also useful for the study of shading devices of complex geometrical shapes such as sun grills.

The shade dial. The study of shading on models can also be done with the sun itself as the light source (Ref. 2). This eliminates the problem of ray divergence. To position the model for a particular situation simulating the conditions of a particular latitude, date and time, the aid of a "shade dial" is needed. The model and the shade dial are put on the same table which is rotated and tilted till the shadow of the ball of the shade dial falls on the required date and time.

Checking of the shadow template by the use of sun machines. The shadow template (see 3.3.2), was checked by the use of the solarscope of the Experimental station and the heliodon of Sydney University. For this purpose, a model of the building with the circular wall of example 3 (3.3.2) was constructed. The photographs (Fig. 36) illustrate that study

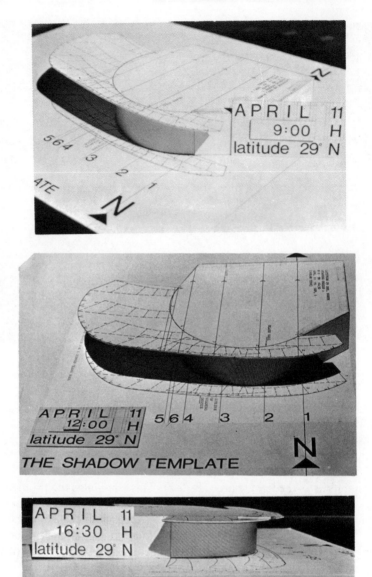

Fig. 36. Shading device for a circular wall: model checking on the
heliodon of Sydney University.

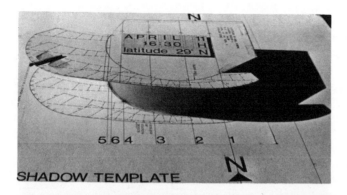

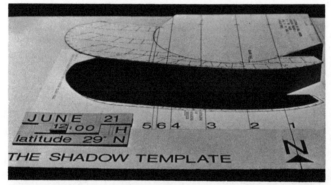

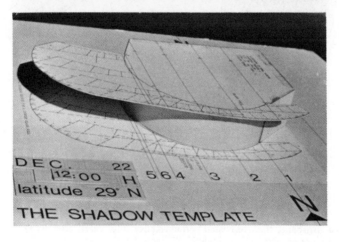

Fig. 36—cont.

which demonstrated that the shading device offers the required protection for the curved glass wall.

3.3.5. The "Combined" Sun Path Diagrams

The combined overheated period-sunpath diagrams ("combined diagrams" for short) are obtained by plotting the overheated periods, as shown by the tables (Fig. 4) on the sunpath diagram as shown in Fig. 9. Fig. 37b shows the combined diagram for Sydney. The data from the

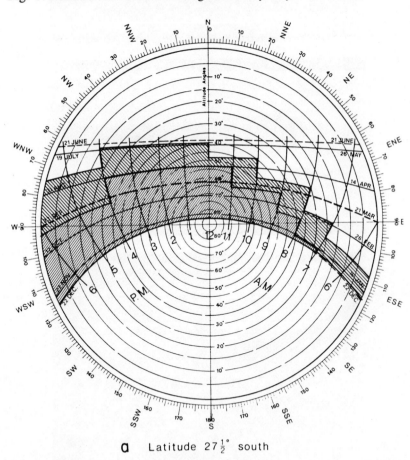

α　　Latitude 27½° south

Fig. 37a. Brisbane: the overheated period. Above solar chart, after R. O. Phillips, is taken to represent Brisbane, latitude 27.5° South. On the chart is added the overheated period, close hatching: September 1 till December 22 approximately, wide hatching: December 22 till June 1 approximately. Shading line taken as 21° Celsius.

table (Fig. 4) for Sydney are plotted on the solar chart for latitude 35°
south, considered close enough to that of Sydney. The combined
diagram for Sydney is more informative since, not only the sun's
positions are given but also the times in which shading is needed. It is
evident that two cities on the same latitude have the same solar chart (if
solar time is used) but have different combined diagrams since these
depend upon the record of the shade temperature for each city.

Symmetry of the solar positions and the combined diagrams. If one

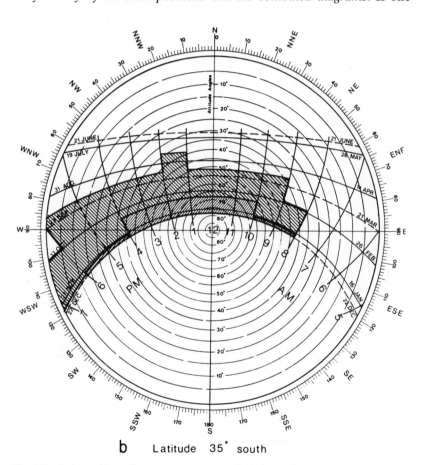

b Latitude 35° south

Fig. 37b. Sydney: the overheated period. Above solar chart, after R. O. Phillips, is taken
to represent Sydney, latitude 33.9° South. On the chart is added the overheated period,
close hatching: November 1 till December 22 approximately, wide hatching: December 22
till April 30 approximately. Shading line taken as 21° Celsius.

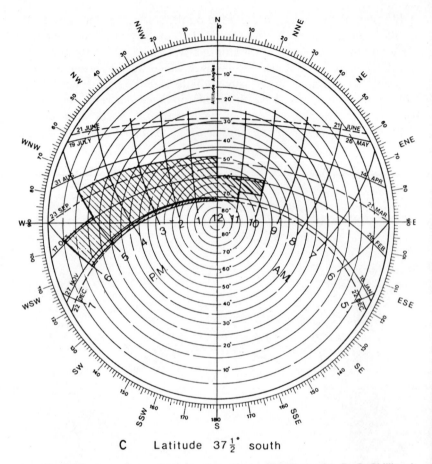

C   Latitude $37\frac{1}{2}°$ south

Fig. 37c. Melbourne: the overheated period. Above solar chart, after R. O. Phillips, is taken to represent Melbourne, latitude 37.8° South. On the chart is added the overheated period, close hatching: December 1 till December 22 approximately, wide hatching: December 22 till March 31 approximately.

examines any solar chart based on solar time, say the one shown in Fig. 9, one notices that the sun position is symmetrical with respect to the summer and winter solstice. Each sunpath line represents two conjugate dates, it follows that a fixed shading device has the same performance on the conjugate dates.

Looking at the temperature tables (Fig. 4) one sees that the overheated periods are not precisely symmetrical. The overheated periods are roughly symmetrical around the month of January. This shift of positions of symmetry from December 22 for the solar positions and a month or more later for the overheated period creates problems for fixed shading devices.

If we look again at the combined diagram for Sydney, (Fig. 37), and take the month of April, we see that a device which shades a window at 13.00 hrs and 14.00 hrs on April 14 automatically cuts the solar rays at the same time on August 31, when insolation is needed, the mean temperatures at 13.00 hrs and 14.00 hrs during August being 16.7° and 16.8°C (21.2°C and 21.1°C in April).

Similarly the device gives shading from 09.00 hrs till sunset on March 21, when the mean shade temperature ranges between 21.2°C to 23.4°C, and automatically gives shading at the same times on September 23 when the temperatures range between 15.3° and 18.7°C, i.e. when shading is not needed (refer to table in Fig. 3 for the mean hourly shade temperatures for Sydney and to 3.1.1 for the definition of 21°C as the limiting temperature for shading). On the table in Fig. 3 for Sydney, the full line encloses the overheated period while the dotted line shows the period when automatic unrequired shading has to be accepted.

Limitations of fixed shading devices. Despite our ability to design shading devices with a reasonable degree of accuracy, the devices we design stop short of achieving the ideal goal to insolate our building during the underheated periods and shade it during the overheated periods. The answer may lie in movable shading devices. However, the fixed shading devices have an advantage from the practical point of view and one has to strike a compromise: if priority is given to shading, and one knows that it is easier and cheaper to heat than to cool, then one elects to shade during the whole of the overheated period, and suffer some loss of insolation during parts of the underheated period.

One can go most of the way, but not all the way, towards shading through the whole of the overheated period. To illustrate this, one can refer to the shadow chart for latitude 29° north (Fig. 38). On the shadow chart is drawn the shading mask for the given set of ambient air temperatures shown in the table in Fig. 39 (with 21°C taken as the limiting temperature). To shade during the month of May through till June 21 gives the shading mask shown by the closely hatched area on the chart, this means automatic shading from June 21 till August 11. To shade for the rest of the overheated period till and including the month of October, we get the shading mask defined by the dotted line on the shadow chart. For a window, 1 metre high and facing south, we need a

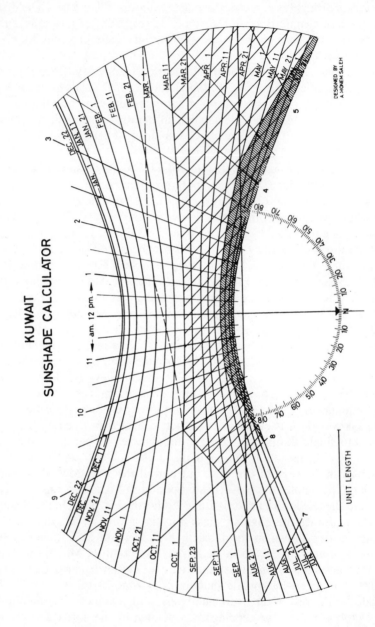

Fig. 38. Latitude 29° North, 21°C shading mask.

HR··MONTH	DEC	JAN	FEB	MAR	APR	MAY	JUN	JUL	AUG	SEP	OCT	NOV
01·········	11·1	10·0	11·2	12·9	15·0	17·1	18·7	20·3	20·1	19·1	16·2	13·6
02·········	10·7	9·4	10·6	12·5	14·6	16·8	18·4	19·8	19·8	18·9	15·8	13·4
03·········	10·4	9·2	10·2	12·1	14·3	16·6	18·1	19·6	19·4	18·7	15·6	13·1
04·········	10·2	8·8	9·9	11·7	14·0	16·2	17·8	19·4	19·2	18·3	15·1	12·6
05·········	10·0	8·6	9·7	11·4	13·7	16·1	17·7	19·2	19·1	18·2	14·9	12·3
06·········	9·8	8·4	9·4	11·2	13·8	16·5	18·2	19·5	19·0	17·9	14·7	12·1
07·········	9·7	8·3	9·4	11·6	14·8	17·8	19·6	20·7	19·8	18·4	14·9	12·1
08·········	10·2	9·1	10·6	13·1	16·7	19·3	21·0	21·9	21·2	19·6	16·2	12·7
09·········	11·6	10·5	12·4	15·3	18·2	20·6	22·2	23·1	22·7	21·2	17·6	14·4
10·········	12·8	11·9	14·1	17·2	19·2	21·3	22·8	23·8	23·5	22·4	18·8	15·2
11·········	14·1	13·5	15·4	18·4	19·9	21·8	23·3	24·2	24·1	22·9	20·3	17·4
12·········	15·6	15·0	16·2	18·7	20·2	22·2	23·4	24·4	24·5	23·4	20·7	18·3
13·········	16·1	15·4	16·7	18·7	20·2	22·0	23·5	24·3	24·6	23·4	21·2	18·7
14·········	16·3	15·6	16·8	18·6	20·2	21·6	23·3	24·3	24·5	23·4	21·1	18·7
15·········	16·2	15·6	16·6	18·6	19·9	21·6	22·9	24·1	24·2	23·1	20·6	18·6
16·········	15·4	15·1	15·9	17·5	19·2	20·4	22·6	23·7	23·6	22·5	20·0	17·9
17·········	14·8	14·1	15·2	16·9	18·6	19·7	22·1	23·1	23·1	21·9	19·5	17·2
18·········	14·2	13·5	14·5	16·2	17·9	19·1	21·6	22·6	22·3	21·4	18·9	16·6
19·········	13·7	12·8	13·7	15·8	17·3	18·4	20·9	21·9	21·9	20·9	18·5	16·2
20·········	13·2	12·3	13·4	15·4	17·1	18·3	20·3	21·5	21·6	20·8	18·2	15·8
21·········	12·8	11·8	12·9	15·0	16·8	18·1	20·2	21·2	21·3	20·6	17·8	15·4
22·········	12·3	11·1	12·4	14·6	16·2	17·7	19·9	20·9	21·1	20·3	17·5	14·9
23·········	11·8	10·6	11·8	13·9	16·1	17·4	19·6	20·7	20·7	19·9	16·9	14·3
24·········	11·4	10·2	11·4	13·5	15·6		19·2	20·4	20·3	19·6	16·5	13·9

Fig. 39. Mean monthly temperatures for a city, latitude 29° North.

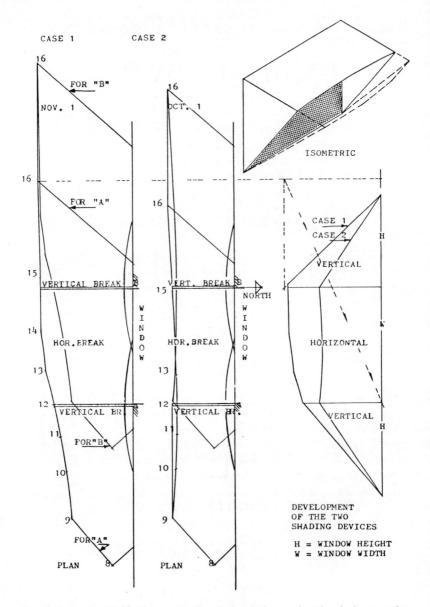

Fig. 40. Latitude 29° North, two shading device designs, using the shadow template.

horizontal shading device projecting about 1 metre to give protection till the end of October (since the dotted line represents the edge of the shading device, refer to 3.3.2).

The table of temperatures (Fig. 39) shows that during October the temperature rises to 21.2°C and 21.1°C for 13.00 hrs and 14.00 hrs only, and we decide to limit the shading till the end of September. This gives the shading mask defined by the widely hatched area on the chart, requiring a horizontal shade projecting by about 0.75 metre only. We exercise our judgement, and decide to shade till the end of September and no more. This not only reduces the cost of the shading device, but also allows the sun to partially strike the facade during February and March when it is needed (north latitude).

One last example illustrates the above approach. Fig. 40 shows as an opening 1.25 × 1.00 metres (width × height) facing true south, 29° north latitude. The shadow chart for that latitude (Fig. 23) is used to draw the horizontal shading device to protect the window till 16.00 hrs. (The ambient air temperatures for the location are those shown in Fig. 39.) The design is then modified to include vertical sunbreaks together with part of the horizontal sunbreak to achieve reasonable dimensions for the shading device.

Two cases are investigated. Case 1 has the protection period between 13.00 hrs and 14.00 hrs on February 11 through to 08.00 hrs and 16.00 hrs on June 21 through to 13.00 hrs and 14.00 hrs on November 1. The period of protection is reduced in Case 2 to start from 09.00 hrs to 16.00 hrs on March 11 and ends on the same hours on October 1. Looking at the temperature table (Fig. 39), one can see that by ignoring the short overheated couple of hours for October, one is not sacrificing too much in terms of protection and yet the advantages gained are: (1) more economical design as can be seen from the developed surface of each design in Fig. 40. (2) Insolation is allowed during the underheated month of February.

3.4. CONCLUSIONS

The shadow chart (or shadow template) can be used to draw up the required shading device directly. The template indicates the periods when complete shading is achieved. The shadow template can be used to draw the shadow of the shading device at different times. The template can be used to design alternative vertical shading elements replacing parts of the horizontal shading device and comparison can be made between the alternatives. The template gives the correct (minimum) shape of the shading device. Shading devices of larger dimensions cut off the needed insolation during the underheated period, apart from being uneconomical materials wise.

It is intended to produce shadow charts for the various latitudes of Australia.

REFERENCES

1. Phillips, R. O., *Sunshine and Shade in Australia,* fourth edition, EBS Bulletin No. 8, AGPS, Sydney, 1975.
2. Olgyay, A. and Olgyay, C. *Solar Control and Shading Devices,* Princeton University Press, Princeton N.J., 1976.
3. Foley, J. C., *A Study at Average Hourly Values of Temperature, Relative Humidity and Saturation Deficit in the Australian Region from Records of Capital City Bureaux,* Bulletin No. 35, Bureau of Meteorology, Melbourne, 1945.
4. *The Nautical Almanac for the Year 1971,* Naval Observatory, Government Printing Office, Washington D.C., 1969.
5. *Handbook of Fundamentals,* second edition, ASHRAE (American Society of Heating, Refrigeration and Air-Conditioning Engineers), New York, 1968.
6. Callender, J. H., *Time-Saver Standards for Architectural Design Data,* fifth edition, McGraw-Hill, New York, 1974.
7. Spencer, J. W., 'Representation of the Position of the Sun,' *Search,* Vol. 2, No. 5.
8. Ramsey, C. H. and Sleeper, H. R. *Architectural Graphic Standards,* fifth edition, John Wiley, New York, 1966.
9. *Control of Sunlight Penetration,* Department of Labor and Immigration, Physical Working Environment Branch (Industrial Data Sheets—A2), AGPS, Sydney, 1975.
10. *Sun Angle Calculator,* Libbey-Owens-Ford Company, Toledo, Ohio, 1974.
11. Watts, S. and Gunn, B., *Sunlight Indicators,* Technical Bulletin No. 13, N.S.W. Planning and Environment Commission, Sydney, 1978.
12. Smith, P. R., *Windows and Sunlight Penetration,* (Physical Environment Report, PR5), Department of Architectural Science, University of Sydney, Sydney, 1973.
13. *Control of Sun Penetration,* Commonwealth Experimental Building Station, RF No. 34, Sydney, 1971.

4

Making the Best Use of Daylight in Buildings

R. O. PHILLIPS

Faculty of Architecture, University of New South Wales, Australia

4.1. INTRODUCTION

With the present interest in the need to conserve energy one aspect which appears to have received little attention in Australia is the possibility of conserving electricity by the greater use of daylight in buildings. The waste of artificial light at times when the windows would be capable of providing the required illuminance can be observed daily in any city.

There are a number of reasons for this situation. Perhaps the most important is that current daylight design methods are based on attempting to provide adequate natural light at virtually all normal working hours; in most multi-storey buildings this is not possible in terms of practical design. This paper attempts to show that better use of daylight might be achieved by the balanced use of supplementary artificial lighting at times and places where the natural lighting is inadequate with consequent cost and energy savings. Another factor is that controls used to exclude direct sunlight frequently reduce the availability of light from the sky to such an extent that artificial lighting becomes essential. It is suggested that it may be possible to exclude direct sun from working areas, but to make satisfactory use of re-directed sunlight.

Before considering these possibilities, a survey is presented of the nature and availability of daylight. In order to keep the presentation free of the relevant mathematical background, all equations have been confined to an appendix.

4.2. LIGHT AND HEAT ENERGY

Light is radiant energy at those wave-lengths which evoke the sensation of vision within the human eye; for practical purposes it may be considered to comprise the range from about 400 to 750 nanometres.

It must be remembered that *all* radiation, whether visible or not, is ultimately converted to heat when retained within the interior of a building. In fact the lighting installed within a room often forms a large part of the summer cooling load to be removed by an air-conditioning system. Hence the most desirable light source is that which produces the greatest amount of light for a given energy input; this is expressed in terms of "luminous efficacy", in lumens per watt (lm/W).

It may not be generally realized that daylight (whether sunlight or skylight) is a highly desirable source from this viewpoint. Values derived from figures given by Moon (Ref. 1) for sunlight show a range of 102–116 lm/W, while measured values for total daylight near London (Ref. 2, p. 27) vary between 110 and 134 lm/W. In contrast, typical values for fluorescent lamps (including the essential control gear) are about 50–60 lm/W; incandescent lamps in common sizes vary between about 10–15 lm/W.

Thus a given amount of light is produced by nature with no more than one-half of the associated total energy input of the artificial light sources used within buildings.

4.3. AVAILABILITY OF DAYLIGHT

4.3.1. Sunlight and Skylight

In the study of daylighting it is conventional to regard the "sky" as a hemisphere surrounding the observer and delimited by his horizontal plane. The sun is the origin of all daylight, but its light is diffused and scattered by the atmosphere, so that the whole sky becomes luminous and it is the resulting "skylight" which becomes the most common source of daylight within buildings.

The level of daylight available from the sun or sky is usually expressed as the total illuminance received on an unobstructed horizontal plane. In the case of direct sunlight this is predictable within fairly close limits, depending primarily on the sun's altitude and secondarily upon the clarity of the atmosphere. Under a clear (cloudless) sky, the level of skylight depends upon the same factors, but is more variable than direct sunlight. Typical values given by Elvegard and Sjostedt (Ref. 3), based on extensive measurement in Scandinavia, are shown on Fig. 1, derived from eqns. (1), (2) and (3).

When the sky is partly or wholly cloud-covered, the level of available skylight varies widely. In general, scattered white clouds or thin cloud layers produce higher levels than the clear sky, whilst a heavy, dense overcast produces lower levels. Fig. 2 shows, in firm line, results for

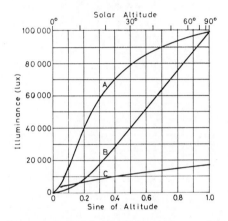

Fig. 1. Illuminance from sun on normal plane (A), and from sun (B) and clear sky (C) on horizontal plane (Ref. 3.).

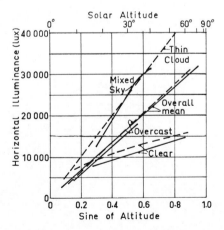

Fig. 2. Horizontal illuminance from various skies. Full-line curves for Paris (Ref. 4.), broken lines for Scandinavia (Ref. 31).

Paris given by Fournol (Ref. 4) for clear, overcast and mixed skies, together with the overall mean. The broken lines show values based on relationships given by Elvegard and Sjostedt—eqns. (3), (4) and (5).

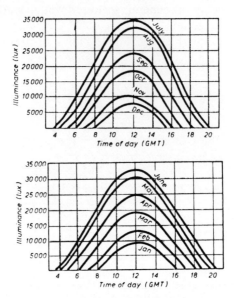

Fig. 3. Average horizontal illuminances for London by month and time of day (Ref. 2.).

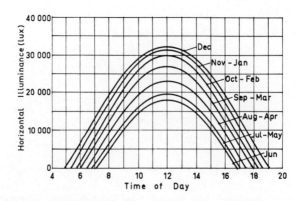

Fig. 4. Estimated horizontal illuminances for Sydney by month and time of day.

On this graph, the line for the overall mean has the equation:

$$E_h = 33\ 000 \times \sin h$$

where E_h=total horizontal illuminance in lux,
   h=altitude of the sun.

Figure 3 (reproduced from Ref. 2) shows monthly averages of horizontal illuminance recorded at Teddington, near London. Values calculated from the above equation at noon for the months of March, June, September and December are approximately 19 400, 29 100, 21 900 and 8500 lux respectively. It can be seen that the agreement is generally quite good. The equation has also been used to estimate values for Sydney (latitude 34°S). The results are presented on Fig. 4.

4.3.2. Frequency of Skylight Levels

Whilst values of average illuminance from the sky are of considerable interest, daylight design is commonly based on the selection of a level of skylight which will be available as a minimum with some specified frequency, such as 90% of working hours. Unfortunately, adequate data of this type is not readily available.

One such set of data, due to Fournol (Ref. 1), appears on Fig. 5, which shows the percentage frequency at which the measured skylight illuminance in Paris falls below the values indicated, at different solar altitudes. Dresler (Ref. 5) has used this data to estimate the frequency of different levels of skylight at various latitudes within normal office hours of 09.00 to 17.00 hrs, as shown on Fig. 6.

Figure 7 presents an analysis of measurements in Belgium by Dogniaux (Ref. 6), which shows the frequency at which the indicated

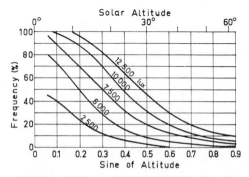

Fig. 5. Frequency at which horizontal illuminance falls *below* given values for different solar altitudes in Paris (Ref. 4)

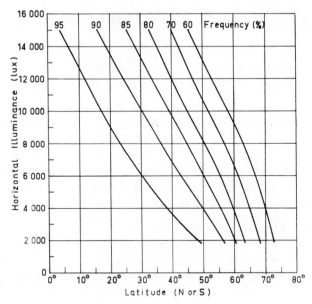

Fig. 6. Estimated frequencies at which horizontal illuminance *exceeds* given values at different latitudes (Ref. 5.).

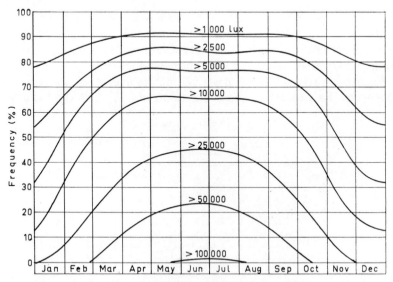

Fig. 7. Frequency at which given horizontal illuminances are exceeded throughout the year in Belgium (Ref. 6.).

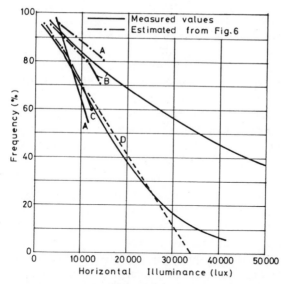

Fig. 8. Frequency at which measured and estimated horizontal illuminations exceed given values at Sydney (lines A), Ann Arbor (lines B) and London (lines C). Line D assumed by Crisp and Hunt (Refs. 15, 16).

levels are exceeded for each month of the year. Since these values apparently apply to all daylight hours from sunrise to sunset, they would tend to under-estimate the frequencies during working hours during the summer months.

A comparison of several sets of data is presented on Fig. 8, which shows the percentage frequency with which the given levels of skylight are exceeded. The full line curves represent measured values during working hours, as follows:

Curve A. Sydney, Australia, latitude 34°S, (Ref. 7)
Curve B. Ann Arbor, Michigan, latitude 42°N, (Ref. 8)
Curve C. London, England, latitude 51.5°N, (Ref. 9)
Line D. Assumed by Crisp (Ref. 15) for calculations.

The broken line curves on the graph represent values taken from Fig. 6 for the appropriate latitudes. It can be seen that the two curves for each of cases B and C agree quite well within the limits shown, but that there is a large and unexplained divergence for case A (Sydney).

4.3.3. Luminance Distribution of the Sky

Early studies in daylight design were based on the assumption that the luminance of an overcast sky was approximately uniform in all directions. Under such a sky the total horizontal illuminance in lux is numerically equal to its luminance in apostilb. Although such skies probably never occur in practice, the above relationship serves as a useful reference base for calculation and comparison.

With the advent of modern photocells and recording equipment it was soon found that real skies departed markedly from the assumed uniform luminance distribution. Moon and Spencer (Ref. 10) in 1942 were the first to develop design methods based on a non-uniform sky and presented a simple relationship describing the luminance distribution of the overcast sky; this has since been adopted internationally as the "Standard CIE Overcast Sky", and is widely used for daylight design. It has the property that the luminance at the zenith is three times that at the horizon, as given by eqns. (6)–(9). The contours of equal luminance (asb) relative to the total horizontal illuminance (lux) are shown on Fig. 9.

More recently it has been found that the luminance distribution of the clear sky can also be described mathematically, the accepted relationship due to Kittler (Ref. 11), being given by eqn. (10). Here, no single set of contours applies, since the pattern changes with the altitude of the sun, but Fig. 10 illustrates a typical distribution with a solar

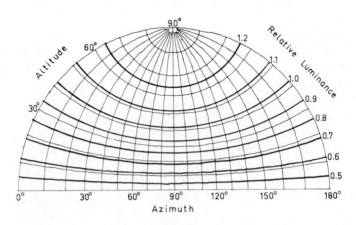

Fig. 9. Contours of equal luminance (asb) relative to horizontal illuminance (lux) for CIE overcast sky—eqn. (8).

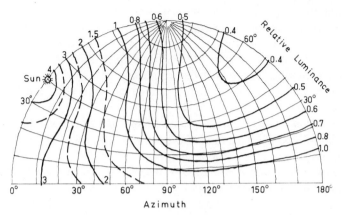

Azimuth

Fig. 10. Contours of equal luminance (asb) relative to horizontal illuminance (lux) for clear sky with sun at 40° altitude—eqn. (10).

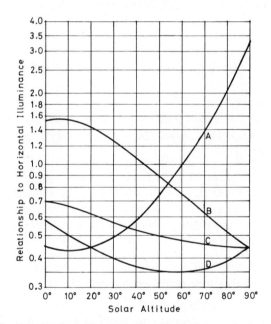

Solar Altitude

Fig. 11. Relationships for clear skies at all solar altitudes between horizontal illuminance and

A: zenith luminance (asb).
B: vertical illuminance facing sun (sky only).
C: vertical illuminance at 90° to sun.
D: vertical illuminance at 180° to sun.

altitude of 40°. The brightest part of the sky adjoins the sun, the luminance generally decreasing as the azimuth of a sky-zone moves away from the sun's position. At azimuths from about 120° to 180° the contours are almost constant with altitude up to about 45° and have the highest luminance at the horizon, *decreasing* at higher altitudes up to a minimum value at a great-circle distance of some 90° from the sun's position.

Thus it can be seen that for orientations approximately 180° from the sun, the luminance pattern of the clear sky essentially reverses that of the overcast sky. Hence the assumption of a uniform distribution may be regarded as an approximation to the average of the two conditions.

Equation (10) is expressed in terms of the zenith luminance, which is not generally available. The equation has therefore been numerically integrated by computer for all solar altitudes to find resulting horizontal and vertical illuminances. Fig. 11 shows the results, where all values are given as ratios of the horizontal illuminance, so that they can be used in conjunction with the normal published data for the latter.

4.4. CONVENTIONAL DAYLIGHT DESIGN

4.4.1. The Daylight Factor

It is conventional in most countries outside America to express the level of skylight illuminance within buildings in terms of the "daylight factor", defined as follows:

The ratio of the daylight illuminance at a point on a given plane due to the light received directly or indirectly from a sky of assumed or known luminance distribution, to the illuminance on a horizontal plane due to an unobstructed hemisphere of this sky. Direct sunlight is excluded from both values of illuminance.

Daylight factors are commonly related to a horizontal working plane at table level, but can also apply to any sloping or vertical plane.

A large variety of methods for the calculation of daylight factors are available, those most commonly used being described in Ref. 2. The usual practice is to determine values at a number of reference points within the room of interest. If these values are then multiplied by an appropriate figure of total external illuminance, the results are the anticipated illuminances at the points.

4.4.2. Design for Daylight
The usual method for designing a building for daylight is essentially as follows:

(a) From an appropriate Lighting Code select the recommended illuminance level for the type of building and visual task (say 500 lux).

(b) Determine a value for the "design sky" in terms of the total external illuminance available for some percentage of working hours (say 5000 lux).

(c) Determine the resulting required daylight factor (%) as (a/b) × 100. For the above values, this is 10%.

(d) After making allowances for dirt on glass, obstruction by window framing etc., select an arrangement of windows or rooflights which will produce the required daylight factor.

The key factor in this procedure is the selection of a value for the "design sky". In the UK this has become a standard overcast sky providing an outdoor illuminance of 5000 lux which "represents average conditions in England over the greater part of winter days, over long periods in late autumn and early spring.... and on wet days in summer" (Ref. 2, p. 2).

The result is that, when this value is selected for design, "most buildings cannot be adequately lit by daylight alone", since it is not practicable to provide the required daylight factor, determined as above. And yet examination of Fig. 3 indicates that for the five-month period from April to August, the average outdoor illuminance mostly exceeds 20 000 lux between 09.00 and 15.00 hrs, and is still at least 10 000 lux until 17.00 hrs. If the 20 000 figure is selected for design, the required daylight factor becomes 2.5%, which can often be provided without much difficulty. At times when the external illuminance drops, interior levels may be supplemented by artificial light, as considered in the next sections.

4.5. MIXED NATURAL AND ARTIFICIAL LIGHT

4.5.1. Psali
In 1959 Hopkinson and Longmore (Ref. 12) introduced the concept of "permanent supplementary artificial lighting of interiors" (psali). This was intended for use in deep rooms, where the rear of the room could

not be adequately lit by daylight. It was proposed that artificial light should be used at all times to illuminate the rear portions. A good deal of attention was directed to selecting a level of light which would blend satisfactorily with the daylit parts. It was found that this was commonly higher than that required at night, so that a separate installation at a lower level was proposed for night-time use.

4.5.2. Non-permanent Supplementary Lighting

A somewhat different concept was used in 1937 by McDermott (Ref. 13) in an experimental investigation. In an office housing eighteen typists each table was provided with supplementary lighting in the form of an individually switched desk-lamp. An automatic recording system registered the level of daylight at which each typist found it necessary to switch on the lamp. It is interesting to note that the average daylight level at which this occurred was approximately 50 lux! An interesting observation made during this study was that "a number of the typists frequently switched on their lamps as soon as they arrived in the morning, although after the lamps had been switched off for the lunch interval, the same typists would work on well into the afternoon, that is until the daylight was steadily decreasing in amount, before using their lamps again".

There is little doubt that similar observations could be made in many buildings in which the daylight is adequate during much of the day. The lights are switched on in the morning, when daylight may be insufficient, but are then left on for the remainder of the day. The remedy for this situation would seem to be photo-electric monitoring of daylight levels with automatic switching-off or dimming at appropriate times, as discussed in the next section.

In this connection, during a study of factory lighting with P. Manning (Ref. 14), the owner of one factory visited, who was very conscious of lighting costs, reported that he used to turn off the lights when he judged the daylight to be adequate; this frequently resulted in complaints from the workers. However, when he installed a photocell to monitor the daylight and a switch to turn the lights on or off at a pre-determined daylight level, the complaints ceased and he made considerable savings.

4.5.3. Automatic Control

More recently Crisp (Ref. 15) and Hunt (Ref. 16) have investigated the feasibility of automatically controlling the level of supplementary artificial lighting by either on-off switching or by dimming of the lights. The basis of this proposal is that a building might be designed to have a daylight factor such that a given level of illuminance would be provided by daylight when the exterior illuminance was at some reasonable level, such as 15 000 to 20 000 lux. The exterior illuminance would be monitored and, when it rose above the design value, the artificial lighting would be automatically switched off; when it fell below the design value the lights would either be switched fully on, or under control of dimmers would be brought up to a level sufficient to provide the required total interior illuminance by a combination of natural and artificial lighting. The relevant equations for electricity savings are given in Appendix 1.

Crisp provides a cost-benefit analysis for several typical buildings, using estimated costs for the dimming equipment and electricity charges. The principal results are given in Table 1 below for two buildings: a traditional classroom with side windows and a small factory with rooflights. In this analysis, both simple on-off switching and dimmer control are considered. Electricity consumption if only the artificial light were used is compared with expected values under automatic control and the resulting annual saving is shown. This is then

TABLE 1.
ANALYSIS OF COSTS AND SAVINGS WITH
LIGHTING CONTROLS

	Classroom		Factory	
Design parameters				
Design interior illuminance (lux)	300		500	
Assumed exterior illuminance (lux)	15 000		20 000	
Required daylight factor (%)	2·0		2·5	
Number of 65 W lamps	50		300	
Savings				
Type of control	*On-off*	*Dimmer*	*On-off*	*Dimmer*
Electricity used p.a. (kWh)				
Without daylight	5600	5600	52 000	52 000
With controls in use	2471	1464	30 575	17 985
Savings with controls	3129	4136	21 425	34 015
Costs				
Cost saving p.a. (£)	62	82	424	680
Present value of savings (£)*	472	624	3225	5172
Cost of controls (new bldg.)	60	475	310	1650
Cost of controls (old bldg.)	460	875	2710	4050

*Discounted at 10% p.a. over 15 years, with no increase in power costs.

reduced to a present value, discounted over 15 years, with no increase in power charges. Estimated capital costs of the control gear are given both for a new building and for the necessary installation costs in modifying an existing building. In these two buildings, the present value of the savings in most cases exceeds the estimated capital costs of the control gear, making the proposal attractive to a building owner. In some other cases, only discounting over a longer period and/or assuming increases in power charges produce favourable financial results. However, in any case it can be seen that substantial savings in energy consumption always occur. Hunt (Ref. 16) considers more elaborate systems, where banks of lighting at the front, centre and rear of a room might be separately controlled, so that only those actually needed to supplement the daylight in a given zone would be switched on.

4.6. CONTROL AND USE OF SUNLIGHT

It is generally accepted that direct sunlight should be excluded from working areas because of the intolerable glare which could be created. This requirement is separate from the heating effect which, though undesirable in summer, can be useful in winter.

However, it is possible that sunlight can usefully augment sky light if properly controlled. Hopkinson and Petherbridge (Ref. 17) have shown that in sunny climates, usually tropical, sunlight reflected from the ground and thence from the ceiling can provide adequate daylight.

Another approach is to arrange that sunlight incident on the window be re-directed on to a white ceiling from which it is reflected to the work-plane. If the sunlight can be made to reach the ceiling near the rear of the room, the reflected light will be received where it is most needed. Most schemes along these lines propose that the window wall should have a vision strip finishing some 2 metres above the floor, protected by a projecting hood with above it a section of window incorporating some means of re-directing sunlight on to the ceiling.

Rosenfeld (Ref. 18), under the name of "beam daylighting", has proposed the use of special venetian blinds with silvered upper surfaces, the slope of the slats being adjusted to reflected incident sun towards the rear of the ceiling. The vertical spacing of the slats would require to be such that no direct sun penetrated between them to the work-plane. This appears to be a practical difficulty and his paper includes a diagram showing different spacings for summer and winter. An earlier proposal for the upper window section was the use of special glass blocks incorporating prismatic faces in their interior, made by Pittsburgh-Corning (Ref. 19). Fig. 12 shows measured values in a typical school classroom with this arrangement, curve A applying to skylight only and curve B with sun on the glass blocks.

The School of Architecture at the University of NSW is currently studying the possibilities of such arrangements, including the use of adjustable mirrors to re-direct the sun. It is apparent that any reflector

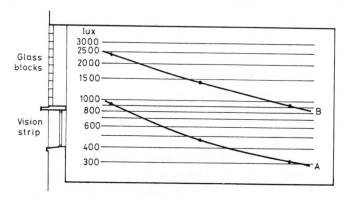

Fig. 12. Measured illuminances in a classroom incorporating prismatic glass blocks above a vision strip.

A: hazy sky, illuminance on glazing 15 600 lux.
B: sun and sky, illuminance on glazing 49 500 lux.

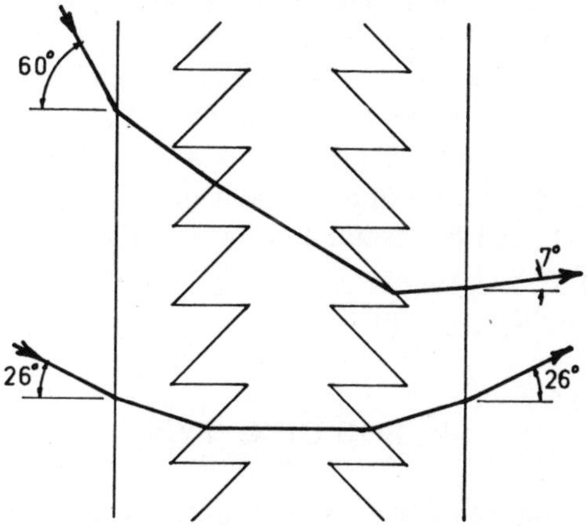

Fig. 13. Typical ray paths through two sheets of prismatic glass.

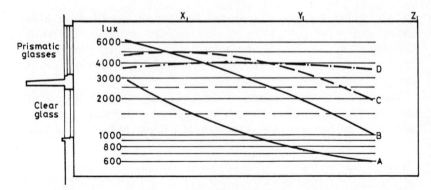

Fig. 14. Estimated illuminances from sky giving 10 000 lux and sun 65 000 lux on the glazing.
A: sky only for normal windows, clear glass from sill to head, without hood.
B, C, D: sun and sky with prismatic glass and hood as shown; refracted sunlight extending to points X, Y and Z respectively.

system can give good control of the direction of the reflected sunlight, but requires periodic adjustment both of the reflector and of any device used to exclude sun from the work area. An alternative is the use of two sheets of prismatic glass with the prismatic faces placed internally to avoid dust collection, as illustrated in Fig. 13, which shows typical ray paths through the system. This method gives less accurate control than reflectors but requires no adjustment.

As a preliminary study, a computer program providing a simplified model of the prism system has been produced, typical results being illustrated on Fig. 14. Here, curve A refers to the result for skylight only, with conventional full-height clear glass windows without the hood. Curves B, C and D are for combined sky and sun with the refracted sunlight extending to the points X, Y and Z respectively. The curves indicate clearly the improvement in uniformity of illuminance when the sunlight can be re-directed towards the rear of the room. A programme of model studies to investigate the possibilities of such arrangements is being planned.

4.7. BUILDING TYPES

From the viewpoint of the provision of daylight, buildings fall into two distinct types: buildings with rooflights and those with side windows.

Fig. 15. Daylit general office at Unilever works, Port Sunlight, England.

Fig. 16. Arrangement of rooflights and trusses for the office of Fig. 15.

Design methods for both types are available in Refs. 3, 20, 21 and elsewhere.

4.7.1. Rooflighting

In general it is not difficult to provide adequate daylight, often of excellent quality, where rooflighting can be used. There are three principal forms of rooflighting.

(1) Sawtooth glazing.
(2) Monitors, with vertical or sloping glass.
(3) Flat or low-pitched roofs with glazing incorporated in the roofiing surface.

With all types in order to secure reasonably uniform lighting it is necessary that the spacing of the glazing panels must not greatly exceed their height above the work-plane. With sawtooth glazing, direct sun can be almost totally excluded. With the other types, sun may fall on the glass, which should then be of a diffusing type, and shielded from normal viewing by some form of louvering or baffles.

An excellent example of rooflighting is illustrated in Figs. 15 and 16

Fig. 17. Daylit export department at Unilever works. Lighting by glass domes above cylindrical upstands.

which show the central office of the Unilever works outside Liverpool in England. This building has a pitched roof incorporating considerable areas of glazing. The roof is supported by trusses with curved lower chords, the trusses being covered with solid material so that they serve as large-scale louvres; the arrangement can be seen in Fig. 16. The export office of the same works is shown in Fig. 17, which is lighted by glass domes on top of cylindrical curbs which prevent direct viewing of the glass.

4.7.2. Side Windows

It is usually more difficult to provide satisfactory daylighting in rooms with side windows. While the light may be adequate near the windows, it falls off fairly rapidly towards the rear of the room. In addition, at points remote from the window the light falls at very glancing angles on the conventional horizontal work-plane. However, not all work is performed on horizontal surfaces and the illuminance on a vertical or sloping surface facing the windows is commonly considerably higher than the usual design methods would suggest. Lynes (Ref. 20) has suggested that the "scalar illuminance" on a small sphere often gives a better measure of the brightness assessed by an observer than does the horizontal illuminance.

As a general guide, it may be taken that satisfactory daylighting can be provided in rooms where the distance to the rear of the room does not exceed some three times the window height, provided that access of light is not obstructed by other buildings. Deeper rooms may require some supplementary lighting, either permanently or with dimmer controls as discussed in Section 5.

4.8. CONCLUSIONS

The previous discussion has indicated that considerable savings can be made in the electrical energy used for the lighting of buildings, with appropriate design. In particular it is suggested that currently adopted values for the "design sky" are needlessly low. If higher values are used in design, the results show that in many buildings especially where rooflighting is possible, adequate daylight can be provided for a considerable portion of working hours. When the daylight becomes inadequate, it can be supplemented by artificial light. One possibility in many office situations is the use of individual desk-lamps, as studied by

McDermott (Ref. 13). Alternatively, the use of monitoring devices to switch off the lights when not needed plus dimmer controls to provide an appropriate level of supplementary lighting when required seems to offer great opportunities for energy savings.

There is also the possibility that re-directed sunlight may improve both the quantity and quality of daylighting when studies of this technique are more advanced.

APPENDIX 1
EQUATIONS

Notation

E_n Illuminance from sun on plane normal to rays (lux)
E_s Illuminance from sun on horizontal plane (lux)
E_c Illuminance from clear sky on horizontal plane (lux)
E_h Illuminance from any sky on horizontal plane (lux)
L_θ Luminance of sky-point at altitude θ (apostilb)
L_z Luminance of the zenith sky (apostilb)
h Altitude of the sun (degrees)
m Air mass, approximately equal to cosec h (dimensionless)
θ Altitude of a sky-point (radians)
ϕ Angle between sun's position and sky-point (radians)
z Angle between sun and zenith (radians)

Equations

(1) Sunlight on plane normal to rays (Ref. 3)
$$E_n = 124\,000e^{-0.23m}$$

(2) Sunlight on horizontal plane (Ref. 3)
$$E_s = E_n \sin h$$

(3) Clear sky illuminance on horizontal plane (Ref. 3)
$$E_c = 16\,250\,(\sin h)^{1/2}$$

(4) Horizontal illuminance from overcast sky (Ref. 3)
$$E_h = 0.26\,E_s + 0.54\,E_c$$

(5) Horizontal illuminance from sky with thin clouds (Ref. 3)
$$E_h = 0.35\,E_s + 0.89\,E_c$$

(6) Relative luminance of CIE standard overcast sky
$$L_\theta = L_z \frac{1 + 2\sin\theta}{3}$$

(7) Horizontal illuminance relative to zenith luminance, CIE sky

$$E_h = \tfrac{7}{9}L_z \text{ or } L_z = \tfrac{9}{7}E_h$$

(8) Relative luminance in terms of horizontal illuminance

$$L_\theta = \tfrac{3}{7}E_h(1 + 2\sin\theta)$$

(9) Illuminance on vertical plane from CIE sky

$$E_v = 0.39E_h$$

(10) Relative luminance of points on clear sky (Ref. 11)

$$L_\theta = L_z \frac{1 - e^{-0.32\operatorname{cosec}\theta}}{0.273\,85} \times \frac{0.91 + 10e^{-3\phi} + 0.45\cos^2\phi}{0.91 + 10e^{-3z} + 0.45\cos^2 z}$$

Note: Zenith luminance and vertical plane illuminances in terms of horizontal illuminance are given on Fig. 11.

Equations for Electricity Savings with Light Controls (Refs. 15, 16)

(11) Savings with on-off controls

$$f = 1 - \frac{100}{d} \cdot \frac{E_d}{E_o}$$

(12) Savings with dimmer controls

$$f = 1 - \frac{50}{d} \cdot \frac{E_d}{E_o}$$

where:

E_d = Interior design illuminance (lux)

E_o = Intercept on horizontal axis of assumed line of sky illuminance versus frequency of occurrence.

d = Daylight factor (%)

f = Fraction of electricity saved when E_d is partly provided by daylight.

Example

Let $d = 2\%$

$\quad E_d = 300$ lux

$\quad E_o = 34\,000$ lux (line D, Fig. 8)

With on-off switching,

$$f = 1 - \frac{100}{2} \times \frac{300}{34\,000} = 1 - 0.44 = 0.56$$

With dimmer control

$$f = 1 - 0.22 = 0.78$$

APPENDIX 2

DAYLIGHT DESIGN AND MEASUREMENT
UNDER DIFFERENT TYPES OF SKY

The usual method for the prediction of daylight levels within buildings is to determine daylight factors at all positions of interest and then to multiply them by an appropriate value of the total external horizontal illuminance. However, as the definition quoted in Section 4.4.1. indicates, the daylight factor at a given point is not constant but varies according to the actual or assumed sky luminance distribution. The most convenient assumption for calculations is that the luminance is uniform, but it has become common practice to base calculations on the CIE overcast sky.

With rooflighting, the choice between these alternatives makes little difference, since only the upper regions of sky provide the light. However, in the critical areas of sidelit rooms remote from the windows the light comes principally from the region of sky near the horizon. As seen on Figs. 9 and 10, the ratio between sky luminance (asb) and horizontal illuminance (lux) in this region for both overcast skies and clear skies away from the sun (although reversed in direction), is generally less than the ratio of unity which applies to uniform skies. Hence calculations based on uniformity usually overestimate the levels found in practice.

Thus difficulties arise when it is required to estimate interior illuminance levels produced by a known (or assumed) exterior illuminance, but from a sky of unspecified luminance distribution. In particular, to apply the automatic control of supplementary artificial light described in Section 4.5.3., it is necessary to decide how the available exterior illuminance is to be monitored.

Some guidance on this question may be found in an experimental investigation by Rapp and Baker (Ref. 22). They made measurements at a number of positions in a test room with windows glazed firstly with clear glass and later with prismatic glass blocks, in some cases with the latter exposed to direct sunlight. The internal measurements were compared with four different types of exterior sky measurement, including total horizontal illuminance (the daylight factor method). Reasonably consistent ratios between internal and external values were found only when the external measurement consisted of the total illuminance *on the vertical plane of the window*. The authors stated that, with this method "it was possible to translate, reliably and with reasonable precision, any interior illumination reading which was made simultaneously with a specific daylight condition, to what it would be for any other outdoor illumination. This was true generally for any point in the room, for any kind of fenestration and for any condition of daylighting".

This evidence suggests that, for sidelit rooms, the prediction of interior light levels and the monitoring of the exterior daylight for control purposes should be based upon the vertical illuminance. It is interesting to note that the generally accepted method for calculating the reflected component of the daylight is based upon this vertical illuminance and that the reflected light often provides a large part of the total at points towards the rear of a room.

If this principle is adopted, it becomes necessary to relate the vertical illuminance to available figures for horizontal illuminance. Under a uniform sky, the ratio between these two values is, of course, 0.5; under the standard overcast sky it is 0.39—eqn.(9). Under a clear sky Fig. 11 indicates that the ratio varies both with the solar altitude and with the orientation of the window relative to the sun. The lowest values occur for windows facing away from the sun, the ratio fluctuating about an average of approximately 0.4, which is close to the overcast value of 0.39.

It is therefore suggested that a reasonable general design method covering the less favourable sky conditions would be to assume that the windows face a region of uniform sky producing a vertical illuminance equal to 0.4 times the actual horizontal illuminance. This is equivalent to basing design on a sky having *a uniform luminance numerically equal to 0.8 times the actual external horizontal illuminance*.

As an example of this method, consider a room with no external obstructions, 4 m wide by 6 m deep and 2.4 m high containing one window with glazing 3 m wide by 1.5 m high. Table 2 below shows calculated sky components of the daylight factor at five points in the room (selected to have convenient angles to the window head) for both an overcast sky and a clear sky facing away from the sun. The calculations are based on the luminance distributions of Figs. 9 and 10 and an average glass transmittance of 0.85. Similar values for a uniform sky multiplied by the proposed factor of 0.8, are also shown for comparison with the mean of the previous values; it is evident that the agreement is generally quite good.

Assuming ceiling, wall and floor reflectances of 80%, 50% and 20%

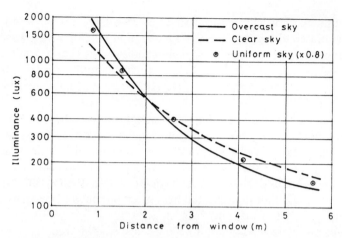

Fig. 18. Calculated illuminances in a room from overcast, clear and uniform skies. External horizontal illuminance 10 000 lux.

respectively, the average and minimum internally reflected components calculated by the BRS split-flux method (Ref. 23) are 1.40 and 1.08. From these figures estimated values at the reference points are added to the Table. The total percentage daylights factors have then been applied to an assumed horizontal illuminance of 10 000 lux. The results are shown on Fig. 18.

In view of the uncertainties associated with actual skies, it is suggested that the values predicted by the convenient assumption of a uniform sky (reduced by the factor of 0.8) are quite adequate for most daylight design.

TABLE 2
CALCULATED DAYLIGHT FACTORS FOR VARIOUS SKIES

Angle to window head	60°	45°	30°	20°	15°
Distance from window (m)	0·87	1·50	2·60	4·12	5·60
Sky components: overcast sky (%)	16·73	7·69	2·33	0·66	0·27
” ” clear sky (%)	10·74	6·17	2·62	1·05	0·52
Sky components: mean values	13·74	6·93	2·48	0·86	0·40
” ” uniform sky (×0·8)	14·96	7·58	2·64	0·85	0·37
Internally reflected components (%)	1·60	1·50	1·40	1·25	1·08

Evidently, in this case some supplementary artificial lighting would be required towards the rear half of the room. For monitoring purposes, the levels shown on Fig. 18 may be expected to occur when the external illuminance on the plane of the window is $0.4 \times 10\ 000$, namely 4000 lux.

REFERENCES

1. Moon, P., 'Proposed solar radiation curves for engineering use,' *J. Franklin Institute*, **230**, 583, 1940.
2. *Daytime Lighting in Buildings*, IES Technical Report No. **4**, London, 1972.
3. Elvegard, E. and Sjostedt, G., 'The calculation of illumination from sun and sky,' *Illuminating Engineering*, **35**, 333, 1940.
4. Fournol, A., 'Resultats français concernant les éclairments naturels,' *CIE Proceedings*, **11**, Paper Q, 1951.
5. Dresler, A., 'The availability of daylight at various latitudes,' *Light and Lighting*, **55**, 10, 1962.
6. Dogniaux, R., 'Ensoleillement et orientation en Belgique. Étude de l'éclairement lumineux naturel,' *Inst. Roy. Met. de Belg. Publ. Series B*, No. 12, 1954.
7. Paix, D., *The Design of Building for Daylight*, Comm. Exp. Building Station, Bulletin No. 7, Sydney, 1962.
8. Boyd, R. A., 'Studies on daylight availability,' *Illuminating Engineering*, **53**, 6, 321, 1958.
9. McDermott, L. H., and Gordon-Smith, G. W., *Daylight Illumination Recorded at Teddington*, Proc. Building Res. Congress, 1951. (Supplementary data extracted from actual records by present author).
10. Moon, P. and Spencer, D. E., 'Illumination from a non-uniform sky,' *Illuminating Engineering*, **37**, 10, 707, 1942.
11. Kittler, R., 'Standardisation of outdoor conditions for the calculation of daylight factors with clear skies,' *Proc. CIE Conference on Sunlight in Buildings*, Boucentrum, Rotterdam, 273, 1967.
12. Hopkinson, R. H. and Longmore, J., 'The permanent supplementary artificial lighting of interiors,' *Trans. Illum. Eng. Soc. (London)*, **24**, 3, 121, 1959.
13. McDermott, L. H., *Daylight Illumination Necessary for Clerical Works*, DSIR Illumination Research Technical Paper No 19, London, 1937.
14. Manning, P. *The Design of Roofs for Single-Storey General-Purpose Factories*, Pilkington Research Unit (England), 1960. (Lighting appendix by R. Phillips).
15. Crisp, V. H. C., 'Preliminary study of automatic daylight control of artificial lighting,' *Lighting Research and Technology*, **9**, 1, 31, 1977.
16. Hunt, D. R. G., 'Simple expressions for predicting energy savings from photo-electric control of lighting,' *Lighting Research and Technology*, **9**, 2, 93, 1977.
17. Hopkinson, R. G., and Petherbridge, P., 'The natural lighting of buildings in sunny climates by sunlight reflected from the ground and from opposite facades,' *Proc. Conf. Tropical Architecture*, London, 1953.
18. Rosenfeld, A. H., 'Beam daylighting—an alternative illumination technique', *Energy and Buildings*, **1**, 1, 43, 1977.
19. *How to Make the Most of Daylight with PC Functional Glass Blocks*, Pittsburgh Corning Corp., Pittsburgh (Pennsylvania), 1951.
20. Lynes, J. A., *Principles of Natural Lighting*, Elsevier, London, 1968.

21. *Natural Lighting of Buildings—Daylight Design Diagrams*, Dept. of Labor and National Service, Australia, Sydney, 1963. (Re-published in modified form as CIE Publication No. 16.)
22. Rapp, G. M. and Baker, A. H., 'Daylight illumination on interiors fenestrated with glass blocks,' *Illuminating Engineering,* **36,** 10, 1129, 1941.
23. Hopkinson, R. G., Longmore, J. and Petherbridge, P., 'An empirical formula for the computation of the indirect components of the daylight factor,' *Trans. Illum. Eng. Society* (London), **19,** 7, 201, 1954.

5

The Thermal Inertia of Buildings, and How to Use it for Energy Conservation

J. J. Greenland

Department of Architecture, New South Wales Institute of Technology, Australia

5.1. INTRODUCTION

One of the major problems in the utilisation of solar energy is its storage so that it can be collected when available and used when needed. The mass and thermal properties of the components of a building are, in the hands of the designers, powerful tools for providing a suitably modified environment for a wide range of climatic conditions. This chapter describes how thermal inertia can be used to best advantage, storing solar energy or avoiding it when required. Elementary empirical theory is presented and a range of examples is described.

5.2. THE NATURE OF THERMAL INERTIA

"Inertia" is a word introduced by Kepler to describe that property of matter whereby it tends to continue in its existing state of rest or uniform motion unless acted upon by an external force. Thus "thermal inertia" has been coined to describe a corresponding response of matter to external heat stress. The property is measured in the S.I. system of units (Ref. 1) as:–

Specific heat capacity (c)—the quantity of heat energy in kilo joules required to raise the temperature of one kilogram of a substance by one kelvin (equivalent to one Celsius degree). The units are abbreviated to kJ/(kgK).

Heat capacity—the quantity of heat energy in kilo joules required to raise the temperature of the whole object by one kelvin, the units in this case being kJ/K.

Volumetric heat capacity—the quantity of heat energy in kilo joules required to raise the temperature of one cubic metre of a substance by one kelvin, the units being $kJ/(m^3K)$.

If the object in question is homogeneous then:

$$\text{heat capacity} = mc$$

where m is the mass in kilograms.

If not, then:

$$\text{heat capacity} = \sum_{i=1}^{n} M_i C_i$$

where the n components of the object have masses $M_1, M_2, \ldots M_n$ and specific heat capacities $C_1, C_2, \ldots C_n$.

These definitions were derived from experiments which showed that the mass of a substance is a necessary factor in its thermal performance, from which it follows that the amount of heat energy q in kilojoules required to raise M kilograms of a substance of specific heat capacity C through a temperature of $\delta\theta$ kelvin, is given by:

$$q = MC\delta\theta$$

The implications of this equation can be seen by considering two bodies of the same mass, A with a large specific heat capacity and B with a small specific heat capacity. If heat is supplied at a constant rate to both, then the temperature of A will rise more slowly than that of B. For a given heat input to both, the temperature of A will rise less than that of B.

Hydraulic Analogy. The thermal behaviour described above is analogous to the behaviour of two tanks A and B shown in Fig. 1, where the volume of the tank is analogous to mass, the cross sectional area analogous to specific heat capacity and hydraulic head to temperature. Thus if both are filled from a constant supply the level of A rises more slowly than that of B, and for a given quantity of water supplied, the level of A will rise less than that of B. Similarly when bodies A and B are cooling, the analogy is that of tanks A and B emptying through tubes of the same size at the bottom of each.

Thermal stress on buildings is generally cyclic with heat tending to enter during the day and escape at night. The effect of thermal inertia is

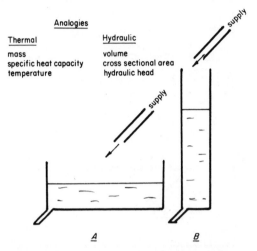

Fig. 1. Hydraulic analogy of thermal capacity.

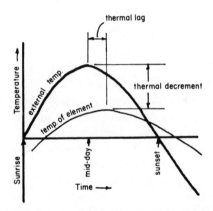

Fig. 2. Response of massive element to cyclical temperature stress.

to reduce the temperature swing (decrement) and delay the peaks (lag). This is illustrated in Fig. 2 for several thermal masses.

Newton's Cooling Law. Newton established the law which described the manner of cooling of a body surrounded by a fluid at a lower temperature. The process is illustrated in Fig. 3. Newton's cooling law applies to an ideal case, but some of its implications carry over to the real world. The rate of cooling decreases as the heat capacity of the

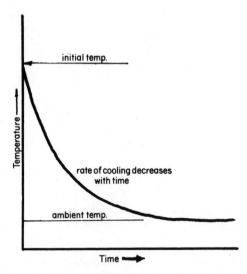

Fig. 3. Newton's law of cooling. A similar curve describes the drop in water level of an emptying tank.

body increases. Tank *A* will empty more slowly than tank *B*. Furthermore, as the rate of heat loss is reduced (e.g. by increasing the thermal resistance) the rate of cooling is also decreased. Increasing the thermal resistance is similar to using smaller supply and draining tubes for the tanks in the hydraulic analogy.

Thus in order to achieve maximum stabilisation of temperature a large heat capacity and insulation against external stress are needed. On the other hand, a rapid response to changing conditions is achieved by using small heat capacity and high transfer rates. Thus light buildings, with light floors and partitions (especially when poorly insulated) cool rapidly when heating is stopped. Massive structures cool slowly and external insulation further reduces the rate at which heat is lost.

Earth's thermal inertia. It is possible to tap an enormous thermal inertia, viz. that of the earth, by integrating the building with the ground. Slab on ground floors, earth berm and underground construction enable this to be achieved. Ground temperature at the surface, if sun penetration is excluded, tends to approach mean annual ambient which is a favourable situation for both summer and winter extremes. Individual applications will be discussed later.

5.3. ROLE OF INERTIA IN THERMAL PERFORMANCE

Buildings are more complex than the ideal bodies discussed so far and heat may be introduced or withdrawn by several means and in a number of places. The role of thermal inertia in providing stable conditions is examined.

5.3.1. Radiation
Solar gain externally and internally. Before the days of widespread cheap air conditioning it was commonly accepted that massive buildings provide better thermal stability than lightweight structures. With no insulation thick-masonry buildings may heat up during extended heat wave conditions or through high-intensity insolation and continue to impose heat stress on the interior for sometime after the external

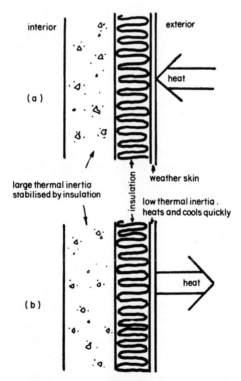

Fig. 4. The most stable temperature is possessed by a large thermal mass protected by a thermal insulation.

conditions have moderated. In these circumstances, high thermal inertia can be a disadvantage.

The fault is overcome by installing thermal insulation on the outside of the massive wall thus cushioning the effect of thermal stress. Practical considerations demand a weatherproofing on the outside of the insulation layer, but this should have as little thermal inertia as is compatible with adequate performance as an external skin. The result is illustrated as a wall in Fig. 4(a). Roofs constructed in this manner are not common, except for multi-level reinforced concrete buildings.

If buildings are constructed deliberately to admit solar radiation for heating purposes, then large thermal inertia on the inside becomes an important design aim. Rays from the sun on penetrating the glazing suffer multiple reflections from floors, walls, ceiling and contents. Measurements of short-wave absorbance of a number of quarter-scale model rooms with north wall glazing show it to be of the order of 0.75–0.84.

Thus it is possible to admit and store a large portion of the incident solar radiation which is available internally after the sun has gone, provided the insulation is adequate.

Exchange of long-wave radiation with the sky and surrounding surfaces. The radiation characteristics of surfaces exposed to large air masses are given by Swinbank (Ref. 2), while the classical theories of Stefan and Boltzmann deal with exchanges between adjacent surfaces. In both cases Fig. 4(b) illustrates that again interior temperature stability is achieved by having large thermal inertia inside surrounded by insulation and a light weatherproof skin on the outside.

5.3.2. Convection
Exchange between building and outside air. Using similar reasoning to above, the type of construction represented in Fig. 4 produces the most stable internal temperature.

Ventilation. The effect of cross ventilation for cooling in very hot weather can be reduced if massive interiors remain higher than air temperature and rob the occupants of a favourable mean radiant temperature. Clearly if cross ventilation is to be effective for the relief of hot conditions, low thermal inertia is indicated.

Exchange with people, lights and equipment. The effect of internal sources of heat is minimised by having high internal inertia.

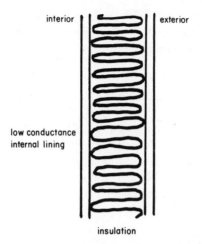

Fig. 5. For intermittent heating, e.g., air conditioned spaces, lightweight structures with low-conductance internal linings save energy.

Air conditioning. When internal environments are manufactured by treating the air, it is costly to heat or cool the frame of the building, especially if the air conditioning is intermittent. In this case lightweight, well insulated external walls should be used (Fig. 5) and even internal rooms should be lined with low-conductance (high-resistance) panelling so that as little of the structure as possible is heated or cooled and the wall surfaces rapidly reach air temperature.

5.3.3. Conduction
Nearly all of the heat exchange by conduction is between the building frame and the ground and this becomes appreciable in very cold climates. It is usual in these cold regions to insulate around the outside of a slab on ground floor and sometimes underneath.

5.3.4. Influence of Thermal Inertia on Comfort
Thermal mass, by maintaining a fairly constant temperature, has the following effects on the comfort of human occupants.

Convection. By influencing the internal air temperature, extremes may be moderated (Ref. 3).

Conduction. Physical contact with massive cool surfaces is a known means of alienating heat stress in the tropics (Ref. 4).

Radiation. Mean radiant temperatures are stabilized and if designed correctly can be a favourable influence on thermal comfort. Ballantyne, Barned and Spencer support this (Ref. 5).

5.4. MATCHING THERMAL INERTIA TO CLIMATE

The designer's resources are vast indeed and the solution area for any given set of restraints is limited only by his ingenuity. Consequently it would be presumptuous to offer a set of "optimum" solutions for various climate types. Herein follow some examples of buildings designed with climate in mind and using thermal inertia as a moderating device.

5.4.1. Hot Climates
Hot arid. Here very high daytime peaks are followed by cold nights. The people of the middle east have for many centuries built heavy clustered structures taking advantage by day of mutual shading and the cooler earth in order to alleviate the effect of high intensity solar radiation and extremely hot winds. Figure 6 shows in diagrammatic form how thermal inertia effects may be combined with other techniques, e.g. evaporative cooling, thermal convection and behavioural response, so that the day's hot peak can be tolerated.

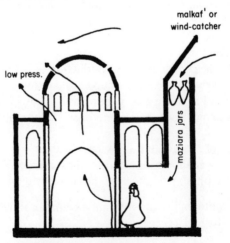

Fig. 6. Wind-catcher with cooling jars. Evaporative cooling, thermal inertia and natural convection combined moderate hot arid climates.

Knowles (Ref. 6) has described the construction of Acoma Indian villages in New Mexico in response to hot arid conditions. Vertical walls are heavy in mass and dark in colour to absorb and hold heat from the low winter sun, while horizontal surfaces are light in mass and colour to absorb as little high angle solar radiation as possible and retain little of it after sundown.

Warm humid. In these areas the temperature swing is not great and humidities are generally high, especially during wet seasons. Slab-on-

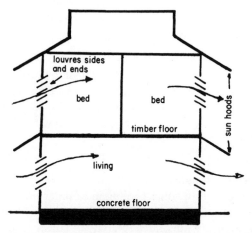

Fig. 7. House in Kedak, Malaysia. Downstairs living has concrete floor on ground, upstairs sleeping has low thermal mass, all rooms have substantial cross ventilation. Suits warm humid climate.

Fig. 8. House on stilts. Low thermal mass enables quick response to cooling sea breeze, suits tropical maritime climate.

ground floors generally remain cooler than the air during the day and can exert a considerable effect on the mean radiant temperature. A common behavioural response in these areas is the custom of removing shoes on entering a building thus enabling the human body to lose heat to a massive floor by conduction.

At night the massive floor remains above air temperature and the job of sleeping is made a little more difficult. It would be an advantage to have bedrooms with fast thermal response in order to cool quickly at night. Figure 7 shows a house in Kedah, Malaysia, where the downstairs living area has a concrete floor and the upstairs sleeping area has a timber floor. Generous allowance for cross ventilation ensures that the upstairs area cools quickly.

Tropical maritime. Here the proximity of large water bodies (themselves exerting the moderating effect of massive thermal inertia on the climate) ensures cool winds and sea breezes. Thus very low thermal masses, lightweight structure with small thermal decrement and negligible lag are indicated. The classical type of construction is illustrated in Fig. 8.

5.4.2. Temperate Climates

These areas may require some cooling in summer and some heating in winter and the inertia of a building can be used to minimise these requirements. Figure 9 illustrates the type of construction which would perform adequately in a warm temperate area while that needed in a cool temperate area is shown in Fig. 10. The main difference between these two designs is the attention given to large glass areas as the nights become colder. The thermal mass of the building may be insufficient for some areas and it is common to see extra storage used, e.g. rock bed or water tank.

5.4.3. Cold Climates

Temperatures in these areas are generally so cold that large window areas are avoided because of excessive losses at night and small compensating gains during the day. Slab-on-ground floors are insulated for some distance around their periphery.

A recent development which makes use of solar energy and thermal inertia without excessive loss of heat through glass is the Trombe-Michel solar wall, an example of which is illustrated in Fig. 11.

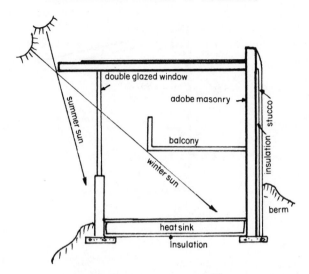

Fig. 9. House in New Mexico (USA) suitable for warm temperate region. Sun heats slab floor in winter and is excluded in summer.

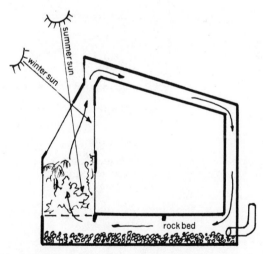

Fig. 10. House near Lake Tahoe (USA) suitable for cool temperate region. Glazing reduced on the east, west and down-sun side. Up-sun side becomes a heat trap.

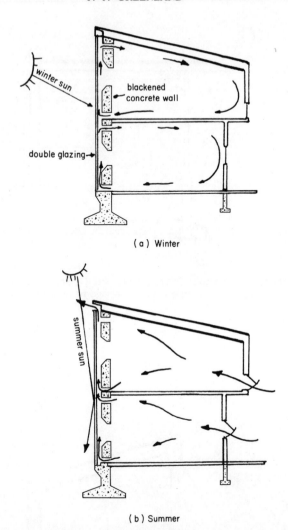

(a) Winter

(b) Summer

Fig. 11. The Trombe-Michel solar wall helps improve conditions in cold climates without losses of heat at night through excessive glass area. It can generate ventilation in the summer time.

5.5. GENERAL

Thermal inertia exerts a great influence on the response of buildings to external stress. Large thermal masses result in considerable temperature decrement and a long time lag. Small thermal masses give quick response and little temperature decrement. The behaviour of the mass is affected by coupling it with thermal insulation and the thermal mass of the earth. By studying the particular climate in which the building is located, the most appropriate combination can be used thus minimising the need for large inputs of external mechanically processed energy to provide the best comfort conditions for the occupants.

REFERENCES

1. *The International System (SI) Units and Their Applications, AS 1000 (1970)*, Standards Association of Australia, Sydney, 1970.
2. Swinbank, W. C., 'Longwave radiation from clear skies', *Journal Roy. Met. Soc.*, **89**, 381, 339–348, July 1963.
3. Williamson, T. and Coldicutt, A. G., 'Utilization of solar energy in dwellings,' *Symposium on Solar Energy Utilization in Dwellings*, Melbourne, 1974.
4. Greenland, J. J., 'Design strategies for achieving thermal comfort with minimum energy input,' *National Symposium on Innovation and Incentives for Conservation in Buildings*, Sydney, 1978.
5. Ballantyne, E. R., Barned, J. R., and Spencer, J. W., *Environmental Assessment of Acclimatised Caucasian Subject at Port Moresby, Papua New Guinea*, Proceedings, Third Australian Building Research Congress, Melbourne, 1967.
6. Knowles, R., *Energy and Form*, MIT Press, Cambridge, Massachusetts, 1974.

6

Available Climatic Data and How to Use Them

R. M. AYNSLEY
*Department of Architectural Science, University
of Sydney, Australia*

6.1. INTRODUCTION

The use of climatic data in building design is associated with two principal goals:

(1) Thermal comfort for building occupants
(2) Protection of a building's occupants and contents during extreme weather conditions.

To achieve the first goal physical data such as dry-bulb air temperature, humidity, mean radiant temperature and rate of air movement are required. Data of this type are then evaluated using a thermal comfort scale, the most commonly used being the 'Corrected Effective Temperature'. An acceptable range of Corrected Effective Temperatures is provided in most texts which will satisfy say 80% of a sample population in a specified region. Regional assessment is essential in order to account for the effects of modes of dress, activity and exposure on acceptable comfort conditions.

Building design in terms of:

(1) Proportions of the envelope,
(2) Solar orientation, shading of roof and walls and location of openings
(3) 'U' value and thermal lag time of construction, and,
(4) Seasonal prevailing winds;

will largely determine the degree of shelter and comfort achieved inside a building which does not rely on mechanical environmental controls. A

134

great deal of effort, technical skill and judgement, gained from experience, is usually required to bridge the gap between the raw climatic data and the appreciation of its effects on the internal environment of a particular building design. In many situations the data one would like are not available, while in other cases one is unsure of an appropriate technique to use in evaluating the effects of available data.

6.2. SOURCES OF GENERAL DATA AND ASSOCIATED QUALITATIVE BUILDING DESIGN AIDS

Climatic data used in the past for building design were extracted from Bureau of Meteorology's records. These, of course, were based on the needs of climatologists and were often inadequate for detailed building design. Formats were principally graphs and tables.

Although the type of data used in building design in recent years has remained unchanged, significant changes have occurred in its frequency of observation and format. Most capital cities, and some larger regional cities, now have hourly data for incident radiation, dry-bulb temperature and wind speed and direction. Much of this data is only available as computer printout or on magnetic tapes for computer use.

6.3. GENERAL DATA

Where designers wish to gain only a general familiarity with the climate at a certain locality, summary data as contained in *Climatic Averages* (Ref. 1) or *RAIA Handbook* (Ref. 2) in tabulated form are probably adequate.

Data provided includes:

1. 09.00 and 15.00 hrs mean wet- and dry-bulb air temperatures, dew point and relative humidity for each calendar month;
2. Mean, 86 percentile and 14 percentile daily maximum dry-bulb air temperatures, for each calendar month;
3. Mean, 86 percentile and 14 percentile daily minimum dry-bulb air temperatures for each calendar month;
4. Mean and median rainfall for calendar month; and
5. Mean number of rain days per calendar month.

No specific sunshine or cloud cover or data on wind characteristics is provided.

More complete data including hours of sunshine and wind frequency and direction are provided in separate booklets for each of the capital cities (Ref. 3) as well as in the Commonwealth Year Books (Ref. 4). Computer printout of hours of sunshine or hourly wind frequency and directions per month are available for a fee for most large towns and cities on request from the Bureau of Meteorology.

Incident solar radiation data is collected by CSIRO, a number of universities and other research establishments. There is no centralised published collection of detailed data; the closest to this would be a series of maps available from the Bureau of Meteorology indicating mean monthly incident radiation based on theoretical calculations, (Ref. 5). Glover and McCulloch (Ref. 6) suggest the following equation as a means of estimating Q, daily total radiation on a horizontal plane.

$$Q = Q_s \left(0.29 \cos \phi + 0.52 \frac{n}{N} \right) \quad \text{MJ/m}^2 \text{ day}$$

where Q_s = solar constant per day taken as 36 MJ/m^2 day
    0.29 = empirical constant to account for transmission properties of the atmosphere,
    ϕ = degrees latitude of location
    n = number of hours of sunshine per day
    N = maximum possible hours of sunshine per day

Incident solar radiation data is used to assess heat entry into a building. Sunshine and shade data is used to assess the need for shading devices as well as potential for daylighting interiors and the obstructing influence of adjacent buildings.

6.4. WIND DATA SOURCES

There are a number of formats used for wind data. Publications such as the Commonwealth Year Book provide tabulated data which include average monthly windspeed, highest mean windspeed in one day, highest gust speed, and prevailing directions at 09.00 and 15.00 hrs.

Annual average windspeeds and extreme gust speed are also indicated. In addition two national maps are provided, one for 09.00 and one for 15.00 hrs observations with wind roses indicating graphically the percentage frequency of winds from eight cardinal points of the compass for each month. Frequency of calms for each month is also indicated.

Separate booklets published by the Bureau of Meteorology for each of the capital cities (Ref. 3) describe the general wind climate and provide mean monthly windspeed and direction frequency data. Although useful for a general appraisal of the wind climate, it is not detailed enough for estimates of airflow through buildings.

Data on prevailing windspeeds and directions is important as infiltration through cracks due to wind can be a major source of heat loss from buildings in cold climates. In warmer climates, particularly when relative humidity is high, indoor air movement is often the only natural method of reducing heat stress. If this is not provided by wind then airflow may have to be   induced by suitable fans.

Humidity data, as well as being essential for evaluation of thermal comfort, is also used in conjunction with temperature profiles through walls to determine dew points and possibility of 'interstitial condensation'.

6.5. DESIGN AIDS

One system for relating general climatic data to appropriate building forms and construction is the Mahoney tables (Ref. 7). These tables can be used manually or as an interactive computer design aid. They are only intended as a subjective guide and do not provide further numerical design data.

Further general guides to climatic design for thermal comfort in buildings have been published by Drysdale (Ref. 8), Givoni (Ref. 9), Van Straaten (Ref. 10), Koenigsberger (Ref. 7), Olgyay (Ref. 11) and Saini (Ref. 12). Of these publications those by Drysdale and Saini relate directly to Australian conditions and include climatic data on sunshine hours, prevailing wind directions and speeds for winter and summer, as well as rainfall, temperature and humidity. These texts cover general climatic considerations, but the indoor environment of many buildings will be influenced by local microclimatic features. An insight into the numerous and complex microclimatic effects can be gained from Geiger's *The Climate near the Ground* (Ref. 13), a standard text on this subject.

6.6. SUNSHADING

Architects have been familiar with Phillips' *Sunshine and Shade in Australia* (Ref. 14) for many years. Just how many designers use the

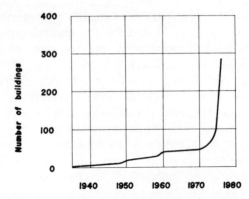

Fig. 1. Cumulative number of solar buildings completed in USA by end of indicated year—after Shurcliff.

data in this book is not clear. However, by the numerous poorly shaded buildings it is probably not many. As the demand for passive solar heated buildings grows, as it certainly has in the USA (Fig. 1), architects will be forced to accept detailed shadow analysis on buildings as a regular routine. For those with the capital to invest there are computer systems currently available to perform such an analysis with output in graphic form. On the other hand, such services could be the basis for a flourishing future service industry.

Data from shadow analysis is fed into computer systems to allow for partial radiation gains on or through building surfaces at various times of the day and year. When computers are not used the shaded or unshaded condition would be taken into account in determining the Sol-air temperatures at external building surfaces in less rigorous manual heat transfer calculations.

6.7. ESTIMATION OF WIND EFFECTS ON THERMAL PERFORMANCE OF BUILDINGS

There are a number of ways wind influences the thermal performance of buildings. One influence common to all buildings is the variation in heat transfer with air speed across the boundary layers of air at the surfaces of building materials (Fig. 2). This consideration is dealt with when selecting air film resistances in U-value calculations or in data input into computer analysis programmes.

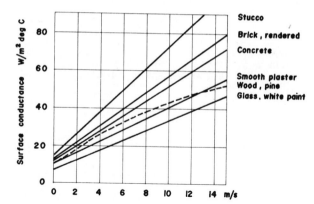

Fig. 2. Surface conductance as a function of wind speed.

'Infiltration' is the entry and exhaust of air through small openings or cracks in buildings. The energy for such airflow in smaller buildings is principally wind pressure, although 'stack effect' due to differences in indoor-outdoor air temperatures has a small effect. In cold climates infiltration is often a major source of heat loss. A worked example of calculations estimating infiltration is provided in *Architectural Aerodynamics* (Ref. 15).

In warmer humid climates with small diurnal air temperature variations indoor air movement is the only way of improving thermal comfort short of mechanical air chilling (Fig. 3). In passive designed buildings this air movement is often achieved by natural ventilation using wind forces, although ceiling fans are often necessary to cope with calm conditions.

There are two methods of estimating airflow through large openings in buildings due to wind. One is to use wind tunnel studies of scaled models to determine windspeed coefficients at critical points inside the model. These coefficients relate an indoor windspeed to an outdoor reference windspeed. By careful selection of the outdoor reference windspeed it can be related to long-term records of windspeed and direction near the building site.

Detailed wind data are now available on request for most cities and towns with airport facilities throughout Australia. Referred to as a Bureau of Meteorology wind frequency analysis, these data usually take the form of a computer output of five years' observations of windspeeds

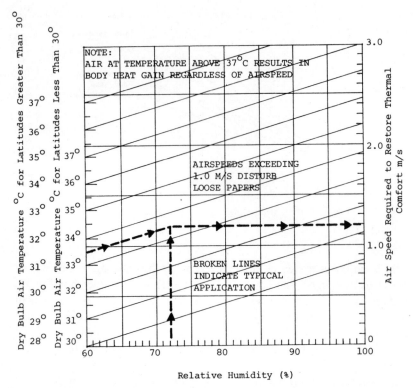

Fig. 3. Graph of estimating minimum air speed required to restore thermal comfort
for a range of dry-bulb temperatures and relative humidity.

and directions over 16 compass points at hourly intervals.

A worked example of the use of wind frequency analysis and
windspeed coefficients to estimate windspeeds through a residential
building is given in *Architectural Aerodynamics* (Ref. 15).

Another method of estimating airflow through buildings with large
openings due to wind is to use wind pressure differences and discharge
coefficients. Wind pressures can be estimated from pressure coefficients
and local windspeed data using techniques described in Australian
Standard 1170, part 2, the current wind loading code. Discharge
coefficients for typical openings and a worked example estimating
airflow through a residential building are given in *Architectural
Aerodynamics* (Ref. 15).

6.8. SPECIFIC DATA FOR COMPUTER SIMULATION

For the many computer thermal simulation models developed at research organizations such as CSIRO and most universities, data on an hourly basis is usually needed. As such data was not readily available in the past, such data was interpolated from the less frequent characteristics available at the time. Typical of recent computer programmes is *TEMPAL* developed by Coldicutt at the University of Melbourne's Department of Architecture and Building. *TEMPAL* simulates the thermal performance of buildings under actual or 'design' external climatic conditions. The output provides information on hourly environmental temperatures and loads on heating and/or cooling plant in terms of frequency of occurrence of loads and temperatures within given ranges. *TEMPAL* also totals energy consumption for heating and/or cooling over specified periods of a fortnight, month or whole season. The *TEMPAL* programme is often used to compare the effects of different constructions and levels of insulations and a range of glass areas. The simulations are based on actual climatic data for a typical year in Melbourne, although other data could be used. A similar programme *ETEMP* developed by Forwood at the University of Sydney's Department of Architectural Science calculates hourly environmental temperature as well as heating or cooling loads.

CSIRO Division of Mechanical Engineering and Division of Building Research are proceeding with the compilation of climatic data suitable for use in computerised heat transfer calculations in buildings and various types of solar energy systems.

An updated bank of solar radiation data has been obtained from the Bureau of Meteorology and is now available to persons with access to the CSIRO computing network. The data bank covers 23 stations. About 60 000 days are available of half-hourly readings of global radiation on the horizontal plane and 17 000 days of half-hourly readings of diffuse radiation on the horizontal plane. In addition magnetic tapes of coincident solar radiation, dry-bulb temperature, wet-bulb temperature, atmospheric pressure, wind speed, wind direction and total cloud cover are being produced for a number of Australian locations. Data are at hourly intervals and several years are available for each location. Where necessary, missing data have been filled in, either by interpolation or averaging. So far tapes for Melbourne, Hobart, Williamstown, Perth, Wagga Wagga, Mildura, Woomera, Port Hedland and Alice Springs have been produced.

6.9. FUTURE BENEFITS OF COMPUTER SIMULATION
MODELS

At present computer programmes for numerical passive solar building design are largely academic research tools. In the near future, however, when more data come from instrumented experimental buildings and reliability of programmes is confirmed it should be a simple matter to produce design nomograms for the major variables in buildings for each basic climatic type.

Coldicutt has begun producing simplified design graphs for Melbourne and Canberra using his *TEMPAL* System (Ref. 16). Others will certainly follow this lead.

6.10. PROBLEMS ASSOCIATED WITH UNITS OF
MEASUREMENT

Conversion from the Imperial system used in the past to the current *Système Internationale* (SI) has been relatively simple for the principal climatic measures such as temperature, rainfall and relative humidity. Other measurements have caused confusion such as wind speeds which still appear in some publications in knots or even miles per hour, while others use kilometres per hour and building standards, such as the wind loading code (Ref. 17) uses metres per second.

A notice in a recent issue of *Solar Energy Progress in Australia and New Zealand* (Ref. 18) indicated further changes in units for radiation measurement:

> "The Bureau of Meteorology will in future use SI units for irradiation data which are issued from its computer archive. The change is expected to be effective from early 1979. Changes to field instruments to convert the raw data will be spread over several years. The SI units of irradiance are watts per square metre and those at present used by the Bureau are
> irradiance: $1 \text{ mW cm}^{-2} = 10 \text{ Wm}^{-2}$
> irradiation: $1 \text{ mW h cm}^{-2} = \text{kJ m}^{-2}$

A Change in Solar Radiation Measurement Reference Standards
Measurements of solar radiation at present are made in the International Pyrheliometric Scale (IPS 1956) which was adopted in 1956 by the Radiation Commission of the International Association

of Meteorology and Atmospheric Physics (IAMAP, a member of ICSU) and by the World Meteorological Organization (WMO). IPS 1956 is a relative scale and in its present form it is the mean of seven designated instruments, maintained by regular comparison at the World Radiation Center at Davos, Switzerland.

In recent years new types of absolute radiometers have been produced. Comparisons between them have shown such good agreement that a new scale has been proposed. This is the World Radiometric Reference (WRR) which represents the absolute units of irradiance within ± 0.3%. Data measured in the IPS 1956 scale are multiplied by 1.022 to convert them to the new WRR scale. It is proposed that the new scale will be maintained by regular comparisons of at least four designated absolute radiometers of different types".

It is to be hoped that with the passage of time more consistency will result which will assist the building designer in gaining an appreciation for the relative meaning of values in the new system of measurement.

6.11. CONCLUSIONS

In the past methods of interpreting climatic data for use in building design were long and tedious with the result that few architects used the tools available. These days computers can flash through the computations involved and present tabulated data on indoor environmental conditions or plot sunshine and shadow patterns indoors and outdoors around our buildings. With such facilities one might think that the climatic design considerations for buildings are well catered for. In fact the opposite is true, many more fundamental errors in climatic design appearing today than in the past. A more thorough understanding of the basic grammar of orientation, shading, insulation etc. is needed so that sketch plans are more carefully considered and final detailed computer analysis is more of a routine final check.

Development of convenient, easily used design aids for use at the sketch planning stage are urgently needed to encourage a widespread consideration of climatic effects on building performance. It is hoped that more effort will be made to develop such design aids, graphs, nomographs, tables, etc. from the abundant output from computer models. If such an approach is not taken, only those with access and the inclination toward computer analysis will have the tools to improve the climatic performance standards of our country's buildings.

REFERENCES

1. *Climatic Averages,* Metric Edition, Department of Science and Consumer Affairs, Bureau of Meteorology, Australian Government Publishing Service, Canberra, 1975.
2. *RAIA Handbook,* Royal Australian Institute of Architects Journal, Section Aa8, Instalment, 1, 1–8, and Section Aa9, Instalment 2, 1–16, 1967.
3. *Climate of Sydney,* 1972, *Climate of Melbourne,* 1975, *Climate of Brisbane,* 1977, *Climate of Perth,* 1977, Series, Department of Science, Bureau of Meteorology, Australian Government Publishing Service, Canberra.
4. *The Year Book—Australia 1977–1978,* Australian Bureau of Statistics, Australian Government Publishing Service, Canberra, 1978.
5. *Climatic Atlas of Australia,* Map set 2, Global Radiation, Australian Government Publishing Service, Canberra, 1975.
6. Glover, J. and McCulloch, J. S. G., 'The empirical relationship between solar radiation and hours of bright sunshine,' *Quarterly Journal of the Royal Meteorological Society,* **84,** 56.
7. Koenigsberger O. H. *et al., Manual of Tropical Housing and Building, Part One: Climatic Design,* Longman, London, 1974.
8. Drysdale, J. W., *Designing Houses For Australian Climates,* Commonwealth Experimental Building Station, Sydney, 1975.
9. Givoni, B., *Man, Climate and Architecture,* Second edition, Applied Science Publishers, London, 1976.
10. Van Straaten, J. F. *Thermal Performance of Buildings,* Elsevier, London, 1967.
11. Olgyay, V., *Design with Climate: Bioclimatic Approach to Architectural Regionalism,* Princeton University Press, Princeton, (New Jersey), 1963.
12. Saini, B., *Architecture in Tropical Australia,* Melbourne University Press, Melbourne 1970.
13. Geiger, R. *The Climate Near the Ground,* translated from the fourth German edition, Harvard University Press, Cambridge, Massachusetts, 1966.
14. Phillips, R. O. *Sunshine and Shade in Australasia,* Fourth edition, Australian Government Publishing Service (Experimental Building Station, Bulletin No. 8), Canberra, 1975.
15. Aynsley, R. M., Melbourne, W. and Vickery, B. J., *Architectural Aerodynamics,* Applied Science, London, 1977.
16. Coldicutt, A., 'Interactive systems for the reduction of heating and cooling loads in houses,' *Thermal Insulation,* **3,** 4, November 1978.
17. *SAA Loading Code, Part 2—Wind Forces, AS 1170,* Standards Association of Australia, Sydney, 1975.
18. 'Solar energy progress in Australia and New Zealand,' *Journal of Aust. and N.Z. Section of the International Solar Energy Society,* Melbourne, No. 17, July 1978.

7

The Use of Computers for Modelling the Physical Environment in Buildings

B. S. A. Forwood

Department of Architectural Science, University of Sydney, Australia

7.1. INTRODUCTION

As a consequence of growing concern about the future of the world's energy resources, building designers are constantly being urged to re-appraise their attitudes to the consumption of energy in buildings and to consider the "energy-economics" of their designs. However, a large gap exists between the rhetoric (which doesn't seem to be in short supply) and the proffering of methods of quantitatively evaluating alternative design strategies.

For the building designer there are basically two problems:

(i) the conservation of energy in existing buildings by either modifying the building enclosure or encouraging different behavioural patterns or comfort standards, and

(ii) the design of new buildings to reduce their dependency upon mechanical means of environmental control and hence the input of external energy.

Until recently there has been a lack of suitable computational tools capable of being applied to all stages of a design process to help designers generate alternative proposals and then choose between them. Existing manual methods lack the computational accuracy to be of any benefit and the vast majority of computer programs available which offer extreme accuracy are too cumbersome to use at all stages of a design.

The fundamental requirement is a greater understanding on the part of designers of the total nature of the physical environment in buildings,

145

how it is created and, in particular, what rôle is played by the building enclosure (i.e. the system of walls, roofs, floors and windows manipulated by the architect) in creating this environment.

This chapter develops the hypothesis that, by generating suitable representations of all the environmental control systems in buildings, it is possible using computer modelling techniques to develop computational tools of sufficient accuracy and flexibility which allow the evaluation of alternative design strategies at all stages of the design process. Before discussing the use of computers for this purpose it is first necessary to explore the interaction between the building enclosure and the physical environment in buildings to formulate a conceptual model of the environmental control systems in buildings from which we can proceed to more detailed discussions.

7.2. ENVIRONMENTAL CONTROL IN BUILDINGS— CONCEPTUAL MODELS

The designer of a building prior to the Industrial Revolution had but one major environmental control mechanism at his disposal, namely the building enclosure. By careful manipulation of its form and construction he modified the transfer of thermal energy and light and sound from the outside to the inside. This conscious use of the enclosure as an environmental filter helps to explain the many regional variations which appear in the historical styles and, of course, is clearly in evidence in much, but by no means all, vernacular architecture. Apart from minor applications of energy such as the burning of coal or wood in open fires and the use of oil lamps and tallow for lighting, the only other form of environmental control available to the occupants of these "pre-technological" buildings was the adaptation of his life style and behaviour to suit a particular climate. Such actions as occupying different parts of a building at certain times of the day or year or manipulating control mechanisms such as shutters, etc., were used (and in some societies still are) to control the environmental comfort of building occupiers. It is sad that many contemporary building designers and users have lost both of these arts.

We can represent this "pre-technological" environmental control system diagrammatically as shown in Fig. 1. This representation shows the major components of the building environmental system, the major energy flow paths into the interior environment and the major control mechanisms available to designers and users for modifying the physical

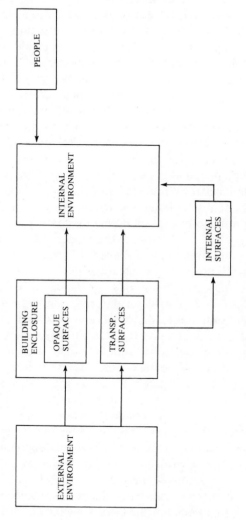

Fig. 1. "Pre-technological" environmental control system.

nature of this environment. We shall consider these mechanisms more closely later.

With the emergence of new technologies during the latter half of the 19th century, several important developments in the design of buildings occurred. Innovations such as gas lighting and, later, incandescent lighting, hot air and steam heating, fan forced ventilation systems and air conditioning meant that more or less satisfactory conditions could be maintained in buildings irrespective of the form or nature of the building enclosure. The development of framed structures removed the structural function of the external enclosure which then became much lighter and thinner as a consequence of the need to reduce the dead loads supported by the structural frame. However, by removing the structural mass from the external enclosure designers also removed its thermal mass and hence its capacity for filtering the extremes of the external environment. Air conditioning and an array of energy intensive lightweight cladding materials provided artificial thermal mass and gave designers the opportunity to develop an entirely new aesthetic vocabulary which they continued to explore during the first six decades of this century, encouraged by the doctrines of the Modern Movement and the examples of the great masters, and fuelled by what seemed to be an abundant supply of cheap, expendable energy.

A diagrammatic representation of this "technological" environmental system is shown in Fig. 2. The major difference between this and the "pre-technological" system is its dependence upon an input of external energy to provide one of the control mechanisms, energy which is rapidly becoming more expensive and, in some cases, scarce. It is difficult to see, even in the medium term, that we will be able to do without building services completely for providing adequate standards of environment in large buildings or that the energy required to power these services can be adequately provided by alternatives to fossil fuels such as solar energy. While these possibly offer long-term solutions, most of our existing building stock and indeed buildings constructed in the next few years have a projected life span which extends past the predicted critical energy supply period and almost all will contain conventional service systems. This particular representation serves well as a general conceptual model of the environmental control systems in buildings and can be used to explore, in more detail, the exact nature of the physical environment in buildings and the mechanisms available to control it.

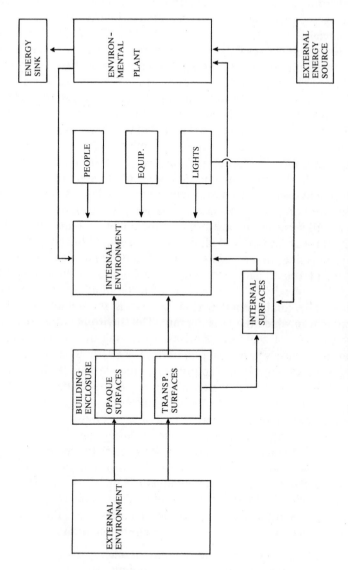

Fig. 2. "Technological" environmental control system.

7.3. THE PHYSICAL ENVIRONMENT IN BUILDINGS

It is unfortunate that, during this century in particular, building design has become compartmented into separate disciplines each with its own set of specialist practitioners, a well defined theoretical framework and hard-and-fast objectives for the achievement of a narrow range of goals with little attention paid to the goals of other practitioners in other disciplines. This has led to the environment in buildings being considered as several separate entities (thermal, visual, aural), each the responsibility of a separate member of the design team.

An inspection of our conceptual model in Fig. 2 will indicate that this is an unrealistic representation of the physical environment within buildings and, more importantly, of the way users of buildings perceive and respond to this environment. People perceive their environments in a multi-model fashion. All of our senses are stimulated simultaneously. We feel warm or cool at the same time as we hear background noise, see the colour of surfaces and are aware of the quality and quantity of light entering through windows. Although we understand the laws of physics which determine the behaviour of the individual elements of the environment (heat, light and sound) we know very little about the apparent complexity of their behaviour in the building environmental situation. The fundamental reason for this is the complexity of the environment in which the laws operate. This environment is created by a large number of building elements interacting in a rather complex manner and clearly what is required, if we are to achieve better standards of design, is an approach to the design of the physical environment in buildings which allows us to model the interactions which take place between the building enclosure design variables and the performance parameters affecting the total physical environment.

A further consequence of developments during this century has been the complete reliance on building services systems to create and control the environment in buildings which has led to the notion that it is an engineering problem and not an architectural problem. Further inspection of Fig. 2 clearly shows that the building services are only one part of a total system and that other control mechanisms exist. Basically there are three mechanisms available to designers and users:

    (i)   control by varying the amount of energy consumed by the environmental plant (heating, cooling, etc.),

   (ii)   control by modifying the characteristics of the building enclosure, and

(iii) control by changing the location of activities to more suitable environments, modifying the behaviour of the occupants by altering occupancy hours, clothing and other behavioural modifications.

It is also obvious that decisions made by the building designer about the building enclosure will have a direct influence on the amount of energy consumed by the environmental plant and could possibly remove the need for external energy completely. So clearly the design of the physical environment in buildings is very much an architectural problem and needs to be considered at the earliest stages of the design process.

7.4. QUANTITATIVE MODELS OF THE ENVIRONMENT

Traditional methods of quantitatively representing and exploring this interactive environmental system are inadequate for providing designers with the evaluative information they require as a basis for decision making. Research techniques involving either laboratory experimentation or the measurement of people's responses are, by themselves, inadequate for, by their nature, they ignore the interactive nature of the environment. Experimentation generally involves making assumptions which simplify either the representation or the behaviour of the factors being observed. In most cases it involves the setting up of artificial conditions in which to monitor the behaviour of isolated environmental parameters. Measurement of responses to environment or to changes in the environment invariably introduces external factors such as the personal biases of the participants, previous conditioning and the chance that a particular response may be distorted by factors not considered relevant by the researcher.

Simplified mathematical models which form the basis of the manual calculation methods currently employed are also inadequate. Because they have to be relatively easy to use, they contain many simplifying assumptions which render them useless except for the very simplest static cases. As a method of detailed exploration they must be viewed with caution. The simplest of these is the steady-state equation for heat transfer.

$$Q = UA(t_1 - t_2)$$

which relates the energy flow through a part of the building enclosure Q to measures of the enclosure's thermal characteristics U, its geometry A

and some measure of the external and internal environmental conditions, expressed as the temperature difference between them (t_1-t_2). More sophisticated versions of this relationship can be developed to include other thermal characteristics of the enclosure, such as its thermal storage capacity. All of these are simple static models of environmental behaviour which allow us to estimate the behaviour of our building under some assumed worst condition.

However, dynamic models are required if we are to understand the response of the building enclosure to changes over time. Several highly sophisticated mathematical procedures have been developed as a direct consequence of the use of computers (Refs. 1 and 2) which allow the modelling of the environmental behaviour of buildings under fluctuating conditions such as they would experience over time in a given climate. These techniques such as the Admittance Procedure, developed in the UK by the Building Research Establishment, the method of finite differences and the Response Factor Method also allow the direct calculation of internal temperatures in buildings which is fundamentally important to building designers in evaluating the effectiveness of the building enclosure in controlling the thermal environment.

Similarly in the areas of lighting and acoustics simple manual analytical techniques are unsuitable for representing the dynamic nature of the visual and aural environments. For instance, daylight calculation methods currently employed are grossly oversimplified in the calculation of the external and internal reflected components of natural light, a severe limitation when modelling the effects of obstructions and of room shape and surface characteristics upon the quantity of natural light available. Recently methods have been developed based upon the calculation of inter-reflections between surfaces (Ref. 3). These provide more accurate results, but again require computers to perform the large number of calculations involved.

7.5. THE USE OF COMPUTERS: FIRST GENERATION

The first generation of environmental design programs has provided some potentially useful techniques for meaningful environmental research. The term "first generation" is applied to those programs which have been available widely since the early 1960s, basically "stand-alone" programs, complete in themselves, concentrating upon one or a few aspects of the environment and generally reflecting an engineering approach to the problem, oriented towards generating design data for the environmental plant.

Computers were applied to building environmental problems some considerable time after they were firmly established in other areas of building design. There are several reasons for this time lag, as follows.

(i) Until recently, environmental design has lacked an adequate formulation as a basis for theoretical studies of the environmental behaviour of buildings.

(ii) The performance of building materials, construction components and services system components depends upon a large amount of data. The unavailability of this data in a suitable form has retarded the development of large-scale computer applications.

(iii) As mentioned earlier, concern for the environmental performance of buildings is of fairly recent origin and this has also slowed progress.

A detailed account of the development of computer applications in this area appears elsewhere (Ref. 4). In this section several typical examples of the types of programs available will be cited together with an assessment of their general characteristics.

7.5.1. Thermal Analysis Programs

There are now numerous thermal analysis programs available which allow the dynamic characteristics of thermal behaviour to be modelled. They are generally classified as either load calculation programs (for the calculation of gains and losses in spaces or heating and cooling loads) or energy analysis programs for simulating the performance of environmental plant over a period of time, usually one year.

The designer wishing to use a computer program is faced with the rather difficult task of selecting the most appropriate program from those available. The choice is made more difficult by a lack of adequate documentation. Another problem in selecting a suitable program is the spread of results obtained by using several programs to solve a similar problem (Ref. 5). The major source of difference between programs is the treatment of the heat transfer through external walls and roof elements, ranging from simple techniques based upon manual procedures to quite sophisticated mathematical models of the heat storage capacity of the structure. The use of the former techniques can result in substantial errors when considering hour-by-hour calculations and non-steady-state conditions.

A further consideration is the type of climatic data representation used. Depending upon the type of analysis required this data may, at one extreme, consist of a single value for each parameter (usually a figure determined statistically as not being exceeded on more than a specified number of days per year) or, at the other extreme, of hourly values of each parameter for each day of the year. For extensive energy analysis the latter is essential, but there are several ways of arriving at this set of data. One could simply pick a typical year for a region and use this year as input data stored on tape. The danger here is that the chosen year might contain periods of extreme non-typical weather which could distort results obtained for long-term planning purposes. Considerable research has been carried out using sampling techniques such as Monte Carlo Methods (Ref. 6) to construct synthetic data. Another approach uses measures such as the mean and standard deviation for each parameter to construct a reference year for any given region or locality (Ref. 7). A further method is to use typical design days for each month of the year or days representing a certain number of similarly occurring days throughout the year (Ref. 8). Thus a whole year can be represented by a small number of days, reducing the amount of data and processing required without seriously reducing the accuracy for long-term purposes.

The most extensive load calculation program available at present is NBSLD, a program developed in the United States by the National Bureau of Standards. It is in fact a suite of programs for calculating heating and cooling loads for a space based upon the Response Factor Method adopted by the ASHRAE Task Group on Energy Requirements and developed in association with the National Research Council of Canada (Ref. 9). Response factors are sets of time-dependent co-efficients which are a measure of the thermal response of a wall or roof element to a randomly fluctuating external environment. They are derived from the number of layers in the element, the thickness and thermal properties of each layer and the internal and external surface characteristics. The number of co-efficients in a particular series is dependent upon the thermal mass or storage capacity of the element. The greater the thermal mass, the greater the number of response factors required to model the transfer of energy.

For a given 24-hour weather pattern the program calculates heat exchanges due to direct and diffuse radiation through windows, conduction through walls and roof, convection due to air infiltration and internally generated heat gains. Calculations are performed for each hour and are converted into cooling and heating loads by the use of weighting factors which model the response of internal surfaces. The program is available from the National Bureau of Standards for a small nominal fee.

An air-conditioning loads program, developed by the CSIRO has recently been made available to the design professions through the bureau services of Control Data Corporation. The program, *TEMPER*, produces hour-by-hour estimates for several specified zones of a building, including an indication of the contribution to the total load made by each heat path into the space (Ref. 10). In addition, hour-by-hour results are tabulated for the whole building. The theoretical basis of the program is a representation of the heat flow paths into a typical building. The program distinguishes between thermally thin sections of the building enclosure and those which are thermally thick. For the former the program assumes a linear heat flow with negligible thermal capacity. For heat flow through thermally thick sections the program uses a finite difference technique to take account of any thermal storage. Input to the program consists of a description of each zone of the building including the properties of all bounding surfaces, climatic data, internal design conditions and operating data. Data collection is via specially prepared coding sheets. Sample output appears in Fig. 3. This program is typical of the style of the majority of load calculation programs available.

Energy analysis programs are generally far more sophisticated than the load calculation programs as they are required to determine hour-by-hour loads imposed upon the environmental plant throughout a typical year and to simulate the operation of the various components of this equipment in response to these loads. Recently there has been an abundance of these programs available and once again intending users are faced with a difficult task in choosing between them. Many authorities, particularly in the USA, are now insisting upon energy calculations as part of the documentation for a building project and the use of a computer is essential to make the computations manageable. However, most of the available programs are very complex which often discourages their use in the small-to-medium-sized design office. Another more serious problem is that different programs often give varying results for the same building which which can cause problems when the program used by a particular authority to check the

JOB NAME USER MANUAL EXAMPLE

CALCULATION FOR MARCH

HOURLY LOAD COMPONENTS FOR ZONE   1 IN WATTS

TIME	LOAD PATH 1	LOAD PATH 2	LOAD PATH 3	LOAD INFILN	ZONE TOT. SENS LOAD	ZONE TOT. LATNT LOAD	TOTAL SENSBLE +LATNT LOAD	FRESH AIR REQTS SENSBLE	FRESH AIR REQTS LATENT
6	2665	-1132	-1870	0	-336	-0	-336	0	-0
7	2115	-1107	-1857	0	-849	-0	-849	0	-0
8	814	-978	-2103	-0	-2268	-0	-2268	0	-0
9	-1132	-850	-4393	-0	-8686	-750	-9436	-191	-798
10	-3426	-732	-7100	-0	-13572	-750	-14322	-579	-798
11	-5725	-628	-9808	-0	-18544	-750	-19294	-967	-798
12	-7671	-538	-12302	-0	-22822	-750	-23572	-1296	-798
13	-8972	-461	-13391	-0	-25135	-750	-25885	-1516	-798
14	-9429	-394	-12848	-0	-24982	-750	-25732	-1593	-798
15	-9314	-337	-11256	-0	-23210	-750	-23968	-1573	-798
16	-8973	-288	-8928	-0	-20492	-750	-21242	-1516	-798
17	-8418	-246	-6613	-0	-17589	-750	-18339	-1422	-798
18	-7672	-211	-4932	-0	-12816	-0	-12816	-8	-0

ZONE TOTAL SENSBLE LOAD INCLUDES
    LOAD DUE TO LIGHTS OF -1560. BETWEEN 830 HOURS AND 1700 HOURS
    LOAD DUE TO OCCUPANCY OF -750. BETWEEN 830 HOURS AND 1700 HOURS
    DIRECT LOAD OF -0. BETWEEN 830 HOURS AND 1700 HOURS

THE ZONE LIGHTING LOAD IS SPLIT INTO CONVECTIVE AND RADIATIVE FRACTIONS
THE CONVECTIVE FRACTION(.500)APPEARS AS THE DIRECT LOAD DUE TO LIGHTS ABOVE
WHILE THE RADIATIVE FRACTION (THE REMAINDER) FALLS ON THE FLOOR OF THE ZONE
AND APPEARS AS A PART OF THE FLOOR CONVECTIVE LOAD

Fig. 3. Program *TEMPER*: typical output.

calculations is different from the one used by the designers to generate them (Ref. 11).

One of the best known energy analysis packages is the US Post Office's *Computer Program for Analysis of Energy Utilisation,* developed by General American Transportation Corporation (Ref. 12). The program package was developed in close co-operation with the ASHRAE Task Group on Energy Analysis and contains many of the load calculation and system simulation algorithms developed by the Task Group and now freely available through ASHRAE. The US Post Office initiated the development of the package in 1967 in order to update its procedures for designing HVAC systems in its new postal installations and to be able to cost the operation of these systems in existing buildings. The computer programs that resulted were designed to be used for:

(i) the pre-design selection of the basic system and energy source,
(ii) the evaluation of specific design concepts during the design stages,
(iii) the evaluation of modifications from the designed system proposed by contractors during the construction stage and
(iv) the evaluation, after the building is completed, of maintenance and operation policies.

The total program consists of seven separate sub-programs, each operating independently, but with the output of one becoming the input for another. These form the three main components of the package; a Load Calculation Sub-program, a Systems Simulation Sub-program and an Economic Analysis Sub-program.

The *Load Calculation Sub-program* is very similar to the NBS Loads program NBSLD. It computes the hourly thermal loads that are generated in each space of the subject building. The Response Factor Method is used to evaluate the instantaneous gains due to solar radiation and heat conduction which are then balanced with those due to infiltration, lighting and other internal sources. Weighting factors are employed to determine the contribution of the lighting, equipment and re-emitted radiation loads to the hourly cooling load.

The other major component, the *Systems Simulation Sub-program,* firstly translates these hourly loads into the actual hourly thermal requirements imposed upon the heating and cooling plant and, secondly, converts these hourly thermal requirements into energy requirements for the system. This component contains 15 subroutines which simulate the operation of fan systems, the heating and cooling coils, the chillers and boilers and size the major components required for each piece of equipment. In addition the monthly energy consumption figures for all energy sources (oil, steam, electricity) are generated.

The Economic Analysis component calculates the annual owning and operating costs for various combinations of equipment based upon the energy consumption generated above. Costs are calculated on a present worth basis. In addition several plotting programs are included to display much of the output graphically.

Although the programs were originally developed for the Post Office, they are now generally available to the HVAC profession. However, user response to the package has been mixed. Most commonly expressed misgivings include the lack of error checking facilities which causes the program to fail whenever an error is encountered, insufficient number of mechanical systems included which necessitated considerable rewriting, errors in the weather tapes provided and excessive man-hours required for data input by staff unfamiliar with the system. Despite these reservations the program seems to be the most successful energy analysis package so far developed.

Oscar Faber and Partners in the UK has recently extended their range of building evaluation programs by the release of program *ENPRO* for energy analysis. For some time Oscar Faber has been involved in the development of interactive graphics techniques for the design of building services (Ref. 13). The Faber system consists of a small low-cost visual display unit (VDU) coupled to a graphics tablet (a flat electronic drawing surface) which is used to input information graphically. Output is displayed to the designer on the VDU. For example, in sizing ductwork the designer draws a schematic layout of the duct network on the graphics tablet, the image of his drawing being displayed simultaneously on the screen. Other information such as air flow volumes for each section of ductwork is entered via the VDU keyboard and the results of the duct analysis are displayed on the VDU for inspection.

Program *ENPRO* is an extension of Faber's previous work. Existing thermal analysis programs have been combined with other programs to simulate various air conditioning and heating systems. The program calculates heating and cooling loads on a building during a year of average temperatures and incident solar radiation. Other internal gains are also taken into account. Standard weather data is supplied by Faber or can be generated by the user. Up to 17 different air conditioning and

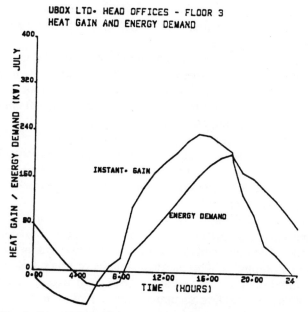

Fig. 4. Oscar Faber Energy Analysis Program: cooling load profile.

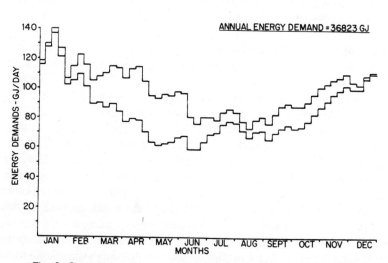

Fig. 5. Oscar Faber Energy Analysis Program: energy demand analysis.

heating systems including dual duct, induction units and variable air volume systems can be analysed for each hour of the day for each month of the year.

Output from the program includes details of the input data and daily, monthly and annual values of energy demands for each system analysed. In addition to conventional output, optional plotted output is available in the form of graphs and histograms representing a summary of the energy demand requirements (Figs. 4 and 5).

Several other energy analysis programs are available including *MACE* developed by the McDonnell Automation Company, *ECUBE* by American Gas Corporation, *AXCESS* by the Edison Electric Institute and *NECAP* developed by the General American Transportation Corporation (Ref. 14).

The Energy Systems Analysis Package, developed by Ross Meriwether and Associates in the United States is available locally through the *Compunet* bureau service and can be used as a complete package or in modules. The package consists of several programs for checking input data, estimating the hour-by-hour energy requirements for a building or building section during a typical year's operation, simulating the performance of various pieces of equipment in a system as they respond to the loads imposed upon them to find monthly and annual energy inputs and an economics package for calculating the monthly utility costs and to perform an economic comparison of several alternate systems.

7.5.2. Lighting Analysis Programs

In this field programs exist for the analysis of daylight in buildings and for the design of artificial lighting systems. Daylight evaluation programs generally adopt one of two approaches to modelling the light flux available within a space. The majority of programs are based upon well accepted but simplified methods such as Hopkinson's method or the BRE *Split-Flux* method for the calculation of the internally reflected component. These methods have limited accuracy and flexibility, but are not computationally demanding and are usually capable of analysing a greater number of alternatives than manual techniques. At the other extreme are programs such as *GLIM* (Ref. 15) which go back to first principles and can produce very accurate results using a very flexible model. This particular program considers the multiple inter-reflections which take place in a room and is suitable for analysing daylight in highly obstructed situations where the major component of light flux is

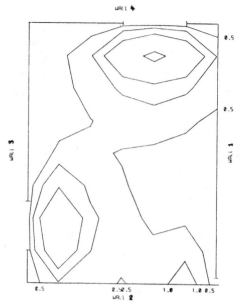

Fig. 6. Daylight factor contours drawn by computer.

the internally reflected light. Output from a typical daylighting program is shown in Fig. 6.

A recent survey of daylighting programs concluded that, although the majority of programs produced results more quickly and more accurately than manual procedures, the manner in which this information was displayed varied greatly and was, on the whole, disappointing (Ref. 16). A significant comment was that most of the programs failed to give the user a feel for the *quality* of the light in a room as many manual procedures were able to do.

Typical of the artificial lighting design programs is APEC's *LIGHT-ING-II* program available in Australia through membership of APEC (Automated Procedures for Engineering Consultants). This group also has a series of Cooling Load and Energy Analysis programs available. *LIGHTING-II* will calculate the number of luminaires of a specific type required to provide a uniform level of illumination over a working.plane and provides cost data for an economic comparison of installations.

Other lighting programs and acoustic programs are available as part of program packages and these will be discussed later.

7.6. SECOND-GENERATION PROGRAMS

The 'first-generation' programs reviewed in the previous section suffer from many of the shortcomings of traditional methods. They tend to concentrate on only one aspect of the environmental control system and do not yield any meaningful information for the designer considering the design of the total environment. Generally they are too detailed and difficult to use at an early stage of the design process when many critical decisions are being made. Usually it is impossible at this stage to generate all of the data required by many of the programs which means that their usage comes all too late to be of any use to the architect. In addition almost all of the programs reflect an engineering approach to environmental design, providing data for the design of environmental plant but giving the architect little information to guide him in his decision making.

However there is a second generation of applications emerging which are characterised by the following qualities.

(i)   They reflect a total-design approach to the problem which is closer to the architect's proper approach than it is to the traditional engineering approach. This approach relates the control hardware to the environmental software.

(ii) More than one aspect of the environmental behaviour of buildings is considered.

(iii) They generate information of a more general nature about the behaviour of buildings and the relationship between design variables and this behaviour.

(iv) Lastly, by the nature of the information they yield, the computer and the designer are no longer in a direct one-to-one relationship, but remote from each other. In fact the designer may not even use the computer but rather the information produced, in the form of design guides.

The first example of this type was the Cambridge Environmental Model developed by the Centre for Land Use and Built Form Studies at the University of Cambridge during the late 1960s. Their aim was to produce a mathematical model which could evaluate several quantitative aspects of the physical environment, namely the thermal, visual and acoustic environments, the main purpose being the definition of the relationships between the physical elements of a building and the environment within. The resulting evaluative model produced statements about the environmental conditions within a building. It was the first successful attempt at integrating the evaluation of several environmental factors within a single description of building form. The evaluative techniques employed by the model were the commonly accepted methodologies of the time. The significant component of the model was its highly ordered geometrical building description procedure which was used to structure the handling of data and the execution of the various evaluative routines (Refs. 17, 18).

A simple Cartesian co-ordinate system is used to describe the geometry with the whole of the building and its surroundings contained within the first quadrant thus ensuring that all dimensional data is positive. The orientation of the subject building is then specified by containing the north point between the X and Y co-ordinates and defining its displacement from the Y axis in degrees. Complicated shapes and obstruction situations can be defined by reducing the shape to a series of rectangular blocks and by specifying the off-set of the origin of each block (left hand bottom corner) from the primary co-ordinate axes and then the length and width of each block, measured parallel to the X and Y axes. Obstructions are treated in exactly the same manner. This process is illustrated in Fig. 7. Basically any complex form composed of rectangular elements (which can be internal courtyards) can be handled by the model.

A secondary co-ordinate system is used to define the dimensions of internal spaces within the overall volume and to define the size and location of windows, thicknesses of walls, dimensions of sun protection devices and the location of reference points within each space. These reference points are used in the daylighting calculations (Fig. 8).

The evaluative part of the model transforms the data as input by the user into forms suitable for each evaluative sub-program. The model evaluates the natural lighting, artificial lighting and thermal performance of each of the subject spaces defined and in the case of thermal performance sums the total gains and losses for the entire building. The original form of the model contained an acoustic evaluation, but this has subsequently been omitted owing to the scarcity of reliable data and procedures in this field. Recently the IHVE Admittance Procedure has been incorporated to calculate internal temperatures in each space. The theoretical basis of the evaluation part of the model has been fully documented (Ref. 19).

The output produced falls into two categories, individual room output and whole building output. As the model is evaluative, the output

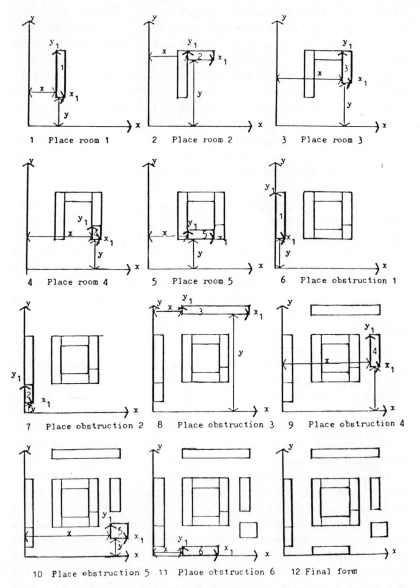

1 Place room 1   2 Place room 2   3 Place room 3

4 Place room 4   5 Place room 5   6 Place obstruction 1

7 Place obstruction 2   8 Place obstruction 3   9 Place obstruction 4

10 Place obstruction 5   11 Place obstruction 6   12 Final form

Fig. 7. Cambridge Environmental Model: procedure for describing a building and its surroundings.

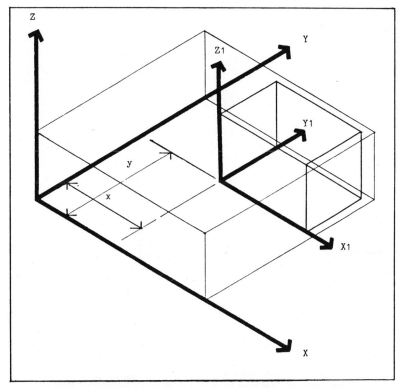

Fig. 8. Cambridge Environmental Model: primary and secondary co-ordinate systems.

consists of a series of statements relating to the environmental conditions in each room. For instance, for each space indicators of daylight quality (daylight factors) are given for a number of points in a room and the total flux required from the artificial lighting and the number of fittings required to produce this flux are given. The thermal analysis, in the original version, begins with the total heat flow through all external surfaces of each room at hourly intervals for each day type considered, followed by an analysis of each surface indicating the gain through the windows and solid surfaces (Fig. 9).

Possibly more important than their application as a direct design aid is the potential that models of this kind posses for explorative studies of built forms to produce information about the relationships between form and environmental behaviour. The Cambridge Model has been used for a series of experiments in which the environmental perform-

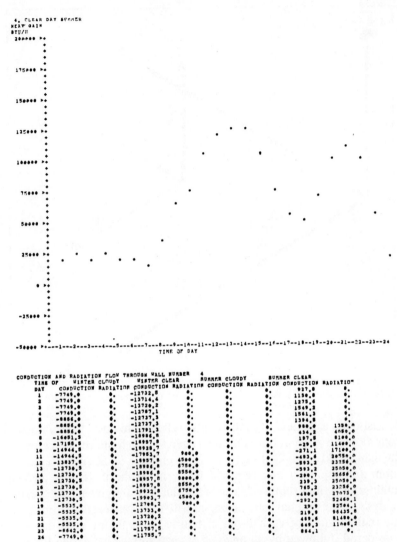

Fig. 9. Cambridge Environmental Model: typical output from thermal evaluation.

ance of a number of built forms was examined when the forms were subjected to varying conditions of obstruction and orientation. Four basic forms were used for the experiment (Fig. 10), each having a gross floor area of 40 000 sq.ft. and one plan dimension of 100 feet. Four alternative wall constructions ranging from completely glazed to

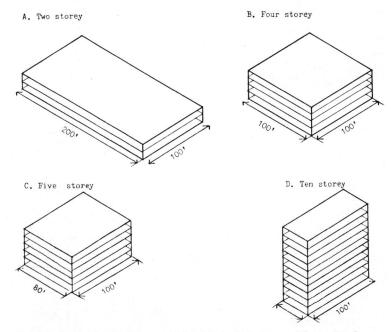

A. Two storey

B. Four storey

200'
100'

100'
100'

C. Five storey

D. Ten storey

80'
100'

100'

Fig. 10. Cambridge Environmental Model: basic forms used in explorations.

completely solid were assumed for each form giving a total of 16 basic buildings (Fig. 11). Each of the forms was first studied separately on unobstructed sites with varying orientations. Then each form was subjected in turn to a series of obstruction situations to investigate the effect of the obstruction on the unobstructed performance. An extract from the results of the experiments is shown in Fig. 12. The particular case illustrated is for fully glazed construction in the unobstructed situation on a clear summer day. The conclusions which can be drawn from studies of this type go beyond the usual 'rule-of-thumb' understanding of buildings and begin to build broadly based design rules for a wide range of archetypes.

Recently work has commenced on an expanded version of this model which includes an attempt to model user response in the environmental control system (Ref. 20).

7.6.1. BEAP: Building Enclosure Analysis Package
This program package has recently been developed by the author as a direct design aid to assist designers with the evaluation of the

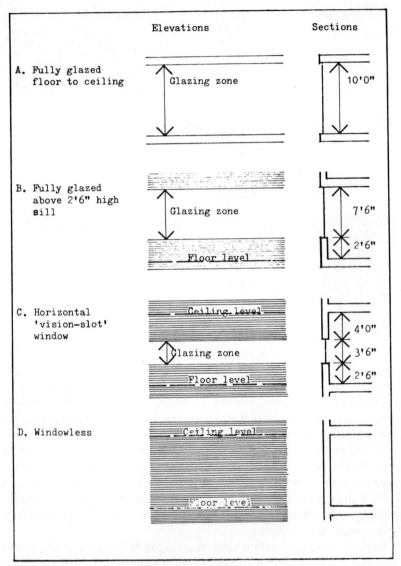

Fig. 11. Cambridge Environmental Model: construction variations used in explorations.

effectiveness of the building enclosure as an environmental control mechanism (refer to Fig. 2). It is seen as a forerunner of more sophisticated models which explore the consequences of decisions made

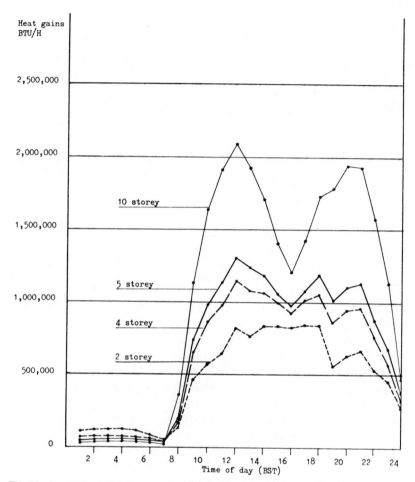

Fig. 12. Cambridge Environmental Model: comparative heat gains from design variations used in explorations.

about various aspects of this enclosure. The formulation of these models is discussed in the next section.

The package consists of a series of program modules which the user can select to evaluate various aspects of the environmental performance of a design proposal. At the present time the following modules have been implemented:

TEMP—   for the calculation of environmental temperatures within a defined space (or spaces),

GAINS—   for the calculation of thermal energy transfer into the internal environment when the space temperature is controlled (via heating or cooling equipment),

LIGHT—   for the calculation of the available daylight at certain defined points within a space, and

SOUND—   for the evaluation of resultant noise levels within spaces due to external noise sources.

In addition the *GAINS* module is sub-divided into three sub-modules, all of which are able to be used separately for detailed design. These are:

GLASS—   for the evaluation of glazing and sun control device combinations,

FABRIC—   for the calculation of energy transfer through the external walls and roof surfaces, and

INT—   for the estimation of energy gains due to lights, people and equipment in the space.

The relationships between these modules and other components of the package are illustrated in Fig. 13.

The package requires that the user first enters a description of the bounding enclosure of each space he wishes to analyse. This is achieved by defining the surface area and construction of each component of the enclosure (wall element, roof, window, floor, ceiling, etc.) and the geometry of any sun control devices used. Construction types need only be specified by a code number as the package contains a master datafile of the relevant physical properties of a large number of common building constructions. An updating facility is available for adding specific construction types to this master file. This cuts down the amount of data required from the user and streamlines the building description process.

The space description created by this process is then stored automatically by the package on a file which the user names. Thus at future sessions this data can be used with any or all of the program modules for further evaluation. All or part of this space description can be changed using an update facility so that various changes in either the geometry or physical properties of the enclosure can be investigated.

All of the modules access a datafile containing climatic data describing one typical day per month for a given region. These datafiles can be constructed using the *PROFILE* module to establish sets of

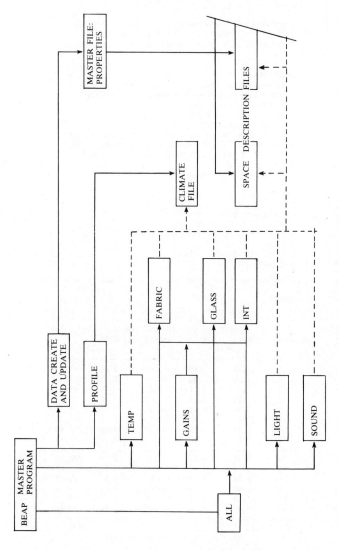

Fig. 13. Basic structure of *BEAP*.

```
WHICH MODULE
? GLASS
DATA SOURCE
? NEW


PROGRAM GLASS - DATA INPUT
THIS PROCESS CREATES AND STORES A DATAFILE.ENTER
INPUT AS DIRECTED WITH A SPACE BETWEEN EACH ITEM


ENTER HEADER TITLE
? WINDOW DESIGN TRIAL 1
ENTER WINDOW HEIGHT,WIDTH,U VALUE,SHADING COEFF.
AND TRANSMISSION FACTOR
? 2.2 1.4 4.6 0.66 0.75
SUN CONTROL DIMENSIONS
DEPTH OF OVERHANG AT HEAD,DEPTH OF OVERHANG AT JAMB
DISTANCE FROM HEAD TO UNDERSIDE OF OVERHANG,DISTANCE
FROM JAMB TO INSIDE EDGE OF OVERHANG(ALL IN METRES
? 0.35 0.35 0 0
INTERNAL AIR TEMPERATURE
? 21
ORIENTATION
? 0
ANOTHER WINDOW
? NO
WHAT IS THE NAME OF THIS FILE
? WIDOW
CLIMATE DATA SOURCE
? CLIMAT

SUNSHADE ANALYSIS : ORIENTATION    0. DEGEES E OF N

SUMMER
```

HOUR	AREAS		PERCENT	INCIDENT	TOTAL GAIN
	SHADED	SUNLIT	SHADED	RADIATION	(WATTS)
	SQ.MTRS				
5	3.08	0.00	100.00	0.00	-18.41
6	3.08	0.00	100.00	0.00	16.16
7	3.08	0.00	100.00	0.00	48.16
8	3.08	0.00	100.00	0.00	73.95
9	3.08	0.00	100.00	0.00	99.03
10	3.06	.02	99.27	2.72	119.24
11	2.53	.55	82.03	93.50	156.95
12	2.22	.86	72.01	158.75	179.44
13	2.66	.42	86.33	67.15	148.46
14	3.08	0.00	100.00	0.00	120.68
15	3.08	0.00	100.00	0.00	109.59
16	3.08	0.00	100.00	0.00	93.62
17	3.08	0.00	100.00	0.00	74.18
18	3.08	0.00	100.00	0.00	48.53
19	3.08	0.00	100.00	0.00	4.91

```
DAILY MEANS
            2.96     .12    95.98    21.47
```

Fig. 14. Extract from a terminal session using *BEAP.*

values for solar radiation, light intensity, diffuse radiation and drybulb temperature for a region. At the present time datafiles exist for Sydney, Melbourne and some NSW country towns.

Having defined the space or spaces to be evaluated, the user then selects the module or modules necessary to perform the particular evaluation he requires. By typing the command 'ALL', all of the program modules are selected and he obtains a simultaneous evaluation of the thermal, visual and aural performance of the building enclosure. Having inspected the results of the evaluation he can then modify the space description and proceed to evaluate the effects of these changes. An extract from a typical session is illustrated in Fig. 14. (It should be noted that at the time of writing (May, 1979) a preliminary version of the package had been implemented and that work is in progress on several modules which will produce output in graphical form).

Figure 15 contains an extract from the output produced by selecting the *TEMP, FABRIC* and *GLASS* modules. The *TEMP* module calculates hourly values of environmental temperature, a weighted mean of the air temperature and mean radiant temperature of the space. This is now an accepted index temperature for thermal comfort assessment. Thus the effectiveness of the enclosure for controlling the internal temperature can be assessed and various alternatives for the construction of the enclosure can be evaluated to determine whether or not any artificial means of environmental control are necessary. The *GAINS* module and its sub-module then allow the designer to explore the effectiveness of his decisions in reducing the heating or cooling load imposed upon the environmental plant.

The *LIGHT* module assesses the amount of daylight available at various points in the room and can be used to evaluate the effects of obstructions, sun control devices and interior surface treatment on this daylight. By default the program produces the illumination in lux available at two points, one near to each window and the other near to the wall furthest from the window. Alternatively the designer can specify a grid of points within the room and calculate the light available at these points. A standard CIE overcast sky is assumed with the option of clear sky conditions also being available. By selecting this module along with either *TEMP* or *GAINS,* a designer can begin to gain a feeling for the consequences of his decisions upon more than one environmental component and learn to appreciate the totality of the physical environment in buildings.

```
SOL AIR TEMPERATURES

HOUR   SOLAIR      AIR

SURFACE NO.   1 ORIENTATION   0 DEGREES E OF N
      1    20.28     20.28
      2    19.78     19.78
      3    19.56     19.56
      4    19.39     19.39
      5    19.93     19.22
      6    22.34     19.50
      7    24.69     20.72
      8    26.63     21.94
      9    30.33     23.11
     10    35.35     23.83
     11    38.49     24.22
     12    39.54     24.44
     13    37.98     24.28
     14    34.62     24.33
     15    30.32     24.11
     16    28.21     23.67
     17    26.80     23.11
     18    24.97     22.56
     19    21.89     21.89
     20    21.50     21.50
     21    21.17     21.17
     22    20.94     20.94
     23    20.72     20.72
     24    20.44     20.44


HOURLY TEMPERATURE ANALYSIS
SUMMER

VALIDATION CHECK DATA

HOUR    INTERNAL     EXTERNAL
-------------------------------
   1    24.18        20.28
   2    24.09        19.78
   3    24.05        19.56
   4    24.02        19.39
   5    23.98        19.22
   6    24.03        19.50
   7    24.25        20.72
   8    24.46        21.94
   9    26.03        23.11
  10    26.15        23.83
  11    26.30        24.22
  12    26.41        24.44
  13    26.33        24.28
  14    26.32        24.33
  15    26.32        24.11
  16    26.29        23.67
  17    26.22        23.11
  18    26.13        22.56
  19    24.64        21.89
  20    24.53        21.50
  21    24.43        21.17
  22    24.37        20.94
  23    24.32        20.72
  24    24.25        20.44
-------------------------------
AVERAGE TEMPERATURES
        25.08        21.86
-------------------------------
```

Fig. 15. Extract from output produced by *BEAP*. Internal temperatures and heat gains through the external envelope.

```
HOURLY HEAT GAIN INTO SPACE


SURFACE NO.   1 ORIENTATION   0 DEGREES E OF N
  HOUR    GLAZING     SOLID    TOTAL GAIN(WATTS)
  100      19.        93.           112.
  200     -15.        87.            72.
  300     -30.        80.            50.
  400     -41.        76.            35.
  500     -52.        63.            10.
  600     -34.        57.            23.
  700      49.        52.           101.
  800     131.        67.           197.
  900     209.       130.           339.
 1000     258.       192.           449.
 1100    1152.       242.          1395.
 1200    1600.       340.          1939.
 1300    2053.       471.          2525.
 1400    2198.       554.          2752.
 1500    1942.       581.          2523.
 1600    1336.       540.          1876.
 1700    1055.       452.          1507.
 1800     172.       339.           511.
 1900     127.       284.           411.
 2000     101.       247.           348.
 2100      78.       199.           277.
 2200      63.       118.           181.
 2300      49.       108.           156.
 2400      30.        99.           129.


TOTAL GAINS(WATTS)
  100       112.
  200        72.
  300        50.
  400        35.
  500        10.
  600        23.
  700       101.
  800       197.
  900       339.
 1000       449.
 1100      1395.
 1200      1939.
 1300      2525.
 1400      2752.
 1500      2523.
 1600      1876.
 1700      1507.
 1800       511.
 1900       411.
 2000       348.
 2100       277.
 2200       181.
 2300       156.
 2400       129.
```

Fig. 15.—contd.

The *SOUND* module calculates the resultant noise level in a space due to external noise sources defined at average frequency and then compares these levels with the maximum acceptable noise level for a space of this type. A further module to calculate reverberation times for special-use spaces such as lecture rooms will be included shortly.

7.7. MODELLING THE CONSEQUENCES OF DECISIONS

The package described above is a prototype for a much larger, more complex simulation model of the environmental control systems in buildings. While some feeling for the totality of the environment and the interactions between this environment and the building enclosure can be gained by using packages such as *BEAP,* it is difficult to fully determine the whole range of consequences which result from making a decision about any particular aspect of the building.

A research project currently in progress in the Department of Architectural Science at the University of Sydney is attempting to develop such a model which is capable of becoming a computer simulation laboratory for performing exploratory studies of the relationships between building enclosure design variables, environmental performance parameters and environmental plant variables, and, more importantly, is capable of modelling the consequences of decisions made about any one component of the building system upon other components. A typical decision consequence chain is shown in Fig. 16, summarising some of the consequences resulting from making decisions about the design of a window. It is this ability to provide designers with the total consequences of their decisions and to automatically take action as a result of an adverse consequence emerging that marks the major difference between this and other simulation models.

The operation of this facility can be demonstrated by a simple example. A decision might be made to decrease the amount of glazing on a facade to reduce the solar load in a space. By tracing the consequences of this decision the model might determine that the reduction in the amount of daylight which follows from the decision requires that the artificial lighting system should be redesigned and will carry out this redesign along with the calculation of the new heat gain produced by this new installation and then determine the effect of this on other components such as the size of ductwork provided, etc. Furthermore it is possible to determine whether or not a particular

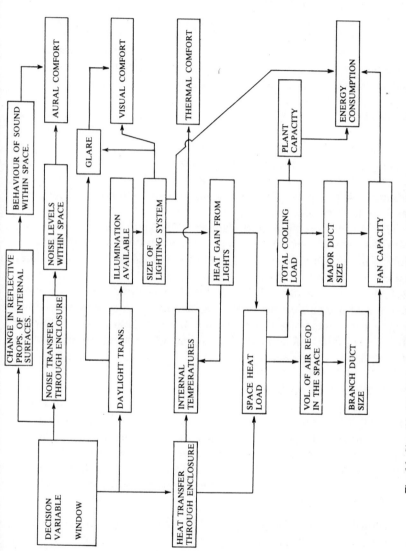

Fig. 16. Simplified decision-consequence graph. The example shown is for a window in a space.

stated goal of the designer (i.e., not to air-condition) may be placed in jeopardy by any particular decision. This Building Environment and Services Systems model (BESS) is being developed with several basic philosophies in mind. It should be applicable to all stages of the design process and particularly the sketch design stage when many critical decisions are made. This requires that the building description procedure should be continual, starting from an initial broad description and moving towards a more detailed description. This necessitates an expandable database capable of accepting descriptions at any level of detail and expanding as the design proceeds. The model should also offer analytical procedures compatible with the level of detail of the building description. Another aim has been to make better use of existing computer software by writing both input and output interfaces which render the programs more usable by architects by providing the designer with a means of communication using terms and methods familiar to him (e.g. graphics).

This approach requires a fundamental change in the program design with the *database* taking on a central organisational role to structure the flow of information to and from a series of individual program modules which process the information being organised by the database. Such systems begin to make full use of the data manipulation and storage facilities of modern computer systems and at the same time extend the real power of the first generation stand-alone program. The structure of the model is illustrated in Fig. 17 and some of the major components of the model are discussed below.

7.7.1. BESS Control System

This forms the operational heart of the model. Because it is unnecessary and undesirable for all of the components of the model to reside in the central memory of the computer all of the time, the major function of this component is to monitor user commands and take appropriate action by calling the appropriate datafiles and program files into the central memory to carry out the functions required by the user. It has the following components.

Control Language Interpreter (CLI). The function of this component is to accept input commands from the user via an interactive terminal and initiate actions required by the commands. The commands are part of a problem-oriented language which the designer uses to communicate with the model. The Command Language Structure has several levels.

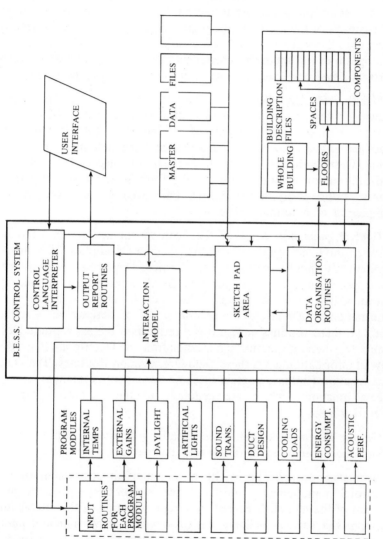

Fig. 17. The Building Environment and Services Systems *(BESS)* model.

At this level, the language consists of a small number of key words which select various modes of operation. The CLI after receiving a valid command assembles the necessary components to produce a sequence of operations and according to the nature of the command will hand over control of the model to the particular area of the model currently executing. Typical Command Words allow a designer to enter a new description of a component, change part of the data structure, select a particular evaluative sequence or request output from a particular file.

Sketch Pad Area (SPA). This can be likened to the architect's drawing board. It is an area of central core in which information generated by other components of the model is stored temporarily together with a copy of the particular building description currently being investigated. This facility allows the user to inspect data, delete or add information without disturbing the Data Structure stored permanently. Information in the Sketch Pad Area is destroyed at the completion of a terminal session.

Data Organization Routines. This component acts as an interface between the Control System and the Building Description Files stored permanently on a Secondary Storage Device. These routines transform the information stored temporarily in the SPA into a form suitable for insertion into the Description Files. For instance, if a piece of information which relates to several levels of description is to be inserted, these routines ensure it is inserted into the appropriate files. Similarly, when information is requested from the Description Files, the flow of information is via these Data Organization Routines. The Data Organization Routines contain machine-dependent permanent storage access functions, which are generally unique to each computer operating system.

Output Report Routines. These routines generate output of the information contained in the Sketch Pad Area.

Interaction Model. This is the most important component of the Control System, being the interface between all of the program files and the rest of the model. It consists of a representation of the interaction between the various building design variables, environmental parameters and environmental plant variables through which the consequences of a decision are established. A trace algorithm establishes a consequence path moving from a description made about a particular component through all components which interact with the initial component. At each node in this path the strength of the consequence is established and the system determines what action, if any, should be taken.

Building Description Files. Outside of the Control System, the Geometrical and Technical Description of the building is stored on a permanent storage device. As illustrated in Fig. 17, the Description is structured conceptually at various levels of detail. Each level has forward and backward pointers establishing connections between data items stored at each level. Four levels of description are possible: Whole Building, Typical Floors, Spaces and Components. Each level represents an increase in the amount of detail required and can be equated to various stages in the development of design proposals.

Master Data Files. These contain major items of data used by the evaluation programs, or required by the user during the building description procedures. Such items as properties of materials, operating data for services systems or components and weather data are stored. An important function of these files is to provide default information to the evaluation programs when this information is not provided by the user.

Evaluation Programs. The Evaluative programs are considered to be modules which can be 'plugged-in' to the system to assemble the required package of operations. The exact configuration depends upon the purpose of the study and the availability of appropriate programs. In theory, existing computer programs from any source may be assembled in this fashion although a certain amount of "interfacing" will be required before the programs can be integrated.

As a design aid the model will allow a designer to describe a given building at various levels of detail and then manipulate the design parameters affecting the envelope design to evaluate the effects of changes in these parameters on the state of the whole system. Decisions such as a change in the U-value of the envelope, a change in the form of the envelope or the amount of glass can be evaluated in this way and their consequences upon the performance of the service systems can be assessed.

When fully developed, the model will allow the various consultants involved to evaluate the effects of their decisions upon other aspects of the environmental behaviour. Thus the lighting designer will learn how his decisions might affect the thermal aspects of the total environment and conversely a decision made to benefit the thermal goals can be analysed for its consequences upon the lighting. For research purposes the model can be used to investigate relationships between sets of design variables and to investigate the effects of changes in design variables upon the system state. By selecting appropriate sets of variables and freezing other variables, one can cycle through a sequence of values for these variables and monitor the system response to these changes to obtain a plot of the relationships existing between sets of system variables.

7.8. CONCLUSION

This paper has attempted to demonstrate that suitable computational tools are becoming available to assist designers in the quantitative evaluation of the physical environment in buildings and to assess the effects of their decisions upon this environment. No longer is it good enough for designers to leave the design of this environment to consultants for it is very much a part of the architecture of a building. Further, in terms of energy conservation, architects can now play an important part in determining the energy efficiency of buildings by designing building enclosures which play a positive rôle in the creation of the internal environment. What is required at the present time to solve many of the energy problems in buildings is alternative attitudes on the part of designers rather than alternative technologies.

REFERENCES

1. Loudon, A. G., Summertime Temperatures in Buildings, Current Paper 47/68, Building Research Establishment (UK), London, 1968.
2. Stephenson, D. G. and Mitalas, G. P., Cooling Load Calculations by Thermal Response Factors, Trans ASHRAE 73, Paper No. 1028, American Society of Heating, Refrigerating and Air Conditioning Engineers, New York, 1969.
3. Plant, C. G. and Archer, D. W., 'A lighting prediction method for complex environments,' Lighting Research and Technology, Research Note, 4(2), 1972.
4. Forwood, B. S., 'Environmental design and building services,' in Gero, J. S. (Ed.): Computer Applications in Architecture, Applied Science Publishers, London, 1977.
5. Nevrala, D. J., Robbie, J. V. and Fitzgerald, D., A Comparison of Five Digital Computer Programs for Calculating Maximum Air Conditioning Loads, Laboratory Report 62, Heating and Ventilating Research Assoc. (UK), London, 1970.
6. Degelman, L., 'Monte Carlo simulation of solar radiation and dry bulb temperatures

for air conditioning purposes,' in Kennedy, M. (Ed.): *Kentucky Workshop on Computer Applications to Environmental Design*, pp 213–223, 1971.

7. Lund, H. 'The Reference Year,' A Set of Climatic Data for Environmental engineering, *Proc second Symposium on the Use of Computers for Environmental Engineering Related to Buildings*, Co. STIC/ASHRAE, Paris, June 1974.

8. Low, D. W., 'A direct weather data filter,' *IBM Journal of Research and Development*, Vol. **22**, No. 5, 485–495, 1978.

9. Kusuda, T. *NBSLD, Computer Program for Heating and Cooling Loads in Buildings*, National Bureau of Standards, Building Science Series 69, US Dept. of Commerce, Washington D.C. 1974.

10. Wooldridge, M. 'Air conditioning load calculation using program *TEMPER*,' *Aust Refrig, Air Conditioning and Heating*, Vol. **27**, 26–28 and 37–38, 1973.

11. Ayres, J. M., 'Predicting building energy requirements,' *Energy and Buildings*, Vol. **1**, No. 1, 11–18, 1977.

12. Lokmanhekim, M. et al, *Computer Program for the Analysis of Energy Utilisation in Postal Facilities*, Research Report RE49–67, General American Transportation Corp., Niles Illinois, 1967.

13. Down, P. G. and Curtis, D., 'Graphical and interactive computer techniques for environmental engineering design,' in Sherratt, A. (Ed.): *Integrated Environment in Building Design*, Applied Science Publishers, London, 1974.

14. Chen, S. Y. S., 'Existing load and energy programs,' *Heating, Piping and Air Conditioning*, Vol. **47**, 35–39, 1975.

15. *GLIM—General Light Interreflection Model*, Applied Research of Cambridge, Cambridge, 1976.

16. Bensasson, S. and Burgess, K. *Computer Programs for Daylighting in Buildings*, Evaluation Report 3, Design Office Consortium, Cambridge, 1978.

17. Hawkes, D. and Stibbs, R. *The Environmental Evaluation of Buildings—1. A Mathematical Model*, Working Paper 15, Land Use and Built Form Studies, Cambridge University, Cambridge, 1969.

18. Hawkes, D., *The Development of an Environmental Model*, Working Paper 55, Land Use and Built Form Studies, Cambridge University, Cambridge 1971.

19. Hawkes, D. 'Modelling the environmental performance of built forms,' in March, L. (Ed.): *The Architecture of Form*, Cambridge Urban and Architectural Studies, Cambridge University Press, London, 1976.

20. Hawkes, D. and Willey, H., 'User response in the environmental control system,' in Steadman, P. (ed.): *Trans. Martin Centre of Architectural and Urban Studies*, Vol. **2**, 111–135, 1977.

8

Computer Programs for the Design of the Physical Environment in Buildings

A. D. RADFORD*

Department of Architectural Science,
University of Sydney, Australia

8.1. INTRODUCTION

There are two practical reasons for turning to computers as an aid in environmental design: they can save the designer effort and time and they can offer the opportunity for him to work with more complete information about the effects of his design decisions. In this chapter I want to examine the forms of information which computer programs can produce and to make a distinction between evaluative programs and generative programs. Evaluative programs will analyse a design solution provided by the designer and are reviewed in the previous chapter. Generative programs will produce design solutions within the computer and are the main subject of this chapter.

8.2. PASSIVE CONTROL OF THE PHYSICAL ENVIRONMENT

Design for passive control of solar energy has direct effects on the thermal and visual environments and indirect effects on the aural environment as well. It is therefore an integral part of design for the physical environment as a whole. To illustrate the scope of the problem consider a typical room in a building (Fig. 1). In acting as a filter between internal and external climates the building enclosure will modify the environment in terms of heat, light and sound and in terms

*Present address: 10 Marchmont Street, Edinburgh EH9 1EL, Scotland.

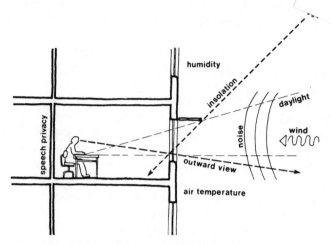

Fig. 1. Environmental attributes for a typical room.

of some psychological factors such as outward view. Some parts of this environment can be regarded, up to an ideal level, as desirable attributes and some as undesirable. The architect may want to allow insolation in winter for both its thermal and psychological benefits and may also want daylight in the room. But if better winter insolation and daylighting is achieved by increasing the size of the window, what will be the effect on temperature in summer? Sun shades will control the period of insolation but reduce the level of daylighting. A horizontal window high in the external wall is efficient for daylighting but no use for outward view. Windows also increase the intrusion of external noise, undesirable in itself but possibly useful as a masking sound to aid speech privacy. The requirements are conflicting and good solutions are not at all clear.

To make any rational design decision the architect must have some kind of information on these likely environmental consequences. At the early stages of design this information comes from previous experience in practice or education and from manuals and reference books which suggest a qualitative approach to the problem. For many aspects of architecture qualitative information is the best that can be obtained. For environmental design, however, some form of quantitative information is needed to make an objective assessment of building proposals. Two- or three-dimensional physical models and simplified mathematical models for manual use have long been used for this purpose. Both approaches are tedious and time consuming for any extensive study and designers tend to work with a minimal amount of information. On the other hand computers are well suited to the fairly complicated and repetitive mathematics involved. Indeed, if one wants to investigate the interacting effects of insolation, temperature and daylighting the problem can be so complex that it cannot be realistically tackled except with the assistance of a computer. Yet computers have not gained the acceptance in architectural offices that one might expect given their impact in other professions, in industry and in commerce. This is partly because many of the early programs produced by research into computer-aided design did not adequately serve the architects needs, but it is also partly because of a fear that the computer and not the architect will emerge in control. Computers can only produce information and it is for the architect to use that information in the design process in the same way as information derived from books, manuals, site investigations or any other source. The advantage of computers is that, because of their ability to carry out complex calculations quickly and relatively cheaply, this information can be pointed directly at the problem and be, if necessary, remarkably detailed. What we are looking for, then, is computer programs that will provide the kind of information that the architect needs for environmental design.

8.3. EVALUATIVE COMPUTER PROGRAMS

The first requirement is for good evaluation programs to analyse specific design proposals (See Chapter 7). This is the area in which most research work has been carried out and some very sophisticated programs have been developed, particularly for calculating thermal loads due to solar energy and other sources. The majority of them are oriented towards the mechanical engineer and an engineering approach to the problem. Because of the level of detail employed in their methods of prediction they require a correspondingly detailed description of the building, surroundings and local climate. This means that they tend not to be used until most, if not all, of the important design decisions are already made, a satisfactory state of affairs if the objective is to determine heating or cooling plant capacity but not very useful for an architect concerned with the design of the building envelope. This lack of effectiveness has been realized and some recent evaluative programs are oriented towards the design stages, requiring a much simpler building description.

Evaluation can be represented as a three-part process where the parameters which describe the design are assembled first, calculations are carried out and the predicted performance is presented. If this performance is unsatisfactory the design is modified and the operation repeated. The great advantage of this approach is that by fixing all the design variables one can examine their effects on as many different aspects of the problem as there are prediction methods available. The disadvantage is that evaluation programs require the user to operate by trial and error. To get any quantitative information the architect must first have a solution and much of the design process therefore involves a cyclical procedure of postulation-evaluation-modification where different possibilities are examined with increasing detail and certainty. Koenigsberger (Ref. 1) has aptly described this approach to design as investigating backwards. Clearly some form of information which prescribed good solutions would often be more useful.

8.4. GENERATIVE COMPUTER PROGRAMS

Let us examine the reverse of this approach. Instead of specifying the design solution and finding the resulting performance, is it possible to specify the required performance and find a design solution which provides it? There are a number of computer programs which generate design solutions but two points must be made about them. The first concerns the nature of the generated solutions. A computer program will make design decisions mechanistically in accordance with the rules set out within it. If these rules do not take account of all the design aspects and aims that the architect would wish to be taken into account then neither will the design decisions. This returns to the notion of computers as providers of information; they can prescribe good solutions in relation to specific criteria for which the program is designed, but it is for the architect to use that information in relation to other criteria. The second point concerns availability. Almost all widely available computer programs which qualify in the category "available tools and methods presently applicable", are evaluation programs. There are very few which carry out design rather than analysis functions. They are worth talking about because the kind of information offered by generative programs can be particularly useful and will, I think, become increasingly important tools in the future. Sometimes the characteristics required of a design solution can be specified directly as an absolute level of performance in some criterion. A familiar example is the lumen method of artificial lighting design which can be carried out manually or by several computer programs; the US *APEC* Lighting Calculation Program is one of them (Ref. 2). A performance is specified as a required design illuminance on the working plane and the design solution is generated in terms of a number and layout of luminaires which will provide this illuminance. The type of luminaire can be either part of the performance specification or part of the solution. Such direct methods are rare in the building sciences; contrast it with daylight design where the only approach is evaluation. More often the desired performance must be expressed in terms of a goal (maximum or minimum) rather than an absolute level of performance. The problem then becomes one of optimization. Optimization techniques are useful because they can be made to operate with methods of analysis which are essentially evaluative in a manner which produces prescriptive information, but they have a number of drawbacks. Architectural problems typically involve non-linear relationships and numerous and complex constraints, just the kind of problem for which most optimization techniques either become cumbersome or fail altogether. Optimization also requires a single specific goal which is to be optimized and this is often difficult to formulate in a design activity characterized by multiple and ill-defined objectives.

Nevertheless formal optimization techniques have been applied to a number of building design problems over the past two decades (Ref. 3). In environmental design all these applications have concerned thermal performance, either for the design of buildings and heating/cooling plant or for policies for plant operation. Comfort, expressed as a function of internal temperature (Ref. 4), energy use (Ref. 5) and monetary cost (Ref. 6) have all been used as criteria and have valid claims for preference. If minimum energy use or cost is the objective, the required comfort conditions become constraints. Such programs produce a target value for performance and an overall policy (in terms of design variables such as thermal insulation, glass area, and plant capacity) for its achievement. The designer's job is to carry out the detailed design in the light of these target values.

In the remainder of this chapter I want to describe three different examples of prescriptive design information produced by computer programs. The first concerns the design of one building element (sun shades) for performance in one environmental component (period of insolation). The second concerns the design of another building element (windows) for a range of levels of performance in each of three environmental components (internal temperature, daylighting and ventilation). The third concerns the design of a range of feasible combinations of performance in two or more environmental components. All three provide a range or field of results which indicate good solutions and from which the architect can choose.

8.4.1. Design Option Diagrams for Sun Shades
A program for the design of fixed external sun shades developed by Shaviv (Ref. 7) provides a classic example of a direct generative design

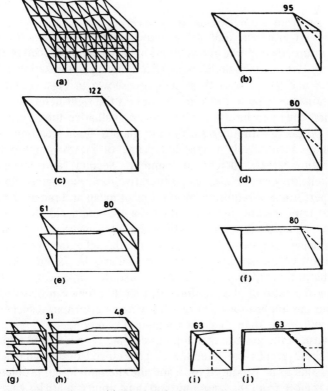

Fig. 2. Axonometric diagram (a) showing shade projection required to shade a window for a specific orientation, period of the year and hours of the day. Some alternative designs are shown in (b)—(h). (Reproduced from Ref. 7).

aid. The traditional approach to sun shade design has been evaluation: the shape of a small roof or shade was assumed and checks carried out to find the extent to which solar penetration was prevented. Shaviv inverts the problem. For each point on a notional grid over a given window the program finds the necessary projection of a shade sufficient to prevent penetration of direct solar radiation on given days and hours. The results are presented graphically and represent the whole field of feasible solutions—Fig. 2(a). Using this information the architect can consider all the possibilities which meet the shading requirements, eg. Fig. 2 (b)–(j), and still retain aesthetic control. Instead of the standardization which allegedly results from computer-aided design, the information makes possible the design of many variations of efficient non-standard shades with a consequent enrichment of building design.

8.4.2. Environmental Design Aid Overlays

A series of graphical aids for window design in relation to internal temperature, daylighting and ventilation have been produced by the UK Building Research Establishment (BRE) using optimization methods (Refs. 8 and 9). Two of these aids are shown in Figs. 3 and 4; the restrictions applying to them are set out on the right hand side of each aid. First they can be used simply as an evaluative tool. Assuming a design proposal with a certain ratio of glass-to-floor area one can find from Fig. 3 the likely mean and range of internal environmental temperature at the height of summer. Second, and much more important, they can be used as a generative tool. For a given floor area and a performance requirement in terms of mean and range of summer internal temperature one can find from the same aid the maximum area of glass. Using Fig. 4 the glass area necessary to meet a performance requirement in terms of daylight factor over some proportion of the working plane can similarly be found. Other aids cover natural ventilation. All of them have the same scale on the axis showing the ratio of glass-to-floor area so that they can be overlaid to examine the implications and feasibility of a performance specification embracing more than one environmental component.

Because of the amount of computer computation required to produce them, these graphs are intended as generalized design guides rather than as aids to be produced for a specific site and design problem. The user is remote from the computer and must approximate his case to the set of values provided; hence the non-dimensional representation of room size in proportional terms. Within their scope and level of detail, however, they represent a major advance on the information previously available.

8.4.3. Environmental Tradeoff Diagrams

The methods described above provide information about design for insolation, thermal conditions or daylighting but no direct information on the relation between them. In architecture there is a long history of research into the separate components of the environment but much less work on the relation of one to another and to the whole. This, though, is the real problem that architects face in the design of a building; they are not concerned about providing the least heat gain or best daylighting or anything else in isolation. Their task is to seek a solution that, taken as a whole, is the best that can be devised (Ref. 10). This implies that there must be some conscious or unconscious process of balancing or trading of performance in the various environmental components one against another. Environmental tradeoff diagrams aid and clarify this process by quantifying the implications of choosing a certain level of performance in one environmental component on the performance that can be achieved in some other component (Ref. 11).

As an example, consider the design problem of a room in a building for which natural lighting is required without a need for air conditioning in summer. To make a comparison of design solutions the environmental components concerned must be interpreted in terms of measurable criteria; these could be daylight factor at the rear of the room for natural lighting and peak internal temperature for summer thermal conditions. Different solutions can provide a (potentially) infinite number of different predicted daylight factors and an infinite number of different predicted peak temperatures. What the designer is interested in is how much worsening of daylight factor must be accepted in return for a bettering of peak internal temperature. This is the information provided by an environmental tradeoff diagram (Fig. 5). It depicts what in the theory of multi-criteria decision making (Ref. 12) is known as the set of efficient or Pareto optimal solutions, that is the set of solutions for which performance in one criterion is better than that given by any other solution which has the same or better performance in the other criteria.

Examining Fig. 5, a daylight factor of d_1 can be achieved with a peak internal temperature of t_1 using two windows of certain dimensions and particular glass and wall construction types. No other solution within a specified acceptable range of window, shading and construction types

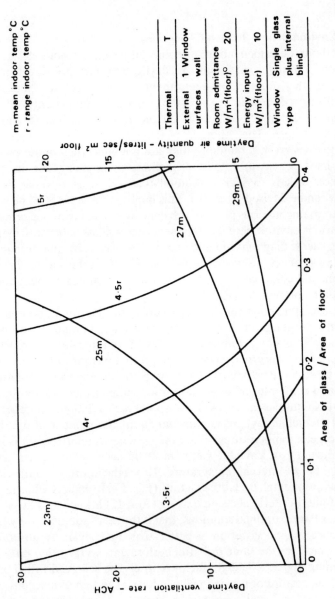

Fig. 3. BRE thermal design aid for small office fitted with internal blinds (Reproduced from Ref. 8).

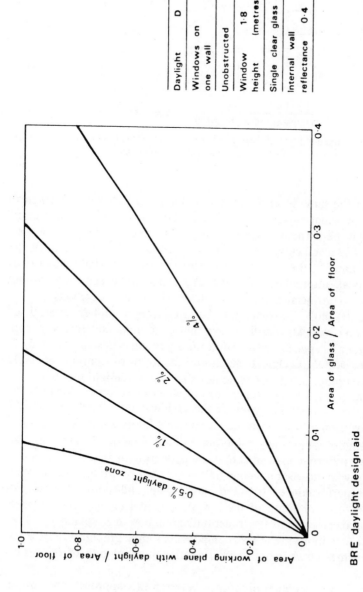

Fig. 4. BRE daylight design aid (Reproduced from Ref. 8).

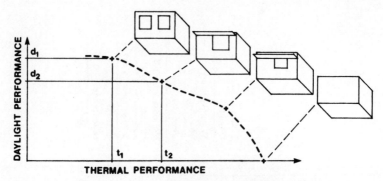

Fig. 5. Environmental tradeoff diagram for thermal and daylight performance in a room with some associated design solutions.

will offer the same level of daylight and a better thermal performance. An improvement in peak internal temperature to t_2 with least worsening of daylight performance can be achieved by another design using one window and a sun shade. A performance combination lying outside the area bounded by the tradeoff curve (for example a daylight factor of d_1 with a peak internal temperature of t_2) cannot be achieved without recourse to artificial services, whatever the design decisions.

These tradeoff diagrams can be produced as either generalized information with standardized external conditions and forms of construction or as specific information for a particular design situation. In the latter case the architect can control the forms of solution generated by the computer programs by nominating a set of design rules to restrict the number, layout and dimensions of windows or other elements and the variety of material types. If the architect only wants to consider solutions using brick construction, concrete floors and single windows, for example, only such solutions will be generated. He can also nominate different environmental components to be taken into account. He may want to examine the tradeoffs between winter and summer thermal performance, between daylighting and noise intrusion or between three or more of these environmental components at once. With three components the tradeoff diagram becomes a plane instead of a curve; with more than three components simple graphical representation becomes cumbersome and computer manipulation of the results desirable.

There is a conceptual difference between this approach and that of the BRE design aid overlays. In the latter, performance in a single environmental component is plotted against a design variable; the proportion of the working plane with daylight factor above certain levels is plotted against the proportion of glazing and internal environmental temperature is plotted in a second graph against the same design variable for various ventilation conditions. Each glazing, shading or construction type results in a different graph. In the tradeoff diagrams the environmental components are plotted directly against each other to describe in a single graph the set of "efficient" solutions to the design problem. To make a good decision the architect needs to know both the environmental tradeoffs and what the resultant design will then be. Indeed, the tradeoff diagram may be used only to indicate a design direction and the chosen design solution may be none of the plotted points. The task of the computer is to provide information; control remains with the architect.

8.5. SUMMARY

In this paper I have emphasized the distinction between computer programs which evaluate a given design solution to predict its performance and those which generate design solutions for a given performance specification. Evaluative and generative programs produce very different kinds of information. Evaluative programs can produce a great deal of information about performance in many aspects of environmental design but for only one solution at a time. They tell the designer nothing about that solution compared with other feasible solutions unless he repeats the analysis with different designs in a process of informal optimization. Generative programs can produce a range of solutions to a given design problem but provide a much smaller amount of performance information. Which approach is appropriate depends on the kind of information being sought. At the early stages of design the prime need is to identify likely good solutions and generative methods are required. Once these solutions are known more information can be obtained about them by evaluation and they can be modified if necessary. The important point I want to make is that rational decision making for the design of the physical environment requires good, concise and pointed information and that many of the more useful forms for this information can only be produced with the assistance of a computer.

REFERENCES

1. Koenigsberger, O., 'Architectural science for practitioners,' *Architectural Science Review*, Vol. **21**, No. 1, 6–7, 1978.
2. Lee, K., *Performance Specification of Computer Aided Environmental Design*, Environmental Design and Research Center, Boston, Mass, 1975.
3. Gero, J. S., 'Architectural optimization —a review,' *Engineering Optimization*, Vol. **1**, 189–199, 1975.
4. Gupta, C. L., 'A systematic approach to optimal thermal design,' *Building Science*, Vol. **5**, 165–173, 1970.
5. Jurovics, S. A., 'Optimization applied to the design of energy efficient building,' *IBM Journal of Research and Development*, Vol. **22**, No. 4, 378–385, 1978.
6. Wilson, A. J. and Templeman, A. B., 'An approach to the optimal design of office buildings,' *Building and Environment*, Vol. **11**, 39–50, 1976.
7. Shaviv, E., 'A method for the design of fixed external sun shades,' *Build International*, Vol. **8**, 121–150, 1975.
8. Milbank, N. O., *A New Approach to Predicting the Thermal Environment in Buildings at the Early Design Stage*, CP2/74, Building Research Establishment UK, London, 1974.
9. Jones, R. H. L., *Computer Optimization for Studying Temperatures in Buildings*, PD 71/74, Building Research Establishment UK, London, 1974.
10. Manning, P., 'Windows, environment and people,' *Interbuild/Arena*, 20–25, Oct. 1967.
11. Radford, A. D. and Gero, J. S., 'Optimization for information in integrated environmental design,' *Proc. Conf. PArC 79*, 447–56, 1979.
12. Cochrane, J. and Zeleny, M. *'Multiple Criteria Decision Making,'* University of South Carolina Press, Columbia, 1973.

9

Tradeoff Diagrams for the Integrated Design of the Physical Environment in Buildings

A. D. Radford† and J. S. Gero‡
Department of Architectural Science,
University of Sydney, Australia

9.1. INTRODUCTION

The traditional approach to design for the physical environment in buildings has been to divide the problem into discrete parts. As means of control, the effects of the building fabric and the effects of installed mechanical services were divorced. One was the domain of the architect and the other the domain of the mechanical engineering consultant. Indeed, in thermal design the effect of the building came to be regarded as part of the problem rather than part of the solution and the whole responsibility for maintaining comfortable thermal conditions was placed on mechanical services. In scope, the design requirements for the principal environmental components of heating, cooling, lighting and ventilation were examined and specified separately. In integrated environmental design a more efficient overall solution is sought by re-placing this compartmentalization by the study and design of the building/environment system as a whole. It is a concept has become increasingly well known and accepted by architects. To date the emphasis has been on integrating the controls, stressing the rôle of the building fabric in reducing the performance required of mechanical plant with a consequent saving of cost and energy. There has been much less emphasis on the integration of design for different environmental components. The subject of this chapter is a more integrated approach to design for different aspects of the environment through the

†Present address: 10 Marchmont Street, Edinburgh EH9 1EL, Scotland.
‡Present address: University of Strathclyde, 131 Rottenrow, Glasgow G4, Scotland.

exploration and clarification of the tradeoffs involved in design decision making.

9.2. THE MULTI-CRITERION PROBLEM

In acting as a filter between internal and external climates the building enclosure will modify the environment in terms of heat, light and sound and in terms of some psychological aspects such as view and insolation. Some parts of this environment can be regarded, up to an ideal level, as desirable attributes and some as undesirable. To illustrate the scope of the problem consider a typical room in a building (see Fig. 1, Chapter 8). The architect may want to allow insolation in winter for both its thermal and psychological benefits and may also want daylight in the room. But if better winter insolation and daylighting is achieved by increasing the size of the window, what will be the effect on temperature in summer? Sun shades will control the period of insolation but reduce the level of daylighting. A horizontal window high in the external wall is efficient for daylighting but no use for outward view. Windows also increase the intrusion of external noise, undesirable in itself but possibly useful as a masking sound to aid speech privacy. The requirements are conflicting and good solutions are not at all clear.

To make any rational design the architect must have some kind of information on at least the most important of these environmental consequences. At the early stages of design this information comes from previous experience in practice or education and from manuals and reference books which suggest a qualitative approach to the problem. For many aspects of architecture, qualitative information is the best that can be obtained. For environmental design, however, some form of quantitative information is needed to make an objective assessment of building proposals. Two- or three-dimensional physical models and simplified mathematical models for manual use have long been used for this purpose. More recently, computer programs providing very detailed simulations of environmental performance have become available. The great advantage of simulation is that by fixing all the design variables one can examine their effects on as many different aspects of the problem as there are prediction methods available. The disadvantage is that simulation programs require the user to operate by trial and error. To get any quantitative information the architect must first have a solution and much of the design process therefore involves a cyclical procedure of postulation, evaluation and modification where different possibilities are examined with increasing detail and precision. Koenigsberger (Ref. 1) has aptly described this approach to design as investigating backwards. Clearly some form of information which prescribed good solutions would often be more useful. Existing simulation techniques also fail to provide any direct information on the relationship between different environmental components, information which is central to the concept of integrated environmental design. In designing a building architects are not seeking to provide only the best daylight or least heat gain or anything else in isolation. Their concern is to find the solution that, taken as a whole, is the best that can be devised. For environmental design this requires some form of prescriptive quantitative information which relates the performance achievable in different environmental attributes not only to the building design but also to each other.

The approach described here traces the implications of choosing a certain level of performance in one environmental attribute on the performance that can be achieved in some other attribute by quantifying the tradeoffs involved. It can best be described by means of an example. Consider a room for which natural lighting is required without a need for air-conditioning in summer. Here two environmental attributes are of principal interest: natural lighting and summer thermal conditions. To make a comparison of design solutions performance in these attributes must be interpreted in terms of measurable criteria. Suitable choices are the daylight factor at the rear of the room with overcast sky conditions and peak internal environmental temperature with predicted external conditions at the height of summer. Different design solutions will provide a (potentially) infinite number of different feasible combinations of predicted daylight factors and peak temperatures. However, these feasible combinations will be restricted by the range of feasible values of the design variables and the physical laws which determine the relationship between internal and external conditions. If they were all plotted on a graph of daylight factor against peak temperature they would lie within some bounded feasible criteria space. Moreover, for any specific value of peak temperature there will be a maximum possible value for the daylight factor. What the designer is interested in is how much worsening of thermal performance must be accepted in return for a bettering of daylight performance. His design options can be made explicit if one can identify the set of performance combinations such that improved levels of daylight factor are always

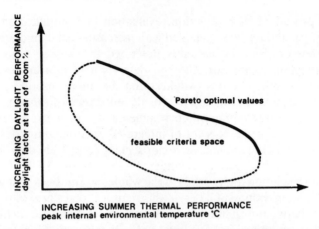

Fig. 1. Feasible criteria space and Pareto optimal values for daylighting and thermal performance

obtained at minimum disadvantage in terms of peak temperature. These values lie along the boundary of the criteria space and in the theory of multi-criteria decision making are known as efficient, non-dominated or Pareto optimal values (Fig. 1).

The corresponding design solutions are known as the class of Pareto optimal solutions (Ref. 2) that is the class of solutions for which performance in one criterion is better than that given by any other solution which has the same or better performance in the other criteria. To trace them requires a mathematical model of building/environment behaviour in the environmental attributes that are of interest and an optimization method to operate on that model.

Although there are other approaches, Pareto optimal values can be derived from the optimization of linear combinations of the criteria with varying weights, that is

$$R = \text{opt} \sum_{p=1}^{P} w_p a_p \qquad (1)$$

where a_p is the performance in the pth of P criteria and the weight, w_p, applied to that performance, ranges over non-negative real numbers and varies with each optimization cycle (Ref. 3). This form of objective function is familiar from its more common application as an additive composition decision model in which the performance of a multi-attributed solution is deemed to equal the sum of the weighted performances of its attributes. Indeed, Yu (Ref. 4) demonstrates that the one-dimensional additive composition model and the Pareto optimality approach are essentially two extreme cases in a domain of domination structures. The former results in a lighter computational burden and a greater burden on the decision maker, requiring him to estimate in advance the impact of the tradeoffs he is making; the latter places a greater burden on the computer and allows the decision maker to make tradeoffs with knowledge of their impacts. The important difference is that for Pareto optimal values only the optimal solution to the objective function (1) is of interest at each iteration, not the weights applied nor the aggregated return achieved. The information that is sought and used is completely independent of any assumptions of either weighting or additivity.

9.3. SYSTEM MODEL

A system model has been developed to provide for a comprehensive set of design variables, including internal and external wall, floor and ceiling construction and surfaces and the position and projection of continuous horizontal and vertical sun shades. Since environmental performance criteria must be related to a specific point or space in order to be meaningful, a model of the building/environment system must be based at a level of individual rooms or areas. Earlier simulation models have followed this same rationale. The effect of any element of the room enclosure on the internal environment depends primarily on two pieces of information, the construction or material of the element and the location of the element. In the model the location variable is systematized by superimposing a notional grid over the plane of the enclosing surfaces (Fig. 2). The external wall is thereby divided into numerous subplanes, while the internal surfaces, which may be required to be of all one construction, are divided coarsely and perhaps as whole planes. Windows, solid and open areas will be made up of numbers of these subplanes and sun shades will be positioned on this grid. Naturally, the finer the grid used the finer the possible definition. The effect of a particular location on the internal environment will be determined by the external environment (solar radiation, external temperature, noise levels, etc.) impinging on it and the properties of the construction form which occupy it. Traditional practice has been followed in choosing criteria and prediction methods for the environmental components (Ref. 5).

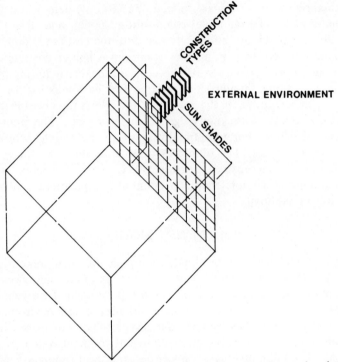

CONSTRUCTION TYPES

EXTERNAL ENVIRONMENT

SUN SHADES

Fig. 2. Decomposition of room enclosing surfaces into discrete locations

Clearly it would be impossible in practice for every location to be occupied by a different construction form even if that situation resulted in good environmental performance. There will be practical restrictions on the way materials can fit together to produce a feasible solution. More important, an architect will often have specific ideas of his own about the form the envelope design can take without violating aesthetic or other requirements. These requirements are modelled by a set of design rules which can be nominated by the architect and which limit the solution space. Closely specified requirements mean a smaller solution space and less computation than with a more open specification. The extreme case is simulation where everything is specified.

The design rules are expressed as three classes of constraint: topology, geometry and materials.

(1) *Topology:* restrictions on the number and spatial relation of windows and other elements.

(2) *Geometry:* restrictions on the position, shape and minimum and maximum lengths and heights of an element.

(3) *Materials:* restrictions on acceptable forms of construction, the number of different materials and the points at which materials can change.

The ability to accept these constraints must be built into an optimization problem formulation for identifying the Pareto optimal solutions. In practice there is no single best approach.

The choice of technique is restricted by the non-linear relationships involved and by the need to handle integer and discontinuous values of the design variables which must correspond with real building construction forms. Exhaustive enumeration is practicable where the number of feasible solutions is relatively small. For more complex situations a dynamic programming optimization formulation has been developed from a dimensioning algorithm which has worked well in another building design application.

9.4. PROBLEM FORMULATION FOR OPTIMIZATION

The dimensioning algorithm can be used to derive an optimal geometry for a given topology of dimensionless spaces by dynamic programming optimization (Ref. 6). Developed for floor plans (Ref. 7), the algorithm is applicable to any group of contiguous rectilinear areas for which a suitable objective function can be formulated in terms of area or boundary length. The enclosing surfaces of a room can be expressed as a series of such contiguous rectilinear areas, Fig. 3. In this example we assume there is one external wall with horizontal sun shades and that the design rules specify no more than two windows with defined minimum and maximum window lengths and heights. Let

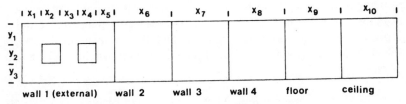

Fig. 3. Room surfaces expressed as contiguous rectilinear areas

H	= room height
W	= room width
D	= room depth
c	= construction type
g	= glazing type
z	= horizontal sun shade projection
x, y	= dimensions defining window and surface lengths
l_{min}, l_{max}	= minimum and maximum window lengths
h_{min}, h_{max}	= minimum and maximum window heights
z_{min}, z_{max}	= minimum and maximum sun shade projections

The room width and height are exogenous variables, while the dimensions and construction types are endogenous variables. The aim is to determine the values of these endogenous variables $x_1, \ldots x_{10}, y_1, y_2, y_3, z, g$ and c in order to optimize the combined return from both window and opaque areas, subject to the constraints:

(1) $\quad x_1 + x_2 + x_3 + x_4 + x_5 = x_7 = W$

(2) $\quad x_6 = x_8 = x_9 = x_{10} = D$

(3) $\quad y_1 + y_2 + y_3 = H$ for wall 1

(4) $\quad y_1 = H, y_2 = y_3 = 0$ for walls 2, 3, 4

(5) $\quad y_1 = W, y_2 = y_3 = 0$ for floor and ceiling

(6) $\quad l_{min} \leq x_2 \leq l_{max}$ or $x_2 = 0$

(7) $\quad l_{min} \leq x_4 \leq l_{max}$ or $x_4 = 0$

(8) $\quad h_{min} \leq y_2 \leq h_{max}$ or $y_2 = 0$

(9) $\quad z_{min} \leq z \leq z_{max}$ or $z = 0$

This can be formulated as a 10-stage sequential decision procedure with j the stage variable and X_j the state vector:

$$X_j = \{x_j, y_1, y_2, c_j, g_j, z_j\} j = 1, \ldots 10 \qquad (2)$$

y_3 being fixed through constraint (3). The stage return is a function $f(X_j)$ at stage j of a form determined by the environmental criteria represented in the objective function and the mathematical models selected for their prediction. The objective function will be additive and of the form

$$\text{opt } R = \sum_{j=1}^{10} \sum_{i=1}^{3} \sum_{p=1}^{P} (w_p a_p)_{i,j} \qquad (3)$$

where w_p is the weight attached for this optimization cycle to the performance a_p associated with the surface area given by the pair (x_j, y_i) for stage j in each of P environmental criteria.

Prima facie it appears that specifying a window topology may often be an unrealistic restriction on the solution space. The reason it is useful is because dynamic programming allows for invariant imbedding, that is the imbedding of solutions to a family of problems within that of the stated problem. Thus the forms of constraints (6), (7) and (8) will result in solutions of no window and one window being generated as part of the solution to the two-window problem. The optimal result in terms of the objective function may be any of these final states. Topology can therefore be determined either outside the optimization by the designer or inside the optimization by selection of the topology which results in the optimal global return. The analysis can be extended to larger numbers of windows simply by increasing the number of stages.

9.5. APPLICATIONS

The remainder of this paper will describe four specific examples to demonstrate the form and usefulness of the information that can be

TABLE 1
FEASIBLE CONSTRUCTION FORMS FOR EXAMPLES 1–4

Code	Description
GLASS TYPES	
1	3 mm Clear float glass
2	2 × 3 mm Clear float glass double glazing
3	6 mm Heat Absorbing glass
EXTERNAL WALL TYPES	
4	300 mm Cavity brick wall, unplastered
5	110 mm Brick/90 mm Air space/50 mm Insulation 12 mm Plasterboard
6	20 mm Weatherboard/25 mm Air Space/75 mm Insulation 12 mm Plasterboard
INTERNAL WALL TYPES	
7	110 mm Brick wall, unplastered
FLOOR/CEILING TYPES	
8	Concrete slab intermediate floor/ceiling, unplastered

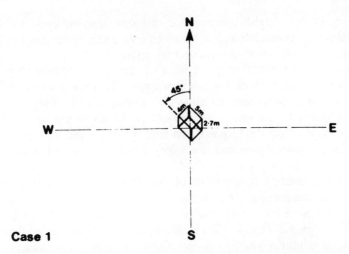

Case 1

**Small office with one external wall and unobstructed horizon
Sydney, Lat. 33°52'S, Long. 151°12'E**

Fig. 4. Design situation for Example 1: small office with one external wall and
unobstructed horizon in Sydney, latitude 33°52'S, longitude 151°12'E.

generated. The first example illustrates the effect of introducing
different controls on the design variables for a straightforward unobstructed situation with two criteria under investigation. The second
example examines a more complex situation where the external
environment is modified by neighbouring buildings. The third example
introduces a third criterion so that the tradeoff diagram becomes a
surface instead of a curve. The final example investigates the design
solutions which result when a larger range of design variables become
involved by examining the design of a room with two external walls.

Initially we return to the two-criteria problem described earlier in this
paper, so that the relevant criteria are daylight factor at the rear of the
room and peak summer internal environmental temperature. The
design variables taken into account are external wall construction types,
glass types, window positions, heights and widths and horizontal sun
shades. In these examples up to three types of external wall construction
and three types of glass are allowed but the internal wall, floor and
ceiling constructions are all fixed. Feasible construction forms are
outlined in Table 1.

9.5.1. Example 1: Unobstructed Situation in Sydney
The first case is a small office with one external wall located in Sydney,
Australia, and oriented north-west (Fig. 4). Consider some very

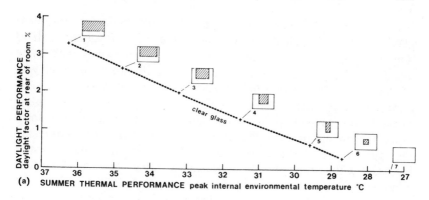

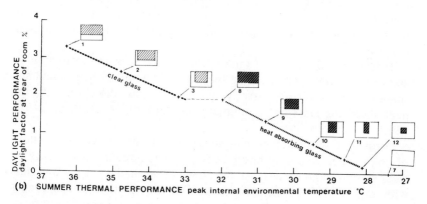

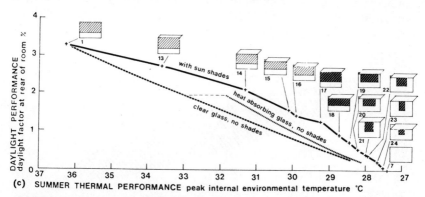

Fig. 5. Environmental tradeoff diagrams for Example 1 with design rules of:
(a) One window, clear glass, sill height 0.9 m, no sun shades,
(b) One window, sill height 0.9 m, no sun shades,
(c) One window, sill height 0.9 m, horizontal sun shade projection up to 1.2 m
Light hatching denotes clear glass (type 1), heavy hatching denotes heat absorbing glass
(type 3). External wall construction is type 4 for all solutions except solution 7 which is
type 6.

restrictive design requirements of one window, ordinary clear float glass, a fixed sill height and no sun shades. The resulting tradeoff diagram (Fig. 5a) is a graph of Pareto optimal values with some associated design solutions represented as sketches of the external wall of the room. The relationship between daylight and thermal performance is close to linear. As one would expect, increasing areas of glass mean better daylight performance and worse thermal performance. Since the effects of solar radiation and external air temperature are uniform over the whole area of wall, whereas the daylight factor increases with window height above the working plane, a tall vertical window is preferred to a long horizontal one. It was also found that the wall construction (type 6) which minimized peak temperature with no window differed from that with any window present (type 4), because of the need to lose heat gain from solar radiation by conduction through the wall.

To examine the effect of relaxing the design rules the restriction on glass type is removed, keeping the restrictions on sill height and sun shades. The tradeoff curve (Fig. 5b) is now discontinuous, the heat-absorbing glass being optimal over the range of daylight factors which it can provide.

For a third set of design rules horizontal sun shades with projections of up to 1.2 m were introduced. In Fig. 5c the three tradeoff curves for clear glass with no shades, for any glass but no shades and for any glass with sun shades are superimposed. The introduction of sun shades influences the curve much more than the introduction of different types of glass.

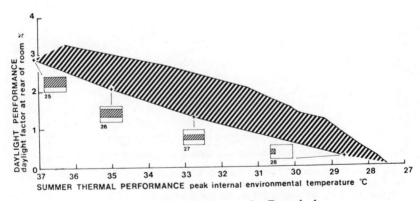

Fig. 6. Feasible criteria space for Example 1

By reversing the optimization parameters (that is minimizing instead of maximizing the daylight factor at any value of peak temperature) the whole criteria space can be outlined (Fig. 6) for the given set of variables and constraints. In this case there is 9° difference in peak internal temperature between the solutions with the best and worst thermal performance. For different solutions offering the same daylight factor there can be up to 4° difference in temperature.

Much information is provided to the designer by these diagrams. First there is information about performance, the combinations of performance values that can be achieved and the possible need for artificial services to supplement these feasible performances. Second, there is information about good solutions and how they change with different performance priorities. For both performance and solutions there is a qualitative level of information and a more detailed quantitative level of information.

Qualitative information about performance is provided by the length and shape of the tradeoff curve and the size and shape of the criteria space. The linear form of Fig. 5a demonstrates that a constant rate of improvement in daylighting is achieved as lower standards of thermal performance are accepted. Contrast this with Fig. 5c where the shape is broadly convex and the rate of improvement in daylighting decreases with increasing sacrifice of thermal standards. The discontinuous form of the curve in Fig. 5b shows that at some Pareto optimal values further decreases in thermal performance produce no improvement in daylighting at all. Certain preference points also emerge, at which further reductions of performance in one criterion within a small range give no improvement or only marginal improvement in the other criterion and which are therefore often good tradeoff choices. Examples are the performances of solution 8 in Fig. 5b and solution 17 in Fig. 5c. On the other hand, the performances of solutions 3 in Fig. 5b and solution 16 in Fig. 5c lie at or close to points where the opposite applies, where a small reduction of performance in one criterion results in a large improvement in the other criterion. They are therefore likely to be poor tradeoff choices. The size and shape of the criteria space show the whole range of feasible performance. Horizontal and vertical sections through it demonstrate graphically the difference between the worst and best values for one criterion that can be combined with a given value of the other criterion.

Quantitative information on performances is provided by reference to the axes of the graphs. Of first interest are the extremes and the range

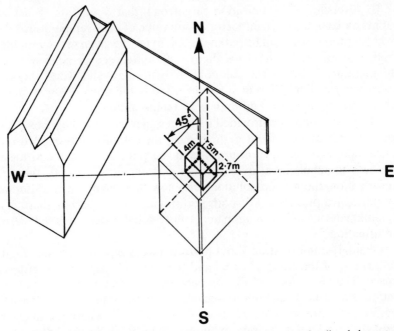

Fig. 7. Design situation for Example 2: Small office with one external wall and obstructed horizon in Sydney, latitude 33°52′S, longitude 151°12′E.

between the extremes, that is the values of the best and worst thermal and daylight performances and the differences between best and worst. Pareto optimal combinations within these extremes show whether desired combinations of performance can be achieved by the use of the building envelope with the given range of design variables and constraints or whether cooling plant would be necessary to maintain acceptable thermal conditions with the desired daylighting level.

The second aspect of the information offered concerns the design solutions associated with these performance combinations. At a qualitative level the changing forms of Pareto optimal solutions along the length of the tradeoff curve is immediately apparent: the increases in window area in Fig. 5a; the increase in window area and change of material in Fig. 5b and the combination of window area, material and shade as it acts in Fig. 5c. These trends are clear without looking at the actual dimensions involved or at details of the construction forms. By superimposing the tradeoff curves with different sets of design variables as in Fig. 5c the potential benefit of adopting different sets of design

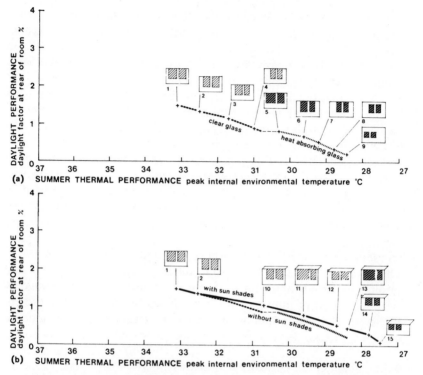

Fig. 8. Environmental tradeoff diagrams for Example 2 with design rules of:

(a) Two windows, minimum margin at wall ends 0.4 m, sill height 0.9 m, no sun shades,
(b) Two windows, minimum margin at wall ends 0.4 m, sill height 0.9 m, horizontal sun shade projection up to 1.2 m.
Light hatching denotes clear glass (type 1), heavy hatching denotes heat absorbing glass (type 3). External wall construction is type 4 for all solutions.

variables becomes clear; the relative benefit of allowing different types of glass, for example, or of introducing sun shades can be seen by their influence on the shape of the tradeoff curve.

Quantitative information on solutions concerns the actual sizes, positions and construction forms which result in Pareto optimal performance combinations in the various regions of the tradeoff curve. Indeed, an architect could directly select one of the plotted points and adopt the solution which provides that performance. But this is not the intention of the diagrams; their purpose is to indicate design trends and directions rather than specific solutions.

It is interesting to examine the benefits of sun protection when compared with an unprotected opening providing a constant daylighting level in place of the usual comparison of an unprotected opening with the same window area. Consider the clear glass window in solution 1 which has a peak summer temperature associated with it of 36.3°C. If that opening is protected by the use of heat absorbing glass (solution 8) the peak temperature is reduced by 4.3° to 32.0°C, but the daylight factor at the rear of the room has also been reduced from 3.3% to 1.9%. If not only the glass type is changed, but also a sun shade is provided (solution 17), then peak internal environmental temperature is reduced to 29.2°C, an overall improvement of 7.1 degrees. However, the daylight factor is now only 1.3%, a level which can be provided by an unshaded clear glass window of much smaller area (solution 4) and which has associated with it a peak temperature of 31.5°C. For the same level of daylighting at the rear of the room, the improvement in peak temperature by using heat-absorbing glass and sun shades is only 2.3°. This may lead to design conclusions different from those which would result from a study of the thermal benefits of shading a constant window area. This kind of information is very difficult to obtain from discrete single-criterion optimization or simulation techniques. It cannot be obtained without some knowledge about the whole field of solutions.

9.5.2. Example 2: Obstructed Situation in Sydney

The same room with the same set of design variables, orientation and location is now set in an obstructed situation (Fig. 7). The design rules for this example are rather different, keeping the fixed sill height but specifying two windows instead of one and requiring returns on the building cross-walls which prevent the windows abutting the edges of the external wall. For clarity, however, the performances will be plotted on the same axis as for the previous diagrams (Fig. 8).

The first point to be evident from this figure is that the spans of the tradeoff curves on both axes are smaller and the best possible daylight factor is only about half that for the unobstructed case. On the other hand, the best thermal performance is almost unchanged. When sun shades are disallowed, the pattern of preferred solutions (Fig. 8a) is similar to that for the first example, a discontinuous Pareto optimal curve with vertical rather than horizontal windows. It is interesting that forms close to the traditional Georgian room elevation are thereby generated (solutions 4 and 7). The heat-absorbing glass is optimal over the lower levels of daylighting.

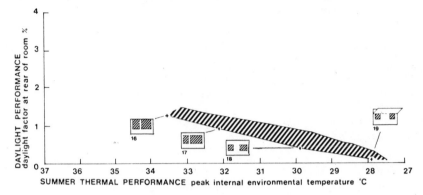

Fig. 9. Feasible criteria space for Example 2.

The introduction of sun shades (Fig. 8b) has a much smaller influence on the shape of the tradeoff curve than in the previous example. The curve is also less steep, indicating that improvements in daylighting entail greater disadvantage in terms of temperature than in the unobstructed situation. At the highest point on the curve solution 1 offers a daylight factor of 1.5% and a peak temperature of 33°C. From Fig. 5c a corresponding daylight factor for the room in Example 1 can be obtained with a peak temperature of about 30°C. If the whole criteria space is traced (Fig. 9), it is found to be very much smaller than in the first example, the difference between peak temperatures offered by solutions with the best and worst thermal performances now being only about 6° instead of the 9° of Fig. 6.

9.5.3. Example 3: Obstructed Situation in Hobart

For the third example, an office with the same range of design variables is oriented due north in an obstructed situation in Hobart, further away from the equator (Fig. 10). The design rules are a single window with a fixed sill height and horizontal sun shade projection of up to 1.2 m.

The shape of the tradeoff curve (Fig. 11) is broadly convex, but steeper than in the earlier cases, allowing increased levels of daylighting at less disadvantage in terms of increasing temperatures. In this case, too, effectively equal performances are achieved by different forms of design solution, whereas in the earlier examples a single design policy tended to dominate at any segment of the curve. Considering solutions 16 and 22, for example, a large window of heat-absorbing glass with small sun shade projection results in similar daylight factor and peak

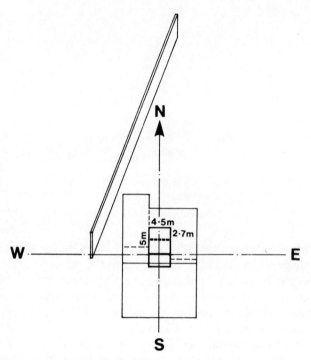

Fig. 10. Design situation for Example 3: small office with one external wall and obstructed horizon in Hobart, latitude 42°53′S, longitude 147°20′E.

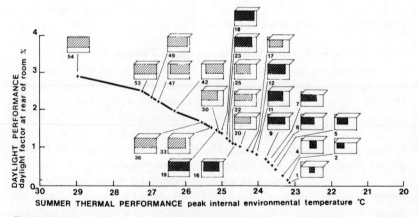

Fig. 11. Environmental tradeoff diagram for Example 3 with design rules of one window, sill height 0.9 m and horizontal sun shade projection up to 1.2 m. Construction forms are given in Table 2.

temperature values to a smaller clear glass with a deeper sun shade window with deeper sun shade. The same wall construction type remains optimal throughout the length of the curve.

The results thus far have shown tradeoffs between two criteria. In this example a third criterion was introduced to represent winter thermal performance. The criterion was minimum internal

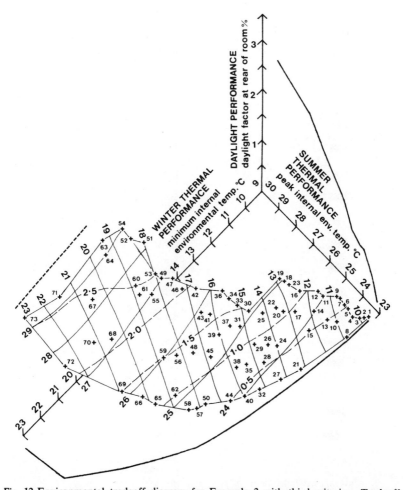

*Fig. 12.*Environmental tradeoff diagram for Example 3 with third criterion. Tradeoff curves relating any two of the three criteria can be obtained by projecting an edge of the surface on to the plane of the relevant pair of axes. Construction forms are given in Table 2.

TABLE 2

PARETO OPTIMAL SOLUTIONS AND PERFORMANCES FOR EXAMPLE 3

Solution Nr.	glass type	wall type	Daylight factor[1] %	Summer temp.[2] peak / mean °C	Winter temp.[3] minimum / mean °C	Noise ingress dB(A)
1	3	4	.07	22.1 / 21.9	9.6 / 9.3	29.4
2	3	4	.14	23.2 / 22.0	9.7 / 9.4	31.0
3	3	4	.16	23.2 / 22.0	10.0 / 9.6	32.7
4	3	4	.28	23.3 / 22.0	10.0 / 9.7	32.7
5	3	4	.46	23.5 / 22.1	10.4 / 10.0	34.9
6	3	4	.54	23.6 / 22.2	10.6 / 10.1	35.6
7	3	4	.63	23.7 / 22.3	10.7 / 10.2	36.3
8	3	6	.07	23.2 / 21.9	10.7 / 10.3	31.8
9	3	4	.63	23.7 / 22.2	10.7 / 10.2	36.3
10	3	6	.28	23.5 / 22.0	11.0 / 10.6	33.9
11	3	4	.83	24.0 / 22.4	11.4 / 10.7	37.5
12	3	4	.92	24.2 / 22.4	11.5 / 10.7	38.1
13	3	4	.51	23.8 / 22.3	11.5 / 10.9	35.7
14	3	5	.67	24.0 / 22.3	11.8 / 11.1	37.6
15	3	5	.51	23.8 / 22.2	12.3 / 11.6	35.7
16	3	4	1.13	24.6 / 22.9	12.3 / 11.5	37.5
17	1	4	.93	24.3 / 22.8	12.8 / 12.2	35.7
18	3	4	1.40	25.0 / 23.1	12.8 / 11.8	38.6
19	3	4	1.49	25.1 / 23.2	12.8 / 11.8	39.1
20	1	4	1.07	24.5 / 22.9	13.3 / 12.6	36.3
21	2	6	.18	23.5 / 22.1	13.2 / 12.7	31.3
22	1	4	1.19	24.7 / 23.0	13.5 / 12.8	36.9
23	3	4	1.20	24.9 / 23.0	12.6 / 11.7	38.1
24	1	4	.70	24.2 / 22.7	13.9 / 13.2	34.6
25	1	4	1.22	24.8 / 23.0	14.2 / 13.6	36.9
26	1	4	.79	24.3 / 22.8	14.3 / 13.6	35.1
27	2	6	.27	23.7 / 22.6	14.2 / 13.7	32.2
28	2	4	.62	24.2 / 22.8	14.5 / 13.9	33.6
29	1	4	.94	24.6 / 23.9	14.8 / 14.0	36.1
30	1	4	1.41	25.1 / 23.3	14.8 / 14.0	37.6
31	1	4	1.22	25.1 / 23.5	15.1 / 14.2	36.3
32	2	6	.37	23.9 / 22.4	15.1 / 14.6	32.9
33	1	4	1.57	25.3 / 23.4	15.1 / 14.2	38.1
34	1	4	1.62	25.5 / 23.5	15.1 / 14.0	38.6
35	2	4	.77	24.4 / 23.0	15.5 / 14.8	34.7
36	1	4	1.82	25.7 / 23.7	15.6 / 14.5	39.1
37	1	4	1.28	25.3 / 23.5	15.6 / 14.8	36.3
38	2	4	.83	24.6 / 23.1	15.9 / 15.1	35.1
39	1	4	1.45	25.5 / 23.7	16.0 / 15.0	36.9
40	2	6	.46	24.0 / 22.5	16.0 / 15.4	33.5

[1] average daylight factor at rear of room.
[2] peak internal environmental temperature approximated by predicted value of 15.00 hrs.
[3] minimum internal environmental temperature during hours of occupation, assumed at 09.00 hrs.
Mean internal environmental temperatures are for 24 hr. period.

TABLE 2—contd.

Solution Nr.	glass type / wall type	Daylight factor [1] %	Summer temp.[2] peak mean °C	Winter temp.[3] minimum mean °C	Noise ingress dB(A)
41	1 / 4	1.58	25.7 / 23.7	16.3 / 15.3	37.4
42	1 / 4	1.99	26.3 / 24.4	16.6 / 15.5	38.1
43	1 / 4	1.68	25.9 / 24.0	16.6 / 15.5	37.8
44	2 / 6	.54	24.2 / 22.6	16.7 / 16.0	34.0
45	2 / 4	1.13	25.2 / 23.6	16.8 / 16.0	35.3
46	1 / 4	2.11	26.5 / 24.5	17.1 / 15.9	38.1
47	1 / 4	2.26	26.8 / 24.7	17.4 / 16.1	38.6
48	2 / 4	1.28	25.5 / 23.8	17.5 / 16.6	35.9
49	1 / 4	2.38	27.0 / 24.8	17.8 / 16.6	38.6
50	2 / 6	.70	24.5 / 22.9	17.8 / 17.0	34.9
51	1 / 4	2.62	28.3 / 25.9	17.6 / 16.2	38.6
52	1 / 4	2.70	28.7 / 26.3	18.0 / 16.6	38.6
53	1 / 4	2.53	27.2 / 25.0	18.0 / 16.7	39.1
54	1 / 4	2.91	29.0 / 26.6	18.2 / 16.8	39.1
55	1 / 6	2.26	27.0 / 24.8	18.3 / 17.0	38.8
56	2 / 4	1.39	25.7 / 24.0	18.2 / 17.2	36.4
57	2 / 6	1.07	25.3 / 23.6	18.9 / 17.9	35.9
58	2 / 6	.83	24.8 / 23.0	18.3 / 17.6	35.7
59	2 / 4	1.49	25.9 / 24.2	18.7 / 17.6	36.9
60	1 / 6	2.53	27.4 / 25.1	18.9 / 17.4	39.2
61	1 / 6	2.38	27.2 / 24.9	18.9 / 17.5	38.8
62	2 / 6	.98	25.2 / 23.5	18.9 / 18.1	35.3
63	1 / 6	2.91	29.2 / 26.7	19.1 / 17.6	39.2
64	1 / 6	2.70	29.0 / 26.5	19.1 / 17.5	38.8
65	2 / 6	1.13	25.5 / 23.9	19.7 / 18.8	35.9
66	2 / 6	1.28	25.8 / 23.9	20.2 / 19.2	36.3
67	2 / 4	2.29	28.5 / 26.5	20.3 / 19.0	37.6
68	2 / 4	2.12	27.1 / 25.1	20.6 / 19.4	37.6
69	2 / 6	1.49	26.2 / 24.3	20.9 / 19.7	37.2
70	2 / 4	2.23	27.4 / 25.3	21.2 / 19.8	38.1
71	2 / 4	2.57	29.2 / 27.0	21.5 / 20.1	38.1
72	2 / 6	2.23	27.6 / 25.5	22.8 / 21.4	38.2
73	2 / 6	2.57	29.6 / 27.2	23.1 / 21.6	38.2

temperature during hours of occupation for the room, assumed to occur at 09.00 hrs. The assumed external conditions were 14 percentile temperature levels (that is temperatures exceeded on 6 days out of 7) and sunshine modified by a cloud cover factor of 0.75 to represent partially cloudy conditions.

For three criteria the Pareto optimal values form a surface (Fig. 12) requiring the identification of many more points for its definition. The corresponding solutions are listed in Table 2. The three projections of the edges of this surface onto the planes of pairs of axes provide the three two criteria tradeoff curves for daylighting and summer thermal performance, daylighting and winter thermal performance and summer and winter thermal performance. Thus the projection of the plane edge onto the axis of daylighting and summer thermal performance produces the tradeoff curve of Fig. 11. The daylighting/winter thermal performance tradeoff curve is unusual in that solutions 63 and 73 together dominate the whole field of feasible solutions, so that the tradeoff diagram reduces to two isolated points. The winter/summer thermal performance tradeoff curve is convex with a steep gradient over much of its length, indicating the potential for considerable gains in winter thermal performance at little disadvantage in summer conditions.

Solutions which are Pareto optimal for a two-criteria problem are generally also Pareto optimal for a three-criteria problem and the easiest approach to generating the surface is to first generate the set of two-dimensional curves. However, solutions which are close on a two-criteria assessment may not be close on a three-criteria assessment. Considering solutions 16 and 22 again, although very close in daylight factors and peak summer temperature, solution 22 is significantly better than 16 in minimum winter temperature (Fig. 12). Thus solution 16 appears to be a good choice only if winter thermal performance is not considered.

Following the contours of this diagram one can identify sets of solutions having the same performance in any one criterion and examine the tradeoffs between the other criteria. Following the 0.5% daylight factor contour, for example, it is apparent that large improvements in winter thermal performance are possible at small disadvantage in terms of summer thermal performance. Solutions 5, 6, 7, 13, 15, 28 and 44 all have daylight factors in the range 0.5% to 0.62% and maximum summer temperatures between 23.5°C and 24.5°C but have winter minimum temperatures ranging from 10.4°C to 16.7°C. A minor reduction in summer thermal performance may be acceptable in return for the

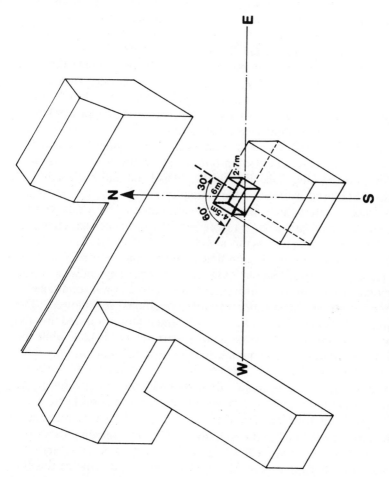

Fig. 13. Design situation for Example 4: small office with two external walls and obstructed horizon in Hobart, latitude 42°53'S, longitude 147°20'E.

improvement in winter. Looking at solutions with equal winter thermal performance, solutions 59 to 64 all have associated with them a minimum winter temperature of about 19°C but have a range of summer peak temperatures of between 25.2°C and 29.2°C and daylight factors of between 1% and 2.9%. Table 2 shows the variation in construction forms which accounts for this range in performance.

9.5.4. Example 4: Obstructed Situation in Hobart

A final example concerns a corner room in an office building situated at an urban street corner in Hobart (Fig. 13). The shorter external wall faces 60° west of north, the longer one 30° east of north. It is assumed that the design rules fix both wall and glass construction types and place restrictions on the minimum and maximum length of windows and on the gap between windows on the same wall. The topology is allowed to vary from one to two windows on the short wall and from one to three windows on the long wall. The sill height is fixed and horizontal sun shades are allowed as in the earlier examples.

The chosen criteria are summer and winter thermal performance with the aim of investigating the tradeoff between the beneficial effects of solar energy in winter and its unwanted effects in summer. The assumed external conditions and criterion times are the same as for Example 3. The resulting tradeoff diagram (Fig. 14) is convex and shows a steady reduction in the rate of improvement in winter thermal conditions as further reductions in summer thermal conditions are allowed. The difference between the peak summer temperatures offered by the solutions with the best and worst summer performance is 12.4° while the equivalent difference of minimum temperature in winter is only 5.8°. Contrast this with Example 3 where the range of achievable temperatures in winter is much greater than summer: the reasons lie in the different orientation, which receives more solar radiation in summer, and the external obstructions which cut out much of the low winter sun.

The form of solutions go through several distinct stages in progressing along the tradeoff curve. The design of the north-west (shorter) wall changes at each plotted point through solutions 1 to 5, holds this for solution 6 and then remains constant for solutions 7 to 10. The design of the north-east (longer) wall is unchanged for solutions 1 through 3, holds a different form for 4 and 5 and is then different for each solution 5 to 10. Only between solutions 3 and 4 (which are relatively far apart in summer performance, although not in winter performance) and

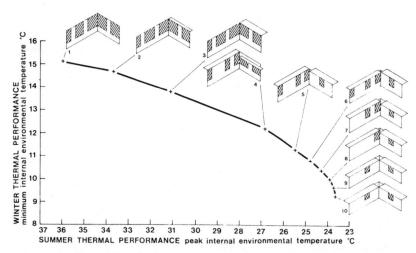

Fig. 14. Environmental tradeoff diagram for Example 4 with design rules of 1 or 2 windows on the shorter wall and 1, 2 or 3 windows on the longer wall, glass type 2 and external wall type 6, sill height 0.9 m, window length 0.9 m to 1.8 m, minimum gap between windows on the same wall of 0.9 m and horizontal sun shade projection of up to 1.2 m.

between solutions 6 and 7 do the designs of both walls change together.

9.6. DISCUSSION

Tradeoff diagrams tackle what we believe to be the central problem in environmental design, the problem of identifying what the real design options are in any situation. There are some disadvantages in the technique, the principal one being the need to express performance in each environmental attribute in the form of a single-valued criterion which is inherent in any use of optimization. In fact the computer programs produce additional performance information, for example mean as well as peak environmental temperatures, but this is not used in plotting the graphs. The choice of environmental components to be taken into account is left to the user. He may want to examine the tradeoffs between winter and summer thermal performances, between daylighting and noise intrusion or between three or more of these environmental components at once. He can also examine the effect of different assumptions of external conditions. For example, the surface in Fig. 12 would be different if the assumed winter conditions were of completely overcast skies with little solar radiation and one useful application is the generation of tradeoff curves for performance at the same time of year with two different assumptions of external conditions.

9.7. CONCLUSION

Environmental tradeoff diagrams offer a new and useful form of prescriptive information for environmental design in buildings. They are intended to have practical application within accepted design procedures as well as being an educational and research tool in the understanding of interactions between different environmental factors. Although there is much potential for further development, the technique can offer the practising architect a form of information which is much more useful at the early stages of design than is offered by either discrete simulation or single objective optimization techniques.

9.8. ACKNOWLEDGEMENTS

This work is directly supported by the Australian Research Grants Committee and the Commonwealth Scholarship and Fellowship Plan. Computing time was provided through the University Research Grant. The material presented here is largely drawn from the thesis entitled, "A Design Model for the Physical Environment in Buildings" by A. D. Radford, submitted for the degree of Doctor of Philosophy in the University of Sydney.

REFERENCES

1. Koenigsberger, O., 'Architectural science for practitioners,' *Architectural Science Review*, **21**, 6–7, 1978.
2. Raiffa, H., *Decision Analysis*, Addison Wesley, Reading, Massachusetts, 1968.
3. Zadeh, L. A., 'Optimality and non-scalar-valued performance criteria,' *IEEE Transactions on Automatic Control*, **AC-8** 59–60, 1963.
4. Yu, P. L., 'Introduction to domination structures in multi-criteria decision problems,' in Cochrane, J. L. and Zeleny, M. (Eds.): *Multiple Criteria Decision Making*, University of South Carolina Press, Columbia (S.C.) 1973.

5. Radford, A. D., *Performance Measurement in Optimal Environmental Design*, Internal Working Paper (unpublished), Department of Architectural Science, University of Sydney, Sydney, 1977.
6. Nemhauser, G. L., *Introduction to Dynamic Programming*, Wiley, New York, 1966.
7. Gero, J. S., 'Note on "Synthesis and Optimization of Small Rectangular Floor Plans" of Mitchell, Steadman and Liggett,' *Environment and Planning B*, **4**, 81–88, 1977.

10

Report on Energy Conservation Research

J. A. BALLINGER
Faculty of Architecture,
University of New South Wales, Australia

10.1. INTRODUCTION

In this chapter I shall confine my discussion of energy conservation to the area of 'passive solar energy', or solar architecture. The recent upsurge of interest in this field seems to gain momentum by the week. However, many do not stop to realize that the concepts involved are far from new. If we look back to the earlier days we find that in the 40s, people such as Drysdale (Ref. 1) at the Experimental Building Station, Olgyay (Ref. 2) in the USA, Givoni (Ref. 3) in Israel and many more were all working in this field. In those days, however, it was research towards improved thermal comfort, rather than the current somewhat inept term 'energy conservation'. In this context it means to use less energy for the task in hand rather than to conserve in the context of the first law of thermodynamics. Perhaps we should say 'low energy consumption' instead.

The Americans coined two terms to describe the two approaches to low energy consumption: 'belt tightening' and 'leak plugging'. The former has more to do with life style and living standards. We accept broader criteria for comfort conditions. The latter is more concerned with our subject here. As it implies it involves reducing the uncontrolled movement or flow of energy (keeping heat in, in winter, and out, in summer, for example).

'Leak plugging' will only be accepted when it is shown to be economically worthwhile, unless the present energy supplies become exhausted. When that happens, it will be too late. We must act now to conserve supplies of energy. Many now believe that energy conservation

224

in terms of passive solar architecture is already economically viable. Much of our research work has a promotional or demonstration component to it. In this paper I have selected a few research development and demonstration houses to illustrate some of the work being undertaken in Australia. Also included in the Appendix are brief summaries of most of the energy conservation research projects being undertaken in this country in the area of passive solar architecture.

Today in this field of research we are not really making any so-called 'major breakthroughs'. Rather we are refining and quantifying systems and techniques which when explained often seem so simple. Many people have said to me 'but such design is just common sense'. While this seems true, it is often very difficult to define in a simple, useful manner. What we are trying to achieve is to quantify passive solar energy and energy conservation techniques in such a way that we can design with assurance and reasonable expectation of performance. Much of this research has been made possible only by the introduction of large-capacity, high-speed computers. Usually the computations involved in temperature calculations and periodic heat flow are too long and cumbersome to attempt without a computer.

The building designer needs a set of guidelines to work with and such guidelines should be performance-oriented rather than prescriptive. To establish these guidelines it is necessary to undertake a considerable amount of research, both theoretical and empirical. We can broadly group current energy conservation research as follows.

10.1.1. Theoretical Studies

Most research work in this area today is computer based. Computer programs are being developed to simulate the thermal behaviour of proposed buildings or evaluate existing buildings for modification. Either some basic-design weather data is used or, as in the case of two programs *TEMPAL* (University of Melbourne) and *SUSTEP* (CSIRO Division of Building Research), actual recorded weather data is used. These programs produce one or more of the following outputs:

(a) Temperature profiles
(b) Thermal Load Calculations
(c) Building operating energy consumption
(d) Optimum size of heating and cooling plant

Computer programs have also been developed to provide theoretical solar radiation data and sun position tables for use by building designers. In addition there is work being undertaken to produce meteorological data in a format that will be useful for building designers. Work is also under way to develop standards for the manufacture and installation of thermal insulation: foam, bulk and reflective foil materials.

In the area of siting, orientation and land use studies there has recently been work undertaken by the Department of Construction, ACT (Ref. 4). Studies were made of optimum siting of houses to take advantage of sunlight in winter. Certain types of land sub-division permitted a greater percentage of houses to be free from overshadowing by objects or buildings on adjacent sites.

10.1.2. Empirical Studies
The range of projects in this area of energy conservation is quite diverse. They are being undertaken mainly by divisions of CSIRO, Universities, Institutes of Technology and some government departments. There are few independent bodies working in this field, due mainly to the limited funding available. Except for CSIRO, whose main charter is to undertake research, and government departments with full-time research units, most research work is operated on a part-time or extra-curricular basis. The projects being undertaken range from component development and testing, the collection of long-term climatic data and its conversion into a useful format for building designers, to the design, construction and monitoring of demonstration buildings as described later.

If research in Australia develops in a similar way to that in the USA—and there is reason to believe it will—then we will see an increase in demonstration projects. Much of the battle for passive solar design is in convincing the general public and our governments that it is not only feasible, but also economical. We need to work towards a set of guidelines that can be tested, validated and then made available to all designers in a usable format. To achieve that aim there remains a great deal of research to be done.

Some areas for continuing research work then, might be:

(a) Development of simple computer-based simulation models to evaluate designs at the design stage.
(b) Collection and reduction of climatic information into a format useful to designers.
(c) Development of cost benefit analysis programs which are fast to use and couple with the simulation models above.

(d) Design, construction and testing of a series of demonstration buildings to help the building industry become more aware of energy conservation techniques and gain expertise. These projects would also provide data for validation of computer models and form the basis of a public education programme.

To conclude, this paper looks briefly at some of the research and demonstration work currently being undertaken. These projects all deal with solar energy utilization using passive techniques as well as energy conservation. The material has been gathered from many sources. The cooperation of those who supplied information regarding their research projects is acknowledged with thanks.

There is work being undertaken in this field by at least four other groups and institutions. Unfortunately it was not possible to obtain information at this time. This report records 25 projects altogether, possibly there are 30–35 projects in total, which for a country of this size is far too few!

10.2. THE CSIRO LOW-ENERGY-CONSUMPTION HOUSE—HIGHETT, VICTORIA

This project is being undertaken jointly by the Divisions of Building Research and Mechanical Engineering. The aim is to build and study a low-energy-consumption house under controlled conditions (Fig. 1). Similar in plan to a standard production house being built throughout Melbourne (Fig. 2), this house has been built at Highett, a suburb of Melbourne. The design has been modified to reduce operational energy consumption as follows.

(a) 'Walls and ceiling are well insulated to reduce heat losses in winter and heat gains in summer' (Ref. 5).

(b) 'Building orientation and careful window placement, together with a floor of high thermal capacity (large mass), provide for "passive" use of solar energy' (Ref. 5).

(c) 'Two "active" solar systems provide hot water and space heating. Space heating is provided by an air-based system using an underfloor bed of small stones as an energy store, while a separate solar domestic water heating system is integrated into the garage roof' (Ref. 5).

Fig. 1. CSIRO low energy consumption house.

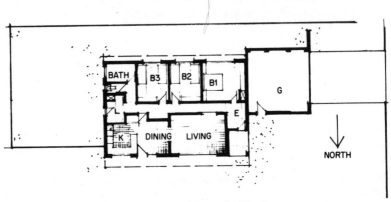

Fig. 2. Plan of house in Fig. 1.

10.2.1. Building Design

'The house has been designed so that solar penetration into the building during winter will contribute to space heating requirements. Window areas on the building's north face have been made large. Winter sun shining onto the concrete slab floor heats the slab, which then acts as a heat store. The living areas, with the highest heating needs, are located on the north side of the house, and bedrooms on the south.

To avoid overheating of the building during summer, eaves are designed to prevent entry of sunlight during the hottest parts of the summer day. A garage protects the western end of the building from the hot afternoon sun.

The building has a high thermal capacity due to its large mass. This is due mainly to the mass of the concrete slab floor, but is assisted by the brick walls. This thermal capacity reduces temperature fluctuations in both summer and winter. In summer the floor acts as a heat sink, and indoor temperatures are not expected to rise above 30°C.

To help prevent heat losses from the building during winter and unwanted heat gain during summer, the house has been well insulated. 100-mm rockwool batts have been installed in the cavity of the brick veneer walls, and 75 mm of rockwool have been installed on the ceiling with double-sided reflective foil laminate installed below the roof cladding' (Ref. 5).

10.2.2. Solar Collectors Storage and Space Heating

There is an area of 19 m² of solar air heated collectors designed as an integral part of the roof. The collector panels are glazed with acrylic formed in a profile to match the roof sheeting. The heated air is passed through a rock-bed heat store located under the concrete floor slab. This bed of 7-mm crushed rock, 500 mm deep, is divided into two sections, living areas and sleeping areas. The rock bed under the living areas will be heated first in preference to the sleeping area's rock bed. An electric convection heater will provide auxiliary heat if needed between 07.00 hrs and 23.00 hrs.

10.2.3. Solar-heated Domestic Hot Water

Integrated into the garage roof is an area of 4.5. m² of conventional black-painted copper tube/plate collectors. This system is also glazed with profiled acrylic. Water is pumped through the collectors from a 315-litre storage tank.

10.2.4. Data Collection

As stated earlier, this house plan is similar to many other houses throughout Melbourne. In the initial monitoring phase it is proposed to monitor a selection of these houses around Melbourne (30–35 units) for comparison with this experimental building. The data monitoring will be controlled by a microprocessor. The data collected will cover various aspects of the house's performance and will be used in a number of independent but inter-related projects. 'The following indicates prime interest areas together with an abridged list of data to be measured or derived from measured data' (Ref. 6).

General assessment:	energy used, conditions for occupants, comparison with current housing.
Underfloor rock-bed:	storage capacity, heat transfer rate to rooms, losses, efficiency of utilization, effect of sensor position and control changes.
Air heater collectors:	weather data, collection efficiency, mass flows temperature gains, effects of control sensor changes.
Water heater:	weather data, collection efficiency, percentage back-up.
Solar air heating: (collector and bed)	effects of control changes, supplementary energy required.
Passive performance:	weather data, internal temperature, alternative building data.
Theoretical comparison:	weather data, internal temperatures, energy used, ventilation rates.

In addition to this the microprocessor is designed to control simulated activities of theoretical occupants and their appliances and equipment.

10.3. UNIVERSITY OF QUEENSLAND ARCHITECTURAL SCIENCE UNIT—SOLAR HOUSE, MOUNT COTTON, QUEENSLAND

This project is the first of a series of dwellings planned for a development referred to as 'Solar City'. The site is located 30 km south-east of Brisbane City Centre (Latitude 27°S). The architectural science unit of the University of Queensland was commissioned by Mt. Cotton Projects Pty. Ltd. to design the building (Fig. 3). It was intended that the house be monitored for approximately 12 months. At this stage the designers are having difficulty obtaining the necessary equipment.

The aim of the project was to gain experience in and test solar-powered air-conditioning systems. At the same time the project provides a valuable demonstration opportunity to familiarise the public and industry with the possibilities of solar-powered air conditioning. Although the project would appear to be in the 'active solar energy' category, it is included because the house itself is designed on "passive" principles.

Fig. 3. Solar house, Mount Cotton, Qld.

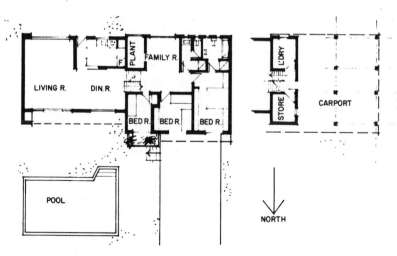

Fig. 4. Plan of house in Fig. 3.

10.3.1. Building Design

The house is approximately 150 m^2 in floor area designed on a split-level plan (Fig. 4). There are living rooms on the lower level and three bedrooms and two bathrooms on the upper level over a carport and storage level. It is built with concrete floors and 270-mm cavity brick external walls and 110-mm single brick internal walls. The wall cavities are filled with 50 mm of urea-formaldehyde foam insulation. The house is oblong in plan oriented to face north. The roof accommodates various solar energy collectors, as follows.

(a) 40 m^2 of flat-plate collector at 10° tilt for the solar-powered air conditioning.

(b) 18 m^2 of flat-plate collector at 35° tilt for swimming pool heating.

(c) 1 m^2 of photovoltaic cells at 35° tilt to provide a token supply of electricity

The windows are restricted to north and south walls. The window area to living rooms is limited to 25% of the floor area and bedrooms to 15% of floor area. Overhangs to north windows exclude sun from September to March but permit various amounts of sun in through the remainder of the year (winter).

The air-conditioning system was designed using program *TEMPER*, developed by Wooldridge (Ref. 7). The design conditions used were:

Indoor: temperature   23°C DB
           relative humidity   50%
Outdoor: temperature, max   30°C DB
                               20°C WB
           diurnal range   10°C

The design temperature conditions used represent a typical hot day and not an extreme day. It was assumed that an increase in maximum indoor temperature to 25°C would be acceptable during summer extremes. From calculations undertaken it was found that with a well designed 'passive solar' structure the peak cooling load was only 5.07 kW and the total daily load 64.6 kWh. A Yazaki Li Br/H$_2$O absorption chiller was used for the air-conditioning system, with a cooling rate of 4.6 kW. The chiller was undersized and coupled with a cold storage buffer tank to avoid intermittent operation, which has been found to be very inefficient.*

10.3.2. Performance Monitoring
It is planned to monitor the performance of the air-conditioning system

---

*Information for this summary was provided by Dr. S. V. Szokolay, Architectural Science Unit, University of Queensland.

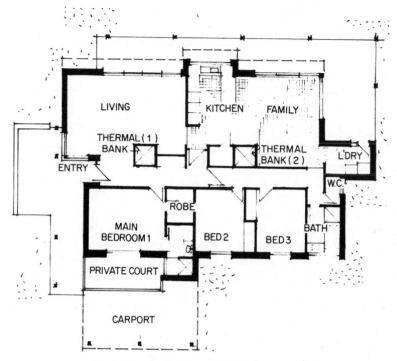

Fig. 5. Plan of solar house Q1, Greenmount, W.A.

and the energy consumption. Further reports will be issued by the University of Queensland Architectural Science Unit.

10.4. SOLAR Q1—GREENMOUNT, W.A. PASSIVE/ACTIVE AIRHEATED SOLAR HOUSE BY SOLARISED DEVELOPMENTS

This project was designed as a passive solar-heated house with active solar air-heated rockbeds for auxiliary heating. The house (Fig. 5), which is 153 m² in area and has three bedrooms and two bathrooms, is being offered on the market in Western Australia as a project house. It has been built with the following broad objectives (Ref. 8):

(a) 'To investigate the potential of current building technology and the existing house market structure to provide efficient and practical energy conservation solutions for housing in the urban content of Western Australia.'

(b) 'To develop stratagies for the introduction and adoption of solar energy in domestic housing.'

(c) 'To provide by demonstration an example of efficient energy use housing, that is compatible with people's traditional image and expectations of existing housing.'

The Solar Q1 house is constructed with brick walls and roof of part tiles and part galvanised-iron deck. The exterior walls have oversized cavities to take thermal insulation. The designers claim a U-value of 0.5 W/m²K for walls and 0.4 W/m²K for the roof. The estimated mean structural heat loss in June with inside temperature held at 20°C is 198 MJ/day. The window size has been estimated to provide the same amount of energy by direct solar heat gain in clear sky conditions. In addition there are four solar-heated air collectors in the roof which are connected to two rock-bed thermal stores. The air collectors are 18 m² in area and are boosted to an equivalent area of 24 m² by reflectors on the roof. It is estimated that the rock-bed thermal stores can hold up to 312 MJ at 55°C heat energy. This represents approximately 36 hours carryover.

The prototype house will be monitored with a 256-point data logger at 10-minute intervals. Of these points 102 will be temperature sensors placed in the ground under the floor slab to monitor the temperature behaviour of the ground throughout the year. The other points will monitor room temperatures, temperature gradients through walls and external weather conditions.

There are a number of similar houses being planned or under construction by Solarised Developments. This example was chosen because it would seem to be their major research project. No doubt many of the others will also be used in part for research.

10.5. THE UNIVERSITY OF NEW SOUTH WALES FACULTY OF ARCHITECTURE AND THE AUSTRALIAN HOUSING RESEARCH COUNCIL PROJECT 22 —SOLARCH EXPERIMENTAL HOUSE MARK I FOWLERS GAP, NEW SOUTH WALES

This experimental house is the first of a series to be built by the Solarch Research Group of the Faculty of Architecture at the University of

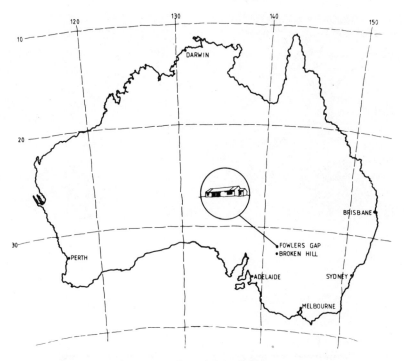

Fig. 6. Location of Solarch house.

New South Wales. The house was prefabricated in the Faculty workshops at Randwick by students and staff. The serviced sections of the house, bathrooms, kitchen and laundry were prefabricated as full room modules, complete with wiring, plumbing and all surface finishes. The remainder of the rooms were prefabricated as a series of flat panels. In November 1976 the completed components were transported to Fowlers Gap, the University of NSW arid-zone field station, located 120 km north of Broken Hill (Fig. 6).

The aim of this design was to produce firstly a house of conventional appearance, suited to the living style of the country (Figs. 7 and 8). Secondly the house should be largely prefabricated to overcome the problems of the lack of skilled labour in remote areas. Thirdly, and most importantly, the house should take advantage of the various characteristics of the arid area climate.

The design was based on a system of well-insulated, pre-fabricated, lightweight roof and wall panels erected on a concrete floor slab, which

Fig. 7. Solarch house.

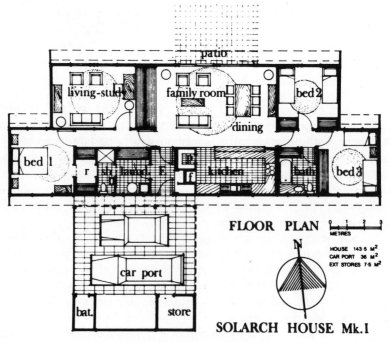

Fig. 8. Plan of house in Fig. 7.

acts as a store for solar energy received through the windows. This is combined with a hydronic solar energy collector and storage system for boosting. The collectors are of the flat-plate trickle-type designed as an integral part of the roof. There is 40 m² for auxiliary space heating and 10 m² for domestic hot water. The traditional trickle-type design has been modified by the group to increase its efficiency and is expected to produce outlet temperatures of up to 70°C. A series of helical coils of plastic tubing have been cast into the concrete floor slab to permit hot water from the storage tank to be circulated through the floor for additional heating as required. Retractable canvas awnings on the north provide shade during summer and deep sun penetration during winter to heat the floor. There are no windows on the east or west walls. The sun's radiation is very intense on the east and west during summer when it is not wanted and very weak in winter when it is wanted.

The assembly and finishing of the building was completed in July 1977, except for the solar energy collectors which were completed early in 1978. A three-year monitoring programme has begun with one or two false starts due to tuning and adjustment of the equipment. Data processing began late in 1978 and it is hoped that performance reports will be issued later in 1979. Monitoring is being conducted with a 26-channel digital data-logger which outputs hourly onto magnetic cassette tape for computer processing. A small weather station has been set up to record wind speed and direction and wet- and dry-bulb screen temperatures for the data-logger. Simultaneously, solar radiation, internal room temperatures and storage tank temperatures are recorded. Platinum resistance probes specially built for each application are used for temperature measurement. In addition, all other operational energy inputs are being monitored either into the data-logger or manually to permit a study of the total energy consumption of the dwelling and its occupants.

Figures 9 and 10 show how the internal temperatures compare with external temperatures during July and December in 1977. These figures show quite clearly the effect of passive solar energy design. Whilst the external temperature range is quite large the daily internal temperature range is relatively small. Figures 11 and 12 show a comparison of measured data and calculated values using program *TEMPER* by the CSIRO Division of Mechanical Engineering.

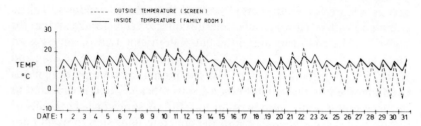

Fig. 9. Daily max. and min. temperatures, July 1977.

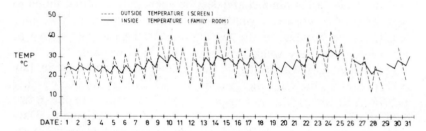

Fig. 10. Daily max. and min. temperatures, December 1977.

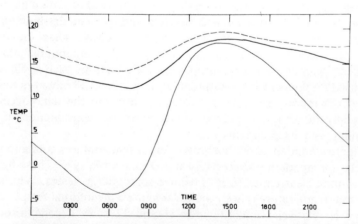

Fig. 11. Thermal performance of living zone—typical cold day (4th July 1977).
- - - - -Calculated internal temperature (includes allowances for occupants, lighting and appliances).
————Measured internal temperature. Note: house closed up and unoccupied (i.e. no internal loads or ventilation).
————Ambient temperature.

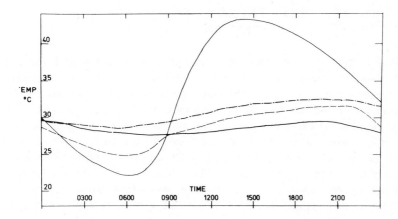

Fig. 12. Thermal performance of living zone—very hot day (11th December 1977).
————Ambient temperature
— · — ·-Calculated internal temperature (includes allowance for occupants, lighting and appliances).
— — — —Calculated internal temperature as above, includes ambient air cooling (18 air ch/hour when ambient temperature less than inside temperature).
————Measured internal temperature. Note: house closed up and unoccupied (i.e. no internal loads or ventilation).

REFERENCES

1. Drysdale, J. W., *Designing Houses for Australian Climates,* Experimental Building Station, Bulletin No. **6,** Sydney, 1952.
2. Olgyay, V., *Design with Climate—Bioclimatic Approach to Architectural Design,* Princeton University Press, Princeton, New Jersey, 1963.
3. Givoni, B., *Man, Climate and Architecture,* Elsevier, London, 1969.
4. *Energy Use in Government Housing,* Part 2, Department of Construction, Canberra, ACT, 1976.
5. *CSIRO Division of Mechanical Engineering Information Service Paper, 12/B/4.* Melbourne, August 1978.
6. Welch, L. W., *Outline of Instrumentation and Control Strategy,* CSIRO Division of Mechanical Engineering. In-house paper, Melbourne, 6th June 1978.
7. Wooldridge, M. J., 'Air-conditioning load calculation using computer program *TEMPER,' Aust. Refrig. Air-Cond. and Heating,* **27,** 12, 1973.
8. Lawrance, R., *Evolution of Energy Conserving Solar Heated Housing for Western Australia,* Private Communication, 1978.

10.6. APPENDIX—ENERGY CONSERVATION RESEARCH PROJECTS (Brief Summaries)

10.6.1. Research Organisation—Australian Housing Research Council
Thermal Performance Standards for Housing in Western Australia.
Investigate the means of achieving optimum thermal performance of housing in the various climatic regions of Western Australia. The proposal is to carry out short-term, intensive monitoring of pairs of similar houses in climatic regions of Western Australia. One house will be of current normal uninsulated construction and one of enhanced thermal resistance. This data will be used to validate a computer program for long-term performance prediction using Bureau of Meteorology data. This analysis should enable design/construction recommendations to be linked to each region.

Energy Requirements, Energy Use and User Satisfaction in Houses. To examine the factors related to energy use and user satisfaction in housing. A questionnaire/interview technique will be used to establish 'normal' patterns of energy use related to family size and income, nature of appliances and thermal details of the houses. The results will be compared with fuel records supplied by the gas and electricity supply authorities. Following a pilot survey a comprehensive consumer survey will be conducted at one housing estate in an outer Melbourne suburb. After the initial survey the introduction of a consumer education and/or household involvement energy conservation program will be evaluated. The effectiveness of the campaign will be tested by comparing the fuel records and consumer satisfaction of the educated group with a control 'uneducated' group.

Thermal Performance of Housing Units in Queensland. To develop thermal performance evaluation guidelines for housing units in Queensland. A detailed analysis by monitoring and computer simulation of a large number of design and construction variations for selected prototype dwellings in a number of climatic regions of Queensland will be undertaken. From this will be developed a simple quantitative method for calculating the thermal performance and resulting comfort conditions covering the climatic variations in Queensland. Representative housing units in Brisbane, Longreach, Townsville and Rockhampton will be monitored. The thermal performance of these dwellings will be simulated using the computer program *TEMPAL*. Design construction alternatives will be investigated. The internal comfort conditions obtained will be described by a habitability index related to climatic conditions. Design guidelines will be developed to cover the range of conditions found in Queensland.

Thermal Performance and Life Costs of Public Housing Units in Victoria and Tasmania. An investigation of means of improving the thermal performance and reducing lifetime costs of public housing in Victoria and Tasmania. A technical study of typical public housing construction in terms of construction and plant type. Computer simulation using actual Melbourne and Hobart weather data will provide information upon energy consumption and comfort conditions of current dwelling designs. A range of modified designs and construction types are examined for capital and lifetime costs, on the basis of thermal performance improvement.

Evaluation of Thermal Performance Computer Programs. To evaluate various thermal performance computer programs against a set of operational criteria. The key to the more efficient use of energy in dwellings is the ability to predict accurately the performance of the building envelope and to assess the consequences of operating the building in different ways. This project aims to evaluate a number of existing programs (both Australian and overseas) in terms of their relevance to specific users, ease of operation, coding, etc., and accuracy in predicting the thermal performance and energy consumption of dwellings. The computer predictions of internal conditions and energy consumption will be compared to measured data obtained from at least five dwellings in various climatic regions of Australia.

10.6.2. Research Organisation—CSIRO Division of Building Research

Climatic Data for Heat Transfer Calculations. To provide concurrent values at hourly intervals of those meteorological parameters required for thermal calculations in buildings, over a period of several years. In addition to values of dry-bulb temperature, direct and diffuse solar irradiance on a horizontal plane, wind velocity and cloud cover, two further parameters are being incorporated with existing tapes for Australian cities. They are wet-bulb temperature and atmospheric pressure for latent load calculations. Another difficulty is that only global solar irradiance is available for some centres. A method of calculating direct and diffuse components from such data has been tested and found adequate.

Thermal Insulation. To examine the properties and performance of thermal insulation and promote the correct use of thermal insulation for reducing the energy required for space heating and cooling while increasing thermal comfort. Assistance to the Standards Association of Australia in preparing draft specifications for thermal insulating materials and a code of practice for their installation in dwellings highlighted the need for apparatus to measure the thermal resistance of loose-fill fibrous materials. A suitable 1-m square apparatus is being manufactured.

Latent Heat Storage. To study methods of storing heat at essentially constant temperature, utilising the latent heat in solid-liquid phase changes. Storage systems employing sensible heat storage, e.g. concrete slab floors, suffer from the disadvantages that the energy stored is limited by the permissible rise in temperature of the slab and by the variation in temperature of the slab and the heated room during the recovery of the stored heat. Storage systems using the latent heat of a phase-transformation store heat at a constant temperature which may be close to that required within the room. This temperature does not vary during the release of the major part of the stored energy. The energy density of latent heat storage is higher than that for sensible heat storage and this should result in a smaller storage volume and weight for the system. Assessment of materials suitable for phase-change heat storage. Methods of containing the phase-change material and transferring heat to and from the storage material will be investigated.

Sirowet (CSIRO Wall Exposure Test). To provide a transportable facility to enable measurement of air infiltration, water penetration, and structural performance of walls under appropriate simulated wind conditions. Penetration of wind-driven rain to indoors in some multi-storey office buildings has in recent times led to some very expensive rectification projects. To try to avoid such problems in future a leading architect encouraged a number of building owners and aluminium companies to sponsor a facility for testing prototype walls. The Division agreed to provide such a facility, and a pressure box of 1-m square modules of glass-fibre-reinforced polyester was fabricated for clamping to test walls up to 5 m high and 7 m wide in steps of 1 m. This box is provided with a water spray system to cover the whole of the test specimen, the water draining from the box being recirculated through a pressure sump, surge tank and petrol-driven pump. A fan provides air pressurization within the box and an adjustable electric-motor-driven crank system fitted to the air pressure control valve enables automatic cycling (simulated gusting). Pressure transducers connected to a recorder measure total pressure drop across the wall, pressures at cavities within the wall and air flow rates into the box using a three-quarter radius pitot measuring system. Dial gauges are used to record deflections of the members under imposed uniform pressure loadings.

Radiation Cooling of Buildings. To determine the feasibility of providing localised cooling within buildings by the use of external cladding materials which have selective radiation properties. The cooling of dwellings, particularly at night time, is essential in many parts of Australia. Capital and operating costs of conventional air-conditioning equipment are relatively high and there is a need for less expensive methods of achieving thermal comfort. One method of achieving this end is to cool the dwelling by radiating heat from the outside cladding. Because of the phenomenon that the earth's atmosphere is essentially transparent to infra-red radiation in the wavelength range 8–13 m, the cooling effect will be greatly enhanced if the surface of the cladding is given selective properties which enable it to radiate in the 8–13 m band but to reflect all radiation outside this band.

Energy Conservation in Buildings. To examine ways in which non-renewable energy resources used for and in buildings can be minimized. The energy required to build a typical brick-veneer dwelling in Australia is only about 5% of the service energy used in its lifetime, taken as 40 years. This indicates that there is greater need for energy conservation measures in the service energy area, particularly in the attainment of thermal comfort. Nevertheless, research into the conservation potential of both areas is required. A joint project with CSIRO Division of Mechanical Engineering aims to use a computer-based analysis procedure for the assessment of building energy usage in the design of low-energy-consumption dwellings suitable for the major population centres of Australia. Eight possible heating and cooling systems have been recommended for modelling in the computer analysis, some of which made use of solar energy. An assessment of the likely cost impact of the low-energy house indicates considerable fuel cost savings to the householder. The energy savings to the nation depend very much upon future energy growth rates and upon the rate at which such houses are built.

Solar Position and Radiation Data. To present solar data in a manner which is easily understood by and useful to the building designer. The solar tables prepared by the Division are well known to building designers wishing to design solar screens or estimate solar heat gains. They are in SI units and also include solar heat gain factors and the effects of horizontal sun breaks of three nominated widths over windows. This is in addition to showing the position of the sun relative to building surfaces of various orientations at hourly intervals of selected days of each month, together with the direct and diffuse solar irradiances for cloudless skies at the same times.

Heat Transfer Calculations. To improve methods of calculating indoor temperatures and air-conditioning loads for a given pattern of outdoor climate and to apply these methods to practical problems. The computer programs *CARE, STEP* and *SUSTEP* are used for theoretical calculations of the thermal performance of buildings. Further work has been undertaken on the representation of the ground in the thermal network. Calculations for house heating by electric cable embedded in concrete slab on ground indicate that under-slab insulation is an economic proposition. Recent analytical work has shown how the programs may be modified to allow for zoning.

10.6.3. Research Organisation—CSIRO Division of Mechanical Engineering

Low Energy Consumption in Buildings. (Refer to earlier description)

    (1) Produce an analysis procedure for building energy assessment.
    (2) Design, build and operate a low energy-consumption house.
    (3) Transfer the design approach to public sector.

    (a) Computer simulation of building with heating and cooling.
    (b) Design studies of alternative proposals for energy conserving equipment and ideas.
    (c) Build home to show low energy consumption technology.

10.6.4. Research Organization—Sydney University Department of Architectural Science

Thermal Inertia of Buildings. To study effects of thermal inertia, especially of floors in single-storey buildings, on thermal comfort. Field experiments and computer simulation.

Solar Heat Loads Through Non-Vertical Glass Surfaces. To study the relative solar heat gains through glass at various angles to the horizontal, (a) as windows, to reduce heat gain, (b) as energy collectors. Experimental procedures and calculations taking into account reflectance at high angles of incidence, and exposure to various proportions of sky and ground.

10.6.5. Research Organization—University of Melbourne Mechanical Engineering Department

Passive Solar Heating Systems. The application of passive solar collector systems to building heating system.

Stage I: computer analysis of "Trombe-Wall" concept applied to typical Australian dwelling complete.

Stage II: construction of test module to verify free convection coefficients (theoretical) used in computer model.

Stage III: construction of test houses to accumulate field performance data for such passive solar systems.

10.6.6. Research Organization—University of Queensland Department of Mechanical Engineering

Modelling of Passive Solar Energy Systems. Devise a mathematical model to simulate the performance of a simple structure and several alternative passive heating and/or cooling devices. Compare the model with the performance of two one-room test buildings. Run the validated model on alternative systems to determine cost-effectiveness. The basic unsteady heat flow in the building structure was calculated by thermal response factors. Building features such as shading, reflection and windows were incorporated as sub-routines as was the roof-pool, a passive solar system. For the model input, a representative year of weather data—hourly values of insolation, wind speed, dry-bulb temperature and wet-bulb temperature—was prepared. Output was the indoor air temperature which was incorporated into a comfort index, $\sum$ PPD, a time averaging of the percentage of people dissatisfied. Comparative measurements were made on two similar buildings, 2.5 m $\times$ 2.5 m $\times$ 2 m, one of which had a particular device and the other without it. Comparisons were also made with the model which could also be run with the measured weather input. At this stage, most work has been done on the roof-pool system. Major conclusions are: the system can be modelled fairly accurately; the roof-pool is useful for low-cost buildings and provides a significant improvement in the indoor climate.

10.6.7. Research Organization—University of New South Wales
Solarch—Solar Energy Research Unit

The Passive Use of Solar Energy for New South Wales Schools. To develop useful guidelines for the design of schools for New South Wales which utilize solar energy in a natural cost effective manner. To establish a level of expertise within the constructing authority and to build and monitor prototype buildings.

Stage 1:   Investigate information and techniques available, climatic data and user parameters. Prepare draft guidelines for design and construction of passive solar energy school buildings.

Stage 2:   Advise and guide the state construction authority in the design and construction of prototype school buildings.

Stage 3:   Monitor the buildings performance and energy consumption, generate student involvement and compare with traditional buildings. Review, revise and complete guidelines for continuing use by the State constructing authority.

Scale Models to Study the Thermal Behaviour of Buildings. To investigate the possibilities of using scale models to study the thermal performance of various passive solar energy systems. The project will first investigate the past work of others in this field and then with the aid of scale models test and extend those concepts to include systems and techniques such as thermal storage walls, solar greenhouses, water walls, etc.

Passive Solar Energy Housing for Sydney Growth Areas. This project is intended to develop, demonstrate and test a variety of passive solar energy techniques appropriate to housing in the major growth areas of Sydney. If houses of the future are to be less wasteful of energy, they must be designed as thermally efficient units. This project does not aim to invent new systems but rather to develop ways in which to integrate known systems into houses. Houses that will be both visually and socially acceptable to the average Australian. We believe this aim to be both practically and economically feasible. Such houses could be termed 'passive solar houses' or 'low-energy houses.' The project will include the design and construction of approximately twelve houses. The houses will be divided into three groups.

(a) Standard public housing design (controls)
(b) Improved standard public housing designs
(c) Modified or new designs which will incorporate novel passive solar energy techniques.

The houses and the external climate will be simultaneously monitored for three years to evaluate energy consumption and thermal performance. The data collected will be analysed by the proponents and also made available for further analytical work by other researchers. The project will also be an active demonstration to the general public of appropriate ways to utilize solar energy in their houses. Techniques and methods which are both practical and economical to implement.

11

Thermal Insulation of Buildings

L. F. O'BRIEN

Division of Building Research, Highett, Victoria, Australia

11.1. INTRODUCTION

Extensive research is being conducted throughout the world to find better ways of utilizing the sun's energy to replace conventional energy sources to heat and cool our buildings. Within Australia the bulk of the effort has been directed at the domestic sector and this is the area to be considered in this chapter. Whether solar utilization for space heating be 'active' or 'passive', it is most important that the energy directed into the interior of a dwelling should not be allowed to escape easily through the building envelope.

Use is made of the mass of a structure to absorb solar radiation and hence the popularity of concrete floors in "solar" houses. The absorbed heat is released slowly and lost through the envelope and by air infiltration and ventilation to outdoors. The rôle of insulation is to slow down the rate of heat loss and to do this effectively a building designer needs a knowledge of the properties of insulants. It is intended to deal with commonly used insulating materials and to give an indication of how much insulation to use.

11.2. INSULATING MATERIALS

11.2.1. Types of Materials
The following materials are commonly used for insulating buildings:

  (a) Glass fibre
  (b) Rock wool

(c) Cellulose fibre
(d) Urea formaldehyde foam
(e) Reflective foil laminate

Of these materials urea formaldehyde foam is relatively new to the market and because of the interest in it, it will be considered along with the other materials, although it is suggested that its market share is small. Other materials such as 'eel grass' and polystyrene are not dealt with because they also are not widely used in the domestic area. Of the materials listed, except for reflective foil laminate (RFL), the materials fall into the class of 'bulk' insulants.

11.2.2. Method of Manufacture

(a) Glass fibre is made in Australia by two processes:

(i) A 'remelt' process in which glass is produced in marbles and stored until required. It is then remelted and released through fine jets forming fibres which are flame attenuated and blown onto a moving conveyor belt. Between the jets and the belt a binder is applied, usually phenolic resin; the fibre then passes through an oven which cures the binder. The glass fibre is then trimmed to size. This is relatively energy expensive as the glass is melted twice.

(ii) The second process starts with raw materials which are converted into glass, some reclaimed glass being added prior to melting in a furnace. The melt is fed to a spinning cylinder with perforated walls through which the liquid glass is extruded by centrifugal force. The material is directed downwards by air jets onto a conveyor belt from where the process is the same as in the remelt process. Due to the single 'melt' this process is less energy intensive than (i) above.

(b) Rock wool. The manufacture of rock wool is similar to the single-melt glass fibre process, the primary material in this case being rocks which when melted and fiberized are similar to glass.

(c) Cellulose fibre. The basic material used for the production of cellulose fibre is reclaimed newsprint. This material is shredded and then fed to a hammer mill where it is reduced to a "fluff", fire retardant being added to produce an acceptable fire performance. Materials commonly used as retardants are borax and boric acid as a mixture and these form about 20% of the finished product by weight.

(d) Urea formaldehyde. Urea formaldehyde foam is relatively new in Australia in the insulation field. It is made from a basic mixture of a resin and an accelerator which are mixed and aerated in a special gun, the mixture setting in a period of seconds, the air bubbles being retained within the set mixture and providing thermal insulation.

(e) Reflective foil laminate. As the name implies reflective foil laminate is typically a laminated material formed by the combination of two layers of kraft paper enclosing a reinforcing web of glass fibre yarn. Outer layers of aluminium foil of thickness around 0.0075 mm are added to each surface. The adhesive used frequently has a fire retardant added to improve the fire performance of the material. Varieties are made with only one surface of aluminium foil, termed single-sided, but this is not recommended for use in buildings as its integrity after repeated wetting and drying is liable to suffer.

11.3. CHOICE OF MATERIALS

11.3.1. Physical Form

The choice of material can depend on the position of that part of the building envelope which is to be insulated.

(a) Glass fibre and rock wool, generally termed mineral wools, are provided as 'batts' or 'loose fill'. Both forms are acceptable for use on horizontal surfaces but a loose fill is liable to have an unacceptable amount of settlement when used in a wall cavity. Batt material is suitable for this application but the Australian Standard being prepared on "Recommended code of practice for the installation of thermal insulation in dwellings" recommends that wire lacing be used to hold batts in position when used in a wall cavity. The "handleability" of these materials is good but the nature of the fibres can cause temporary skin irritation and therefore protective clothing should be worn whilst handling them.

The question of health risks associated with fibrous materials, in particular cancer, has been raised, but extensive and continuing investigations have not shown any link between cancer and domestic mineral wool insulation. Such a link has been shown with asbestos fibres, but in these the fibre diameter which is an important factor is less than 2 μm, whereas for mineral wools fibre diameters are around 5 to 10 μm.

(b) *Cellulose fibre* is only available as a loose fill material in Australia and is not recommended for vertical cavities. It is generally pneumatically applied onto ceilings, but hand spreading is simple.

(c) *Urea formaldehyde* can be supplied in batt form or may be foamed *in situ.* In batt form its handleability is poor and it is marketed with aluminium foil facings to provide adequate strength. Its ability to be foamed *in situ* makes it a useful retrofit material in the cavities of double brick walls in sheltered situations.

(d) *Reflective foil laminate* is mostly supplied in roll form in widths of 1400 mm. It is used for both wall and ceiling insulation and is more easily applied as ceiling insulation during construction. It has properties which make it available for use as thermal insulation, sarking and as a vapour barrier.

11.3.2. Thermal Resistance
Bulk Materials. The potential of a bulk material to resist the flow of heat has been judged by its thermal conductivity, *k*, which may be defined as the quantity of heat which flows through unit area of a homogeneous material of unit thickness when unit temperature gradient exists between its faces.

$$k = \frac{QL}{A(t_1 - t_2)}$$

where
k = thermal conductivity (W/m K)
L = thickness of material (m)
A = area of material (m²)
$(t_1 - t_2)$ = temperature difference between faces (K)

The reciprocal of *k* gives the thermal resistivity of the material or the resistance of unit thickness (1 m in SI units). The thermal resistance, *R*, of a given thickness is found from

$$R = \frac{L}{k}$$

and this has been referred to in the industry as the *R* value—units m²K/W.

The thermal conductivity of insulation can be controlled by varying density and fibre diameter or particle size, the optimum density for

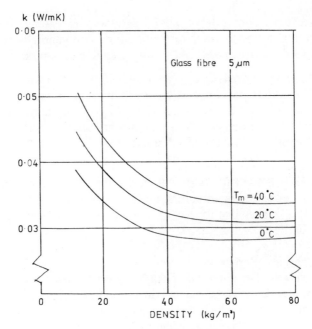

Fig. 1. Variation of *k* with density.

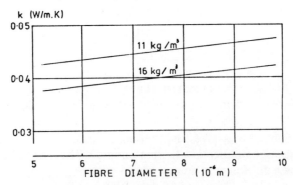

Fig. 2. Variation of thermal conductivity with fibre diameter.

minimum thermal conductivity being around 50 kg/m³ for mineral wools. Figure 1 illustrates the variation of *k* with density for a typical glass fibre material with a fibre diameter of 5 μm for a range of temperatures. It can be seen that at low densities a small change in density produces a large variation in *k*, but around the optimum where rock wools are produced density is not so important. Figure 2 illustrates,

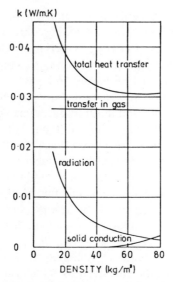

Fig. 3. Mechanisms of heat transfer.

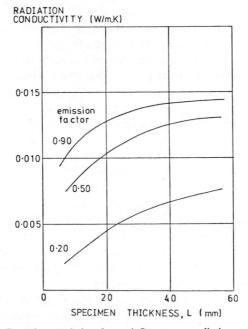

Fig. 4. Boundary emission factor influence on radiation conductivity.

for a typical case, the dependence of k on fibre diameter for two densities. The importance of controlling fibre diameter during the manufacture of fibrous insulating materials is demonstrated with a change in fibre diameter of 3 μm producing a change in k from 0.038 to 0.041 W/mK for a material of density 16 kg/m^3.

For reasons of economics manufacturers of glass fibre operate at densities around 10 kg/m^3 and this introduces changes in the magnitudes of the modes of heat transfer. Bankvall (Ref. 1) has produced the data for Fig. 3 and the ever increasing importance of radiation is shown at the low densities. Conduction of heat by conduction through the gas is still the most important mode with fibre conduction being negligible. Transfer by convection is also negligible this being demonstrated by the measurement of heat transfer in an upward and downward direction through a sample. Bankvall found virtually no difference in the thermal conductivities of each case.

The increasing importance of radiation at low densities offers the possibility of increasing the effectiveness of the insulation by the addition of surfaces of low emission factor, reflective foil, on one or both sides of the material, or even within the material. Bankvall has studied this possibility and his results are presented in Fig. 4. It can be seen that at small thicknesses great improvement can be obtained in the resistance; e.g. at $L = 40$ mm changing the emission factor of a bounding surface from 0.9 to 0.2 alters the contribution of radiation from 0.014 to 0.007 W/mK for a material of 16 kg/m^3. The effect would be even more dramatic at lower densities. The benefit decreases rather rapidly as L increases.

Current practice is to manufacture low-density fibrous materials to a required R value which implies a given thickness. Improvement in performance for a given thickness could be obtained by interposing radiation blocking layers at regular intervals throughout the thickness of material, say each 25 mm. The layer need not necessarily have appreciable thermal resistance but as evidenced by Fig. 4 a material with a low emission factor offers scope for considerable lowering of the radiational conductivity. A practical problem is the adhering of the glass fibre to this layer and at the same time retaining the low emission factor. The above considerations refer primarily to glass fibre. Rock wool and cellulose fibre have higher densities.

Tye (Ref. 2) has studied some aspects of cellulose fibre and Fig. 5 presents results of his observations on the effect of density on thermal conductivity. The curve was obtained from studies on materials from

k (W/mK)

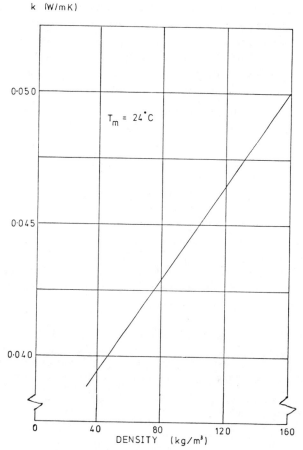

Fig. 5. Variation of thermal conductivity with density for cellulose fibre.

one source, but when results were studied from more than one source there is an indication of a minimum in thermal conductivity at approximately 40 kg/m³.

Little work has been done on urea formaldehyde but increasing use of the material has been responsible for initiation of research projects. Unless correct formulation of the foam is achieved, appreciable shrinkage can occur leading to fissures appearing with a consequent loss in insulating performance. The only feasible way of determining the effect of such fissures is by full-scale measurement, but at present such facilities are not available in Australia.

Concern has been expressed at the possibility of water transmission from the outer skin of an external wall through fissures in urea formaldehyde to the inner skin. The UK experience has shown that for cavity brick walls which have the cavity filled the problem is minimal provided the building does not experience high levels of wind-driven rain. It is reasonable to expect the same situation locally.

Reflective foil laminate. Reflective foil laminate provides resistance to heat flow by virtue of the surface characteristics of the aluminium foil. For long wavelength radiation, the type encountered in buildings, the high reflection factor, ρ, of the surface and its complementary property of low emission factor ε ($\rho + \varepsilon = 1$ in this case) makes this material suitable for retarding horizontal or downward heat flow. Tables 1 and 2 give values of resistance of this material when used in conjunction with the airspaces encountered in buildings, along with values when RFL is not used (i.e. surface of high emission factor).

Attention needs to be paid to the possibility of condensation occurring on the surface of RFL as a layer of water increases the emission factor from 0.05 to that for ordinary building materials.

TABLE 1
THERMAL RESISTANCE OF AIRSPACES

Nature of bounding surfaces	Position of airspace	Direction of heat flow	Resistance (m^2K/W)	
			20 mm width	100 mm width
High emittance surfaces	Horizontal	Up	0·15	0·17
	,,	Down	0·15	0·17
	45° Slope	Up	0·17	0·17
	,,	Down	0·15	0·16
	Vertical	Horizontal	0·15*	0·16
One surface of low emittance	Horizontal	Up	0·39	0·48
	,,	Down	0·57	1·42
	45° Slope	Up	0·49	0·53
	,,	Down	0·57	0·77
	Vertical	Horizontal	0·58*	0·61
Two surfaces of low emittance	Horizontal	Up	0·41	0·51
	,,	Down	0·63	1·75
	45° Slope	Up	0·52	0·56
	,,	Down	0·62	0·85
	Vertical	Horizontal	0·62*	0·66

*For vertical airspaces greater than 20 mm, with horizontal heat flow, the value of resistance for 100 mm should be used.

TABLE 2
THERMAL RESISTANCE OF PITCHED ROOF SPACES

	Direction of heat flow	Resistance ($m^2 K/W$)	
		High emittance surface	Low emittance sarking
Ventilated roof space	Up	nil	0·34
	Down	0·46	1·36
Non-ventilated roof space	Up	0·18	0·56
	Down	0·28	1·09

11.3.3. Energy of Production

With the ever increasing concern with energy resources considerable attention has been paid to the energy consumed in producing building materials and in particular Hill (Ref. 3) has examined various types of insulating materials. The method of calculation has aroused some controversy as the energy is expressed as the Gross Energy Requirement and is defined as the sum of the fuel energy supplied to drive all the process stages within the system boundary chosen, plus the gross heats of combustion of those inputs which have alternative uses as fuels.

When considering building systems, such energy accounting acts adversely for timber and in the field of insulation adversely affects 'eel grass', a seaweed which has some potential as a fuel, and cellulose fibre made from recycled newspaper. The payback periods required to recover the energy for six insulating materials have been calculated for the Melbourne winter climate, Table 3, and it can be seen that in all cases energy payback is less than one heating season. For Sydney which has 209 kelvin days as compared to Melbourne with 681 (base 15°C) the payback period would be approximately in the ratio of these kelvin days.

11.3.4. Fire Performance

Bulk insulating materials are usually graded for fire performance by AS 1530, Part 3, Early Fire Hazard Properties of Materials. This test gives four indexes:

(1) Ignitability (Range 0–20)
(2) Heat evolved (Range 0–10)

TABLE 3
ENERGY PAYBACK PERIODS FOR SIX THERMAL
INSULATIONS

	None	Rock-wool (75 mm batt)	Glass-fibre (75 mm batt)	Cellulose fibre (100 mm loose)	Eel-grass (100 mm loose)	Urea-formal-dehyde (65 mm foam)	Reflective foil laminate (double-sided)
GER of insulation (MJ)	—	11 480	15 640	11 000	4490	5350	4400
Seasonal heating load (MJ)	59 090	35 540	35 320	33 980	34 490	35 200	49 420
Reduction in heating load due to insulation (MJ)	—	24 550	23 770	25 110	24 600	23 890	9670
Payback period (heating seasons)	—	0·5	0·7	0·4	0·2	0·2	0·5

(3)   Spread of flame (Range 0–10)
(4)   Smoke developed (Range 0–10)

It is considered that for the purposes of assessing and controlling the fire performance of insulating materials, the two most suitable indexes are the 'spread of flame' and 'smoke developed'. The proposed Australian Standard for cellulose fibre quotes these two indexes only. Other methods of gauging the fire performance of this material are under investigation. The most likely consist of imposing a radiant load on a horizontal situation rather than vertical as in AS 1530 Part 3 and observing the spread of flame after ignition.

The question of whether AS 1530 Part 3 gives a true picture of the full-scale performance of insulating materials has been investigated and reported by the Experimental Building Station (Ref. 4). This has shown that the ranking obtained for spread of flame, heat evolved and smoke developed agrees with real fire exposure where flames penetrate the eaves and are deflected under the roof sheeting.

RFL is tested for combustion properties according to AS 1530 Part 2. *Ad hoc* full-scale tests have shown qualitatively that the flammability indexes obtained give a true representation of the fire performance of the materials.

11.4. PERFORMANCE CONSIDERATIONS

Insulation within buildings has not been the general practice and when used wall insulation has largely been limited to RFL and ceilings to 50 mm of batt material or 75 to 100 mm of loose-fill insulation. The calculation of resistance of the element of a building has traditionally ignored the effect of timber framing. The error involved has been small for small thicknesses of insulation but becomes larger with increasing thicknesses. Further error is involved in assuming still-air conditions in the cavity, but the error involved here is not known. Frequently the resistance of the air space is halved to make some attempt at greater accuracy.

Table 4 gives the overall heat transfer coefficients (U values) for brick veneer walls to show the range of values obtained by various methods of calculation. A similar situation exists for insulated ceilings but Table 2 does give values for ventilated ceilings.

It is obvious that at high levels of insulation serious errors in calculations of heat transfer through brick veneer walls can occur if ventilation and framing are not taken into account, e.g. for wall insulation of 2 m^2K/W. If the wall is considered as being not ventilated, a U value of 0.41 is obtained, but allowing for framing and ventilation a U value of 0.47 is obtained, the error involved being 13%.

Calculation of U values for ceilings normally takes no account of framing timbers and similar errors can occur, but in this case they are not as serious because in the winter calculation the roof space is frequently not brought into the calculation. The effects of wind in roof

TABLE 4
U VALUES FOR BRICK VENEER WALLS

Wall Insulation, R	U value (W/m²K)			
	Normal Calculation		Framing Allowance	
(m²K/W)	Not Ventilated	Ventilated	Not Ventilated	Ventilated
0	2·19	2·65	2·02	2·42
1·2	0·61	0·63	0·63	0·67
1·6	0·49	0·51	0·53	0·55
1·8	0·44	0·46	0·49	0·51
2·0	0·41	0·42	0·45	0·47

spaces and wall cavities and its influence on the thermal resistance of fibrous materials is not well known. Likewise the effects of damage to RFL after installation are not well known. Damage can occur by following tradesmen tearing the material and thereby making possible increased heat losses by convection.

11.5. LEVELS OF INSULATION

For the climate in the major cities of the temperate zone of Australia, air conditioning of dwellings could hardly be regarded as a necessity and with proper design and appropriate building materials the need could be virtually eliminated. To determine optimum levels of insulation often then becomes concerned with the financial benefits accruing from its use in the cold season.

One method of examining the situation is to take a standard house and calculate the cost of energy required to maintain the internal temperature at some desired level. This has been done for Sydney for ceiling insulation making use of the computer program *STEP*.

A present worth analysis has been performed with the following assumptions:

(a) Period of investigation: 40 years
(b) Discount rate: 10%
(c) Insulation repayment period: 20 years
(d) Insulation repayment interest rate: 12%
(e) Annual rate of increase of fuel cost (above inflation): 1%

TABLE 5
OPTIMUM ECONOMIC CEILING INSULATION FOR
SYDNEY (R VALUES)

Insulation Cost $(Unit R.m^2)$	R value $(m^2 K/W)$ for Fuel Price (c/MJ) shown				
	0·5	0·75	1·0	1·5	1·75
1·0	0·95	1·23	1·47	1·87	2·06
1·5	0·74	0·95	1·15	1·47	1·62
2·0	0·59	0·79	0·95	1·23	1·36
2·5	0·51	0·68	0·82	1·08	1·18
3·0	0·46	0·59	0·74	0·95	1·05

Optimum economic values of thermal resistance (R values) obtained for various initial fuel costs are given in Table 5 for various insulation costs expressed in terms of dollars per m^2 for unit thermal resistance.

At current fuel and insulation costs the optimum R value for ceilings in Sydney is between 0.7 and 1.0 m^2K/W. Richards (Ref. 5) has shown the improvement in summer comfort achieved by reflective foil laminate sarking (which is equivalent to adding thermal resistance of a similar value to the optimum given above). It should be noted that the insulating value of foil used in ceilings is considerably less than this for upward heat flow, i.e. winter conditions.

In the present situation with increasing fuel prices the economics of solar heating must become more attractive and the examination of the economics of insulation could alter considerably. The benefits of more insulation rather than more collectors needs examination.

REFERENCES

1. Bankvall, C. G., *Heat Transfer in Fibrous Materials*, Document D4, The National Swedish Institute for Building, Stockholm, 1972.
2. Tye, R. P., 'Heat transmission in cellulosic fibre insulation materials,' *Journal of Testing and Evaluation*, **2**, 3, 176–179, May 1974.
3. Hill, R. K., 'Energy requirements for thermal insulation,' *Thermal Insulation*, **3**, 3, 101–12, July 1978.
4. Moulen, A. W. and Grubits, S. J., *Fire Spread in Ceiling Insulation Materials*, TR 44/153/430, Experimental Building Station, Sydney, p. 10.
5. Richards, F. R., 'Field test of reflective foil laminate insulation,' *Thermal Insulation*, **4**, 1, 10–13, Feb. 1979.

12

Solar Energy Systems in Australia and Overseas

P. R. SMITH

Department of Architectural Science,
University of Sydney, Australia

12.1. INTRODUCTION

The number of overseas examples of solar energy utilisation which can be found in the literature is large and it grows with every new issue of the many 'energy' periodicals now available. In 1977 Kaiman Lee listed 391 examples of energy-efficient buildings—mainly in the USA— (Ref. 1). A substantial number of these used aspects of solar energy technology and, of course, the list could not have hoped to be exhaustive. By comparison, the number in Australia seems to be very small. This can be largely explained by reference to relative populations, to climate and to the availability of combustion fuels.

In order to derive some benefit from describing examples found in Australia and elsewhere, they need to be put into a context. Therefore, let us begin by establishing some descriptive headings under which systems or examples can be classified and then describe the geographic and economic conditions under which they operate.

12.2. DESCRIPTORS FOR SOLAR ENERGY SYSTEMS

It is not the intention here to develop a taxonomy of solar energy systems, but to make the best use of commonly used classifications. There are several axes along which examples can be classified. Two which are useful at this stage are a 'system' axis and a 'development' axis. Typical descriptive terms which might be used along these axes might be:

System axis: passive—domestic hot water—space heating—space cooling—process heat—electricity generation.

Development axis: theoretical study—R and D—demonstration—assessment—standards and criteria—commercial production.

Different descriptive terms might be added or substituted, but those listed suggest the range and some rank-ordering of characteristics.

Another which is commonly used is a *hardware axis:* direct gain—flat plate—evacuated tube—concentrating collectors might be the values along this axis. A *temperature axis* is closely related to both the hardware and the system axes, but in some cases it might give more readily useful information.

12.3. GEOGRAPHY, CLIMATE AND ECONOMICS

Two principles which affect the viability of solar energy systems can be stated in simple terms:

(i) Solar energy is free, but the devices to collect it are not free.

(ii) Solar energy is only available when the sun is shining.

It can readily be shown that (i) is not true in some cases of direct gain and that (ii) is not true when diffuse radiation is collected or nocturnal radiation is used as a source of cooling. Nevertheless, within their limitations, these two principles provide the basis for studying geography, climate and economics in relation to solar energy systems.

Principle (i) indicates that solar energy is unique among energy sources in having a zero marginal cost. The fixed costs are spread over the energy collected and therefore the more one uses the system, the better. The amount of usage is limited to the intersection of two sets: one defined by the availability as described in principle (ii) and the other defined by the demand pattern of the end use. (Thermal or other storage may be used to shift one of the sets to increase the intersection).

It happens that domestic hot water is a popular application of solar energy for several reasons: the low temperatures needed allow simple equipment to be used and also the demand is fairly continuous around the year. There is an increase in winter as the feed-water temperature falls and system losses increase, but this is not a great effect. At latitudes up to the high 40s, it is possible to install sloping collectors which have only marginally less capacity in winter than in summer and are therefore well utilised for the full 12 months. Industrial process heating follows a similar demand pattern, and is only recently receiving some much-deserved attention from the solar industry. It is, however, outside the usual definition of energy consumed by buildings.

Space heating and cooling is another avenue for solar energy use. Space heating suffers from the mismatch of supply and demand suggested by principle (ii), but can utilise easily-produced low-temperature energy. Space cooling exhibits good correspondence between supply and demand, but for small buildings the *area of the intersection* may be small if cooling is only needed for a small part of the year. (Larger buildings usually need some cooling year-round.) The temperatures needed for cooling are inconveniently high for trouble-free operation on a commercial basis using first-generation collectors. 'Second-generation' collectors now going into production promise to meet these temperatures more easily, although at higher initial cost.

Electricity generation on medium to large scale could be considered at least a third-generation stage of solar utilisation. It is generally considered that electricity shortfall in the short term might be made up by conservation; in the medium term by coal and nuclear thermal stations; and in the longer term by solar (thermal or direct-conversion) and fusion, if the technology can be solved. For the building industry, production of electricity in central solar power stations has much to commend it. Buildings last longer than most other goods and their ability to accept electricity from whatever external source is favoured by the technology of the time is a great advantage.

The principles so far discussed form a basis for considering examples of solar energy utilisation in various regions.

12.4. NORTH AMERICA

North America has a tradition of high-technology HVAC systems and high standards of thermal comfort in buildings of all types. In the past few years there have been official efforts to relax these standards in the interests of energy conservation. Nevertheless it is easier to justify the cost of a solar-powered installation if it is compared with a traditionally elaborate system, rather than with the less expensive systems used in other countries.

Compared to Europe, North America has cities with similar heating loads, but 10° nearer the equator. (See Fig. 1 and Table 1) By reference

TABLE 1
ANNUAL HEATING REQUIREMENTS FOR SELECTED
CITIES

City	Latitude °N or °S	Elevation (m)	K-Days Heating (re 18°C)	Extreme Temps. °C † Winter	Summer
New Orleans, La	30	*	700	2	33
El Paso, TX	31	1200	1500	−4	37
Dallas, TX	33	*	1300	−4	37
Los Angeles, CA	34	*	750	7	32
San Francisco, CA	37	*	1700	7	25
St. Louis, MO	38	*	2500	−12	35
Denver, CO	39	1600	3100	−16	32
Chicago, IL	41	*	3300	−17	33
New York, NY	41	*	2700	−9	33
Halifax, NS	44	*	4100	−9	27
Montreal, QUE	45	*	4400	−9	33
Vancouver, BC	49	*	3100	−7	26
Winnipeg, MAN	49	250	5900	−32	31
Tokyo, Japan	36	*		−2	31
London, England	51	*	2950	−3	26
Hamburg, Germany	54	*	3550	−9	24
Copenhagen, Denmark	56	*	3800	−7	24
Moscow, USSR	56	*	5350	−21	27
Sydney, NSW	34	*	750	5	29
Canberra, ACT	35	800	1900		
Melbourne, VIC	38	*	1500	3	33

Values taken from Ref. 2 and 3 (rounded).

*Altitudes less than 200 m are not listed.
†Winter temperatures exceeded on 97½% of days, summer on 2½%.

to Fig. 2 (energy available year round at latitudes 40° and 60°) it can be seen that year-round solar collection is feasible at latitude 40°, but the energy available in midwinter at latitude 60° is so small that very substantial supplementation will be needed from other sources. (These diagrams are based on clear weather. All locations will suffer from some cloudy days, but America has certain areas at high altitude where clear winter days are frequent.)

Compared to Australia, North America has a much more severe climate, with longer heating and cooling seasons, so that solar equipment for space heating and cooling will be utilised for longer

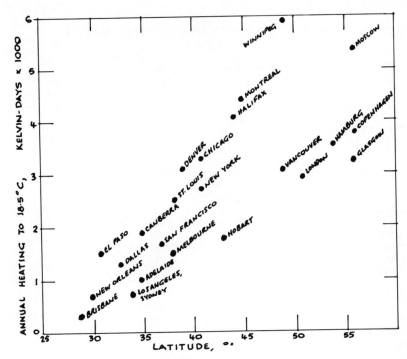

Fig. 1. The relationship between annual heating requirements (*K*-days per year re 18.5°C) and latitude, for selected cities. The cities tend to group along two lines, indicating maritime and continental climates.

periods. There are also substantial taxation incentives for the installation of energy-conserving devices. This is of the greatest importance, since many of the installations would not be economically viable without it at the present state of fuel costs.

Much solar hardware is now at the commercial production stage of development, i.e. in the catalogues and available through the normal HVAC contractors. This also is important. Firstly, it removes the 'unusual' connotation from the equipment. Secondly (at the domestic scale) it implies that there is a contractor who would be installing the furnace (and perhaps air conditioning) in any case. This trade is usually absent from Sydney houses, and many builders would be reluctant to introduce such an additional trade.

Solaron air collectors (Fig. 3) are produced by a Denver company headed by Dr. George Löf, one of the pioneers of solar energy in the

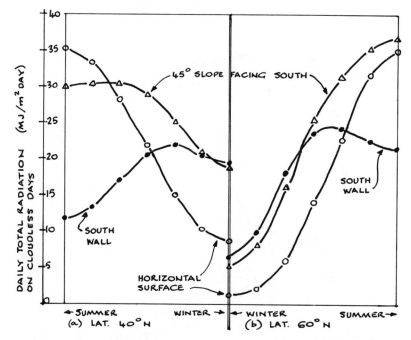

Fig. 2. Monthly solar energy incident on various surfaces, (a) at lat. 40°, and (b) at lat.60°, assuming clear sky conditions. (After Ref. 4).

USA. The product is now well into the commercial stage, having been listed in Sweet's Catalogue for some years. Development of the design has been carried out with the ordinary user in mind. The connections between adjacent panels are built-in, so that the units can be simply butted together. Air will not freeze or evaporate and slight leaks will not cause any damage. By way of contrast, the plumbing cost of connecting up liquid-filled collectors can approach the cost of the units themselves; serious damage can be done to the units if the liquid freezes or runs dry; and leaks can damage ceilings and furnishings. As a result, the air collectors (although a little less efficient than comparable liquid collectors), are cheaper to buy, install and maintain.

Northrup concentrating collectors (Fig. 4) are also at the commercial stage. They are produced in Dallas and used both in the USA and overseas to provide higher temperatures than can be reliably obtained from flat-plate collectors under field conditions. Temperatures around

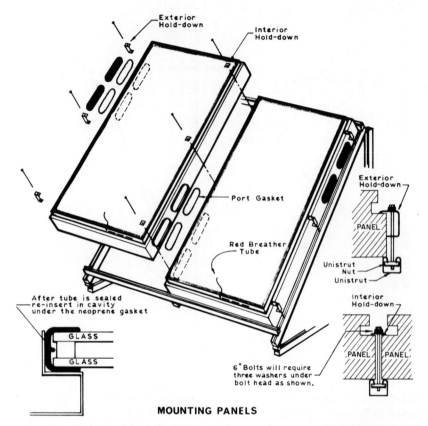

Exterior
Hold-down

Interior
Hold-down

Port Gasket

Red Breather
Tube

Exterior
Hold-down

PANEL

Unistrut
Nut
Unistrut

After tube is sealed
re-insert in cavity
under the neoprene gasket

GLASS

GLASS

Interior
Hold-down

PANEL   PANEL

6" Bolts will require
three washers under
bolt head as shown.

MOUNTING PANELS

Fig. 3. Solaron solar collectors, using air as the heat transfer medium.

130°C will comfortably operate absorption-refrigeration machines and
will supply process heat to conventional steam-operated equipment, as
well as allowing for easy storage of sensible heat for space heating.
These functions can be performed in the laboratory using special
equipment operating at around 90°C, from flat-plate collectors, but
large areas are required for heat-exchange surfaces and the margin for
deterioration of performance is small. The higher temperatures available from the concentrating collectors make the design of the remainder
of the system much easier. These linear concentrators use a linear
Fresnel lens to concentrate the solar beam on to a tube. They track
continuously throughout the day in one plane, but no seasonal
adjustment is made in the other plane.

Fig. 4. Northrup linear Fresnel lens concentrating collector (cross section).

One installation of 1200 m² of collectors on a resort hotel in the Virgin Islands will provide all the energy for the space conditioning. This is particularly appropriate in a region without an electricity supply, but in the USA the company lists (in 1977) 28 installations, usually providing heating, cooling and hot water. The Northrup corporation was already in the HVAC industry and therefore found little difficulty in integrating its solar products with the rest of its activities. It deals mainly in commercial and industrial applications.

The National Security and Resources Study Center at Los Alamos NM (Fig. 5) is one of many demonstration projects funded by the Federal Government to study and demonstrate solar energy technology in a practical situation. The three-storey conference and library building has a sloping roof on one end, 750 m² in area, devoted to solar collection. The collectors are an integral design (i.e. they form the roof surface and insulation) and use paraffin as the collecting fluid. This has the advantages of not freezing and of inhibiting corrosion so that cheaper materials can be used.

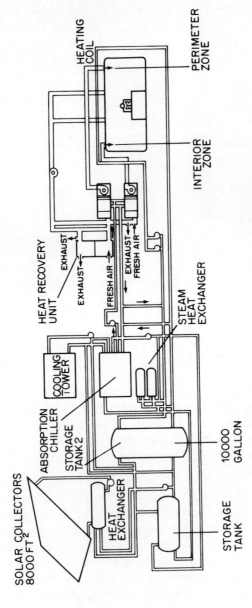

Fig. 5. National Resources and Study Center, Los Alamos, NM.

Skytherm and Energy Roof Systems are at the developmental stage at present. They are somewhere between passive and active systems, useful for single-storey domestic or commercial buildings. *Skytherm*, designed by Harold Hay of Los Angeles, uses a layer of water on the roof, contained in a plastic envelope (Fig. 6). The plastic bags are

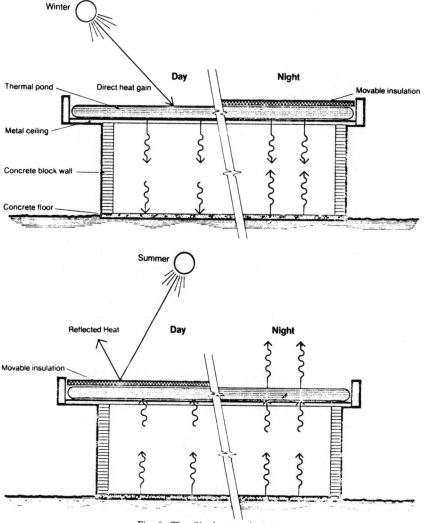

Fig. 6. The *Skytherm* principle.

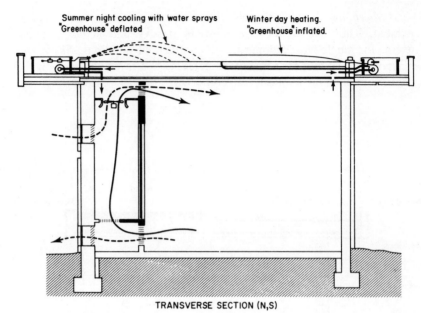

Fig. 7. The "energy roof" principle (Arizona State University).

covered by removable insulation panels, so that when they are uncovered they either gain heat (in daytime) or lose heat (at night). The ceiling is simply a roll-formed steel decking, so that heat is readily transferred between the water bags and the interior. The thermal storage provided by the water and the gain or loss available by operating the insulation ensures a reasonably uniform internal condition.

The *Energy Roof* is an adaptation developed at Arizona State University. Instead of moving the insulation panels (which necessitates a place on the roof to store them), a panel of foam insulation floats on the water within the plastic envelope (Fig. 7). When this floats to the top, the water is insulated from the exterior climate. A circulating pump can pump water on to the top of the insulation panel when it is desired to expose the water to the climate. The operation is similar in principle to *Skytherm*. For additional night cooling, water can be sprayed on to the outside of the plastic envelope to evaporatively cool it.

There is extensive interest in *passive systems* and some specialists in the field have a substantial following. *Steve Baer,* (Ref. 5) who runs

Zomeworks in Albuquerque, NM, designs and sells many types of automatic or manually operated devices to control sunlight penetration, ventilation and heat loss. One such device is the 'Skylid', a roof shutter which opens or closes automatically by the transfer of refrigerant from one cylinder to another due to thermal differences. Another is the 'beadwall', a double-glazed window in which the cavity between the glass is filled with expanded polystyrene beads. The beads are pumped in and out by a small electric fan, to vary the thermal properties of the window.

Detailed theoretical and experimental studies of passive behaviour have been carried out at *Los Alamos Scientific Laboratories*. Dr. Douglas Balcomb (Ref. 6) is among the chief researchers interested in this work. An interesting development at present is the preparation of simple design charts which can be used to predict the percentage of total heating load which will be supplied by a given area of glass, related to a particular climate (Ref. 7). These charts depend upon very extensive computer simulation of building behaviour under recorded weather patterns, but the results are combined to form much simpler predictive methods which can be economically used in the design of individual buildings.

The development of simple design methods is important to the whole solar energy industry. Relatively simple methods have been developed for conventional mechanical systems, where the climate is a variable on the load side but the supply of energy is constantly available. With solar energy both the load and the supply are variables and any solution will have to be based on many statistics, or simulation, or real-time experience. Balcomb has already shown that mathematical modelling techniques can produce acceptable, simple design methods for active systems (Ref. 8). In all cases, however, the records which meteorologists will be asked to keep will be more detailed than they usually have available at present.

Underground construction has received considerable attention in the USA. *Frank Moreland* (Ref. 9) is one of the researchers active in this area. There is already a substantial list of underground or partly earth-insulated buildings in many parts of the country. With a little imagination it can be thought of as one way of modifying solar energy inputs on a yearly time-scale.

Underground construction implies a strong structural system and effective waterproofing and is therefore likely to be more costly than conventional construction. It is advantageous in very harsh climates (where the heating or cooling costs can be reduced by an order of magnitude) and for 24-hour operations such as a library stack or food cold-store. There are many fringe benefits: additional security against storms, explosion and unauthorised entry; reduced external maintenance and the availability of urban parkland on top of the building. It is interesting to note that many urban parking stations and transport terminals are constructed underground on the strength of the latter point alone. The Domain parking station and Wynyard railway station are two examples in Sydney.

12.5. EUROPE

Northern Europe, with latitudes in the 50s and often extended periods of cloud cover in winter, presents great difficulties for using solar space heating. Most energy-conservation measures have been in the areas of reducing heat losses and more efficient use of equipment, with a few systems attempting seasonal heat storage.

Heat pumps have received much interest in Europe, as well as in North America. They are a means of multiplying the heating effect of electricity by a factor, usually between 3 and 5, depending on the source temperature. In some installations the heat pump uses various items of waste heat as its source and sometimes a solar collector panel as well. A solar-sourced heat pump has several advantages: the collector panel operates at fairly low temperatures and is therefore not subject to the large losses of a normal collector; because it can operate above ambient air temperature rather than below it, the coefficient of performance is much better than for an air-sourced heat pump; and when the sun is not shining, it will still operate with the reduced coefficient of performance (COP), so that a separate booster is not required.

The Danish *Zero-Energy-House* is representative of several European experiments aimed at reducing energy consumption of a building at all costs. The result is about as practical as using a racing-car for everyday motoring, and rather more expensive. Nevertheless, just as ideas developed in competition eventually result in improvements to the everyday product, so some of the lessons learned from these elaborate buildings will be adapted for more general use.

The house is heavily insulated (with 300 mm of insulation in the walls,

400 mm in the roof and floor) and has shutters to protect the double-glazed windows from heat loss at night. There is 40 m^2 of vertical solar collector, feeding a 30 m^3 storage tank. The tank reaches about 80°C during the summer and in a good year will supply the shortfall of solar input during the winter. During the 1976–77 winter, below-average sunlight reduced the available solar input and the house did not act quite as economically as expected, so that additional heat from a furnace was needed during the winter.

The efficiency of the insulation, reduced infiltration and waste heat recovery systems is such that the total requirement for space heating is reduced from 19 450 kWh for a typical well insulated house to 2300 kWh for this house (i.e. only 12% of the typical value). Whether this reduced amount is supplied by solar or other means, it is already a substantial reduction.

In England, *St. George's School at Wallasey* constructed in 1962, raised considerable interest because of its large south-facing glass wall, combined with good insulation on other surfaces and reduced ventilation rates, all designed to eliminate the need for supplementary heating. It has been the subject of numerous articles, a useful recent review being given by Davies (Ref. 10). Winter temperatures of 16°C and above are reported, while summer daily means reach 24½° and peaks exceed this figure. Because of the special hours of schools (shorter than office hours) and the long summer vacation, it is easier to achieve tolerable conditions by solar gain in schools than in other buildings. Nevertheless it is generally conceded that the summer conditions in direct-gain type schools can be quite unpleasant (especially if the ventilation is insufficient) and the presence of sunlight in the teaching spaces can be visually unpleasant.

Domestic solar water heating in the UK is into the commercial phase, although evaluations are still being carried out. As in all countries, its economy depends upon the price of other energy sources. Used in conjunction with a site-stored booster fuel (oil, coal or bottled gas) it also provides a measure of protection against strikes in the energy supply industry.

Houses heated by active solar systems include one (widely reported) at Milton Keynes, which has 38 m^2 of collector and 4.5 m^3 of hot water storage, and several being constructed at BRE, one with the larger storage volume of 36 m^3 (Ref. 11). These must be regarded as being at the R and D or development stages. In fact Courtney reported in 1976 the 'major' projects in Britain as consisting of seven houses, two schools and a commercial building, with future proposals of about the same number. There were also, however, a dozen major theoretical or experimental studies under way, many of them aimed at optimising systems or evaluating the performance of components.

12.6. JAPAN AND THE EAST

Some of the highly industrialised nations such as Japan and Singapore are particularly deficient in indigenous energy resources and therefore very anxious to develop solar energy systems. In 1974 the Japanese Government started 'Project Sunshine', to encourage long-range research into new energy sources.

Solar water heaters are used in considerable numbers in Japan. In 1976, Kimura (Ref. 12) estimated the annual sales at 100 000 units, mostly of the cheap black-plastic-tube type. Since then, with rising fuel prices, more elaborate flat-plate collector systems have been used.

Fig. 8. A "solar house" in Japan (K. Kimura, architect).

Many experimental houses have been constructed using *solar space heating* and in some cases cooling as well (Fig. 8). It is generally accepted that the cooling technology is too complicated to operate satisfactorily at the scale of a single house under field conditions. Solar space heating alone is a little simpler. The Japan Housing Corporation is experimenting with flat-plate collectors for space heating in some of its apartments.

The *Kent Ridge Teaching Hospital* in Singapore (Ref. 13) was designed to reduce energy consumption without sacrificing comfort. Many of the rooms are not air-conditioned relying on overhangs, North-South orientation and cross ventilation. Because of the need for ventilation, the building has a very spread-out plan. *Domestic hot water* is provided primarily by eight separate solar collector/storage systems, totalling 1227 m^2 of collectors and located close to the points of use. The conventional flat-plate collectors work efficiently in the Singapore climate in producing water at 45° C for general purposes. It was decided not to use solar heat for the higher-temperature water needed for kitchens, laundries and sterilisation.

12.7. AUSTRALIA

A national competition sponsored by ACI and a group of professional institutions in 1978 (Ref. 14) drew a few dozen entries from around the nation. Most were houses, using passive or active solar collection or both, as well as wind generators and wood stoves. There were only a handful of non-residential buildings submitted, and these did not incorporate solar energy devices (apart from attention to orientation and shading).

There is no clear economic reason why solar energy should be limited to housing, apart from the separation of capital cost (paid by building owners) and running cost (paid by occupiers) in the commercial arena. In Sydney householders pay about 2½ cents for a kWh of electricity, about the same for gas, while oil or off-peak electricity is just over half this price. Industry pays almost twice as much for electricity, substantially less for gas, and has access to very cheap fuel oil if it can use the heavy residual grades. In other parts of the country the figures and the relativities change.

The mild coastal climate is particularly well suited to simple passive

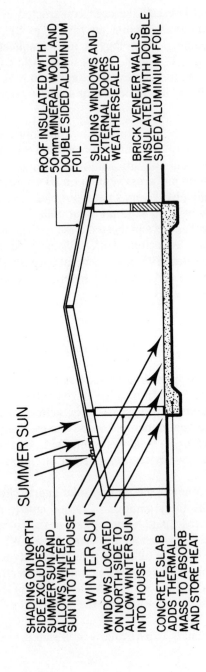

ROOF INSULATED WITH 50mm MINERAL WOOL AND DOUBLE SIDED ALUMINIUM FOIL

SLIDING WINDOWS AND EXTERNAL DOORS WEATHERSEALED

BRICK VENEER WALLS INSULATED WITH DOUBLE SIDED ALUMINIUM FOIL

SUMMER SUN

SHADING ON NORTH SIDE EXCLUDES SUMMER SUN AND ALLOWS WINTER SUN INTO THE HOUSE

WINTER SUN

WINDOWS LOCATED ON NORTH SIDE TO ALLOW WINTER SUN INTO HOUSE

CONCRETE SLAB ADDS THERMAL MASS TO ABSORB AND STORE HEAT

Fig. 9. Merchant Builders Pty. Ltd. "energy saving" project house (cross section).

design measures, because at minimum cost they can provide reasonable comfort. Cheap electric radiators can be used to top-up a passive house if they don't have to be used for long periods. The heating bill for a conventional house is not great enough to justify costly solar collectors and storage for space heating purely on economic grounds.

An example of fairly simple passive design is an entry in the competition by *Merchant Builders Pty. Ltd.* (Fig. 9) in which a popular project house design was modified in terms of orientation, floor materials and window design to become a collector of solar heat in winter, but to shade itself in summer. Many innovations of architectural style in the last two decades have found their way into the mainstream of Australian usage by way of the project house industry, and it is encouraging to see an appreciation of solar energy being introduced to the wider house-buying public in this way.

In a more elaborate example passive and active solar systems are combined in the *Cole Residence,* under construction in Sydney (Fig. 10).

Fig. 10. Cole Residence, Sydney (I. G. Cole, Architect).

Fig. 11. Solar collectors on camping ground amenities block, Wilcannia, NSW.

The house uses thick stone and brick walls for thermal inertia to overcome hot weather and incorporates solar collector panels with water storage for space heating, as well as domestic hot water.

The *solar hot water* industry is well into the commercial phase in Australia with solar systems being normal in most new construction in the tropics, and quite popular in most regions except the major east-coast population centres (Fig. 11). Here the availability of cheap alternative fuels (off-peak electricity is attractive because the winter climate and the peak transport loads combine to give the supply authority a peaky load profile and gas is also cheap in Melbourne) combines with the cloudiness of a maritime climate to reduce the attractiveness of solar units.

Apparently the only example in Australia of a commercial-scale building heated and cooled by solar energy is the *Eldridge Medical Centre* in Sydney (Ref. 15, Fig. 12). It is a two-storey building with a sawtooth roof. The sloping panels face North, and have 474 m^2 of collectors covering virtually the whole of the roof area. The collectors were specially designed for the project, using dimpled stainless-steel panels with a selective surface. Narrow sections of conventional roofing are located between adjacent collectors for walkway access, but apart from this the collectors form the roof surface and insulation.

Fig. 12. Eldridge Medical Centre, Sydney: the sloping parts of the sawtooth roof carry solar collectors to supply heating and cooling to the building.

The collectors feed a water-storage tank and gas-fired booster boiler. Heating is achieved by circulating this water through fan coil units, while cooling is obtained with a bank of lithium bromide-water absorption chillers. The absorption machines will operate on 74°C water, but achieve full performance at 88°C. The water is returned to the collectors (or the gas booster) at 70°C, which means that the collectors are required to perform at quite a high average temperature in the cooling season.

The project was financed and constructed by private enterprise without direct Government subsidy for the solar installation. A payback period of 14 years was indicated, using a 70% solar contribution and no increase in fuel prices. If fuel prices increase, one would expect the economics to work out more favourably.

These figures may not appeal to the average investor who is seeking short-term returns, but for Government and institutional buildings with a long life and essentially owner-occupied, it appears that such figures would be within the bounds of possibility, if there was a definite energy policy which encouraged the use of renewable energy sources in buildings.

REFERENCES

1. Lee, K., *Encyclopedia of Energy-Efficient Building Design: 391 Practical Case Studies.* Environmental Design and Research Center, Boston, Massachusetts 1977.
2. ASHRAE, *Handbook of Fundamentals,* 373–392, New york, 1967.
3. McGuinness, W. and Stein, B. *Mechanical and Electrical Services for Buildings,* 213–216, Wiley, New York, 1971.
4. Ballantyne, E. R., private communication.
5. Baer, S. *Sunspots,* Zomeworks, Albuquerque, 1977.
6. Balcomb, J. D. and Reller M. H. (Eds.), *Passive Solar Heating and Cooling Conference and Workshop Proceedings,* U.S. Dept. of Commerce, Publication LA-6637-C, Albuquerque, 1976.
7. Balcomb, J. D., private communication. A publication is in course of preparation.
8. Balcomb, J. D. and Hedstrom, J. C., *Sizing Solar Collectors for Space Heating,* Los Alamos Scientific Laboratories Publ. LA-UR-76-1334, Los Alamos, NM, 1976.
9. Moreland, F. (Ed.), *Alternatives in Energy Conservation—the Use of Earth Covered Buildings,* Conference in Fort Worth, Texas, 1975. National Science Foundation Publ., NSF-RA-760006.
10. Davies, M. G., 'The contribution of solar gain to space heating,' *Sun at Work in Britain,* 3, 11–20, June 1976.
11. Courtney, R. G., 'Solar energy utilisation in the U.K.—Current Research and Future Prospects,' *Architectural Science Review,* **19**, 2, 44–49, June 1976.
12. Kimura, K., 'Present technologies of solar heating, cooling and hot water supply in Japan,' *Architectural Science Review,* **19**, 2, 41–43, June 1976.
13. Stedman, R., 'The Kent Ridge Teaching Hospital, Singapore, *National Symposium on Energy Conservation in Buildings,* Institution of Engineers' Australia, 70–74, Sydney 1978.
14. Kent, J. H. (Ed.), *National Symposium on Energy Conservation in Buildings,* I. E. Aust, Sydney, 1978.
15. Chilman, K. F., 'Australia's first solar air-conditioned building,' *Solar Energy—For Buildings?,* Conf. of Building Science Forum of Australia, Sydney, 1978.

13

Sun Shading Devices

E. L. HARKNESS

Department of Architecture, University of Newcastle, Australia

13.1. INTRODUCTION

The most efficient way of maximising management of the influx of solar heat gain through the building envelope is to:

(a) protect the glazing against both the direct and the diffuse components of solar radiation heat gain in summer; and

(b) admit both the direct and diffuse components in winter.

The above can be achieved with greatest efficacy by using movable external sunscreens.

13.2. SUN SHADING DEVICES USED IN NATURALLY VENTILATED BUILDINGS IN SOUTH AMERICA

13.2.1. Louvred Doors

Delightfully direct in the application of these principles is the delicate detailing in the design of the Grand Hotel, Buenos Aires, the Western facade of which is illustrated in Fig. 1. The void to solid ratio is small and the glazed areas are protected with louvred timber shutters.

On a summer's afternoon the shutters may be closed to exclude a heat load in the order of 800 W/m^2 at 16.00 hrs. In winter the shutters may be opened to admit a heat load in the order of 460 W/m^2 at 15.00 hrs. On a quiet winter's afternoon free from cold winds, the glazing could be opened to admit a maximum heat load. If the glazing is closed only 70% of the diffuse component would be admitted and the quantity of direct component admitted would be proportional to the angle of incidence.

Fig. 1. Grand Hotel, Buenos Aires, Argentina. Latitude 34½° South. View of the western facade.

13.2.2. Hooded Canvas Screens

The hooded canvas screens illustrated in Fig. 2 would not be as efficient as the timber louvred shutters of the Grand Hotel because they cannot shade the entire glazed area from heat load; nor are they as effective in attenuating the air speed over the glazed areas on a cold winter's night. They do, however, when in use, permit a view down to the street.

Figure 2 shows the use of hooded canvas blinds on the southern reveal of this old building. In summer this blind would give protection from a heat load from the diffuse component of solar radiation of more than 50 watts/m^2 from 09.00 hrs. to 12.00 hrs. (allowing for shading from the building itself) and a diffuse load greater than 100 watts/m^2 from 12.00 hrs. to 15.00 hrs. Without a sunscreen at 16.00 hrs. the heat load from the direct component on the glass would be in the order of 100 W/m^2 and at 17.00 and 18.00 hrs. greater than 150 W/m^2.

In winter this south-facing hood, if opened, would permit to be incident on the glass no direct component, but a diffuse component greater than 12.5 W/m^2 from 09.00 to 12.00 hrs. and greater than 25 W/m^2 from 12.00 to 15.00 hrs. of which only 8.7 and 17.5 W/m^2 would

Fig. 2. Hooded canvas screen, Buenos Aires, Argentina. Latitude 34½° South.

be transmitted if the glass windows were closed. If the hooded blinds on the western facade were opened in the morning in winter, the diffuse heat load on the glass would be 52 W/m^2 at 10.00 hrs., 70 W/m^2 at 11.00 hrs. and 86 W/m^2 at 12.00 hrs. In the afternoon these opened blinds would permit a heat load of 460 Watts/m^2 to be incident on the glass.

The hooded canvas blinds are a major and large-scale element in the fenestration design. A significant thermal advantage of canvas blinds over most alternatives is their low thermal conductivity and low thermal capacity—they do not present a problem of reradiating heat into the building. If canvas blinds are used, the architect should submit to his client a maintenance schedule which should include replacement of the blinds. The cost of replacing the canvas blinds needs to be offset against the saving of not air-conditioning the building and, of course, thermal comfort for the occupants. Examples of the use of canvas and other external movable blinds applied in retrofitting existing buildings may be seen in San Francisco, where their application can be seen to be both functional, decorative and in scale with the buildings.

13.2.3. Roller Shutters

In the Hotel Republica (Fig. 3), roller shutters on the eastern facade may be closed in summer to protect the glazing in summer at 08.00 hrs. from a heat load of 800 W/m². These roller shutters can be opened in the

Fig. 3. Hotel Republica, Buenos Aires, Argentina. Latitude 34½° South. View of the eastern facade.

afternoon to afford a view. At 13.00 hrs. the heat load from the diffuse component would be 100 W/m^2. It is noteworthy that in summer in Buenos Aires most shutters remained closed throughout almost the entire day, even at times when no direct solar radiation would be incident on the shutters. It would appear that protection from the diffuse component is important and that protective devices are used for this purpose where fitted.

In autumn and spring the occupants may choose to adjust the shutters to protect against some of the influx of solar heat gain in the morning and open the shutters in the afternoon to admit the diffuse component.

Fig. 4. Residential building, Neuquen, Argentina. Latitude 39° South. View of the eastern facade.

In winter the roller shutters of the Hotel Republica could be opened to allow 470 W/m² to be incident on the glass at 09.00 hrs. Given that the building has shallow balconies, it could be argued that it would be more rational if the roller shutters were inverted to permit the top to be opened progressively as the sun rises. In this way more daylight illumination and a view could be achieved for a greater percentage of the morning hours.

The horizontal strips of the roller shutters in the Hotel Republica are in harmony with the horizontality of other elements used in this fenestration design. The character of the building is crisp and ordered. The architect will maintain long-term control over the appearance of the building. The sunscreening devices, i.e. the shallow balconies and the roller shutters, constitute the major design elements in the facade. The sunscreening elements do not appear to be added on as an after-thought but have been effectively synthesised into the design.

Roller shutters were also used on a residential building in Neuquen, Argentina, (Fig. 4). The effectiveness of external roller shutters in excluding direct and diffuse solar radiation during a summer's day, and their effectiveness in reducing heat loss from the building on a cold winter's night is unquestioned.

13.2.4. Articulated Roller Shutters

Figure 5 illustrates the use of articulated external roller shutters on the Gran Hotel Roma, Bariloche, Argentina which increases the amount of control which the occupant has over the quality of his thermal and illuminated environment. In this example the articulated roller shutters have been used on the northern facade. The shutters may be adjusted to project out from the facade giving less protection from the direct component of solar radiation, but permitting a greater view down to the street for a given amount of direct heat gain than simple un-articulated roller shutters.

13.2.5. Horizontal Adjustable Louvres

Horizontal adjustable louvres used in the Compania Financiera Central Building, Buenos Aires (Fig. 6), enable the occupant a considerable amount of control over the interior thermal and illuminated environment. Given that a west facing facade was not avoidable, the horizontal louvres may be adjusted to admit a maximum of heat gain on a winter's afternoon or to close off afternoon heat gain in summer at which time a relatively even distribution of daylight could be

Fig. 5. Gran Hotel Roma, Bariloche, Argentina. Latitude 41° South. View of northern facade.

achieved within the building. The major inconvenience of horizontal louvres on the western or eastern facade is that, in order to maximise their efficiency, they need to be adjusted frequently. Vertical louvres, on the other hand need adjustment much less frequently. It is noteworthy that a number of louvres are missing in this photograph. One of the consequences of using adjustable louvres is maintenance —acceptance of the need for which needs to be taken into account in the architect's design. Access to carry out maintenance of sunscreening devices must be considered at the design stage as an inevitable cost. Designing a building in which access for maintenance purposes is dangerous will add to the building's recurrent through-life costs. The architect of the Compania Financiera Central building has not provided

Fig. 6. Compania Financiera Central Building, Buenos Aires. Latitude 34½° South.
View of western facade.

easy access for maintenance of the louvres, which has resulted in the
building now having the appearance of needing maintenance and the
architect is beginning to lose long-term control over the appearance of
his building.

13.2.6. Fixed Vertical Louvres

An exotic piece of architecture, the Banco Provincial De Salta,
Argentina, Latitude 25°S (Fig. 7), illustrates that the architect is not
aware of the functional dependency which fenestration design for a
particular facade has on orientation. In this example the architect has
used similar elements on each facade irrespective of orientation. On the
northern and western facades the direct component of solar radiation
will be incident on the glazing whenever the sun is at a normal to the
facade because the vertical louvres used are at a normal to each facade.
The use of vertical louvres spaced to provide a horizontal shadow angle
of 60° on the southern facade would be effective. The fixed vertical
louvres on the western facade could have been effective if they had been
designed to provide a horizontal shadow angle of 30° south of west. The
sunscreening elements on the Banco Provincial De Salta are major
elements in the fenestration design, are heavy in appearance and are not

Fig. 7. Banco Provincial De Salta, Salta, Argentina. Latitude 25° South. View from the south west.

functionally designed. Had the architect an understanding for the design of non-redundant sunscreens, he could have designed an equally exotic building in which the fenestration treatment of each facade would have been a function of its orientation, and in which he could have exercised more control over the interior thermal and illuminated environment.

13.2.7. Horizontal Sliding Louvres
Fenestration of the Hotel Presidente, Rosario, Argentina (Fig. 8), includes the use of horizontally sliding louvres on its western facade. In being effective against the influx of solar heat gain, the louvres exclude a view.

13.2.8. Sculptural and Kinetic Sunscreens
The building illustrated in Fig. 9 is on the campus of the Universidade De Brasilia, Latitude 16°S. This building shows an approach to fenestration design that is far removed from that of the early exhibition architecture of Brasilia. In this example the windows in the upper floor are hooded from the northern sun and oriented towards the south. The

Fig. 8. Hotel Presidente, Rosario, Argentina. Latitude 33° South. View of western facade

Fig. 9. Universidade De Brasilia, Brazil. Latitude 16° South.

Fig. 10. Palacio da Alvorada, (official presidential residence), Brasilia, Latitude 16°
South. View of western facade.

'Mobile' is interesting but difficult to rationalise at this stage of completion.

To illustrate that architects are willing to make a commitment to exotic fenestration design, the western elevation of the Palácio da Alvorada (Official Presidential Residence), Brasilia, Latitude 16°S is included (Fig. 10). In summer the direct component of solar radiation will be incident on the glass from 15.00 hrs. to sunset. Combined with the effect of the diffuse component of solar radiation incident on the glass, the internal thermal environment may be expected to be unacceptable. Had the architect an understanding for the design of non-redundant sunscreens, he could have produced an equally exotic piece of architecture, but which would have been thermally more comfortable and in which the lighted environment would also be better controlled.

Another sculptural example may be seen on the Mendoza Campus building illustrated in Fig. 11. Mendoza, Argentina, is at a latitude of 33°S. A study of this northern facade detail indicates that it would exclude the direct component in summer and admit some of the direct component in winter. The truncated concrete pyramids would scatter the direct and diffuse components of solar radiation, produce a constant illuminated environment throughout the length of the building and be more even throughout the depth of the room, than would be so in the former illustration, i.e. in the Palácio da Alvorada.

In the above mentioned sunscreens, movable external sunscreens enable the occupant to exercise considerable control over the quality of

Fig. 11. Mendoza Campus Building, Argentina. Latitude 33° South. View of the northern facade.

the interior thermal and illuminated environment. There are few examples of fixed sunscreens, whose designs can be shown to be a function of solar geometry, which are efficient at controlling the penetration of the direct component of solar radiation and which permit a view.

A more detailed review of fenestration design of modern buildings was published in the *Architectural Science Review* in 1977 (Ref. 1).

13.3. NON-REDUNDANT SUNSCREENS

13.3.1. Introduction

For want of a better term the author has coined the phrase 'non-redundant sunscreen' as meaning a sunscreen which has been designed to possess no redundancy on a selected design day in terms of its shading a window for a specified period throughout that day. The author's first published comment on redundancy in sunscreens appeared in a paper presented to the August 1976 Australian and New Zealand Architectural Science Association Conference in Canberra. (Ref. 2). Refinement of procedures for the design of non-redundant sunscreens has resulted in a complete chapter of fully worked solutions being published in the book *Solar Radiation Control in Buildings* (Ref. 3).

13.3.2. Design Procedures

The design procedures enable a free-form line drawn, say, in plan, to be projected into a position in three-dimensional space such that that line represents the outer extremity of the shading device and will shade the window for the period specified. Alternatively, a particular geometric form may be superimposed over the window and the redundancy plotted upon that form. The redundant part may then be removed and the developed surface of the remaining portion drawn. It is only through experience that the designer can come to an early appropriate decision about the geometry to be used. The appropriateness of the geometry selected as a basis for design will be a function of the orientation of the facade being studied. It is possible—even likely—that a novice's first selection of geometry may not be suitable.

In brief, the design procedure is as follows:

(a) Given the orientation of the facade for which a sunscreening device is to be designed, make a decision (which might later be modified) as to the design day and the period of time on that design day during which the window is to be shaded.

(b) List the corresponding pairs of vertical and horizontal shadow angles which define the movement of the sun relative to a normal projected from the face of the facade. These VSAs and HSAs may be calculated from first principles for greatest accuracy, or may be found by using a shadow-angle protractor and a solar chart—design aids first made available to architects in Ralph Phillips' book, *Sunshine and Shade in Australasia* (Ref. 4). If a complex form is to be used—particularly if a curvilinear form is to be used, then the time intervals between pairs of HSAs and VSAs will need to be closer than if simple forms are used.

(c) Decide whether the design will be free-form or geometric.

(d) Decide on the maximum projections of the sunscreen from the face of the building and also on its extension beyond each side and above the window. The greater the projection and extension beyond the boundaries of the window, the greater will be the cone of vision which may be provided from within the building.

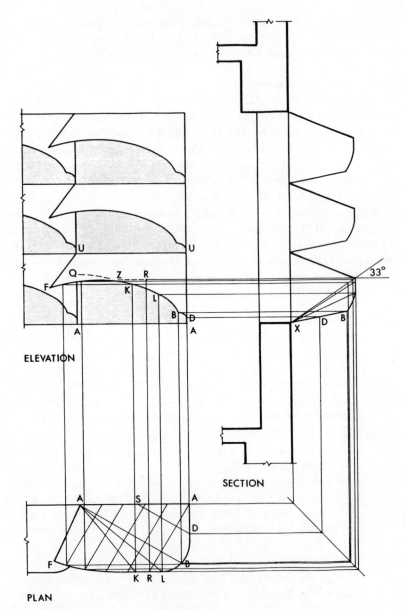

Fig. 12. Free-form sunscreen. (One of many examples from "Solar Radiation Control in Buildings" by E. L. Harkness and M. L. Mehta, Applied Science Publishers, London, 1978).

This projection will, of course, be a function of the material used.

(e) The next step of plotting the sun's movement relative to the building facade, upon the geometry of the sunscreening device selected, may best be illustrated by a few examples.

(i) Figure 12 shows the orthographic development of a free-form sunscreen. It is a sunscreen on the northern facade of a building at latitude 32½°S designed to exclude direct solar radiation throughout the year except in the period from May 26 to July 19. On May 26 and July 19, direct sunlight may fall on the glass from sunrise to 10.00 hrs. and from 16.30 hrs. to sunset. The designer first drew a free-form line on plan which became the curved line FKRLBDA. Using the HSAs the sun's positions relative to a normal to the wall were plotted in plan. The sun's morning movement was plotted from the western-most lower edge of the window. The sun's afternoon movement was plotted from the eastern-most lower edge of the window. The points of intersection between the free-form line and the HSAs in plan were then projected into the section where the points of intersection of those points with the VSAs projected from the lower edge of the window were noted. These points were then projected onto the elevation. These points jointed, delineate the lower edge of the sunscreen. The next design decision to be made is to decide how the form of the sunscreen is to be developed. In this case a point was selected on the outer extremity of the sunscreen in plan and the portion of sunscreen defined in elevation by UZU was defined as a simple planar triangle. The remainder of the form was developed as a conoid about the upper corners of the window.

(ii) Figure 13 is a photograph of a sunscreen designed for a northern facade at latitude 32°54′S in which direct sunlight is to be excluded from the glazing for the period October 17 to February 26.

The geometric form upon which the solar geometry was superimposed, was a simple pyramid with its base in the plane of the window wall. Using a simple sundial a

Fig. 13. Geometric Sunscreen. Pyramid with base in plane of the window wall. Redundancy removed.

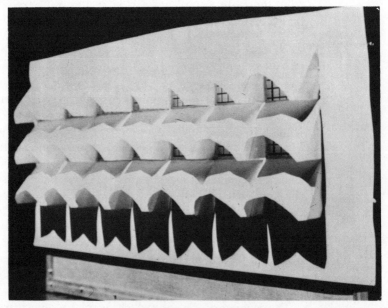

Fig. 14. Geometric Sunscreen. Parabolic conoid with parabola in horizontal plane at window sill level and form generated as a conoid from a pair of points one-third of the window height above the sill. Redundancy removed.

model of the sunscreen may be set up with a graphed board in the plane of the glazing from which may be counted the number of area units exposed to the direct component of solar radiation. This is a useful method of determining the precise area of glass exposed to the direct component when complex sunscreens are designed.

(iii) Figure 14 illustrates a sunscreen designed to exclude direct sunlight from the northern facade of a building at latitude 32°54'S for the entire year.

The geometric form upon which the solar geometry was superimposed, was a parabolic conoid—with the parabola being in the horizontal plane at window sill level.

13.3.3. Summary

The examples shown in Figs. 12, 13 and 14 were designed by second-year architecture students at the University of Newcastle and serve to illustrate that the geometric concepts involved can be managed by young minds newly acquainted with geometry. These examples also serve to illustrate that the fenestration design of a building can be functionally designed to perform a specified task; that the process can be creative and the result, refreshingly sculptural . . . a reason for texture on the facades of buildings.

13.3.4. Note

A step-by-step, line-by-line description of the design of non-redundant sunscreens, including orthographics, development of surfaces and models and assessment of heat loads is included in the author's book, *Solar Radiation Control in Buildings*. The book includes complete design descriptions of the examples in Figs. 12, 13 and 14 plus many others including spherical surfaces and flat-plane geometry. All of the examples include developed surfaces which may be photocopied from the book, folded up to make a model and tested on a heliodon.

13.4. QUANTIFICATION OF HEAT LOADS

As a service to architects in the Newcastle region, Harkness and Malcolm have published a 62-page handbook entitled *Solar Radiation Intensities in Newcastle*, which includes charts of solar radiation

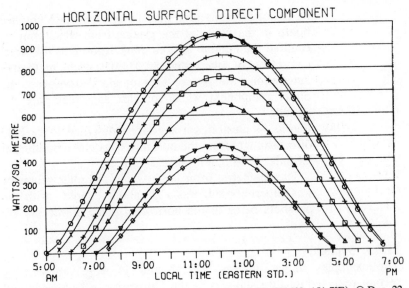

Fig. 15. Solar radiation intensities. For Newcastle N.S.W. (32.9°S, 151.7°E). ○ Dec. 22. × Jan. 16/Nov. 27. + Feb. 26/Oct. 17. □ Mar. 21/Sep. 23. △ Apr. 14/Aug. 31 ▽ May 26/Jul. 19. ◇ Jun. 21.

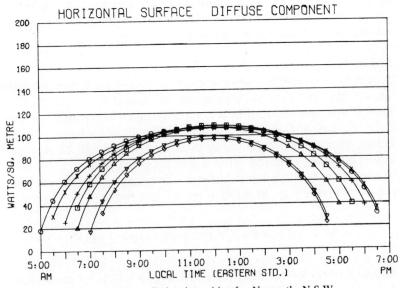

Fig. 16. Solar radiation intensities for Newcastle N.S.W.

intensities (direct and diffuse components) on the horizontal and vertical planes at Newcastle, NSW (latitude 32.9°S) for each month of the year at half-hourly intervals in the Australian Eastern Standard Time zone (Ref. 5). The solar radiation intensities on the vertical plane have been plotted in a form similar to the familiar solar charts which give the sun's position. Figures 15, 16, 17 and 18 are examples of the kind of charts included.

These charts enable the architect to estimate the sol-air temperatures on opaque surfaces and the heat load on the glazed surfaces of a building. Given that the architect has established the areas of glass exposed to direct solar radiation and that he has the manufacturer's data on the transmissivity of the particular type of glass being used, he may calculate the instantaneous heat gain through the glass due to the direct and diffuse components of solar radiation. With the current availability of computer-aided design, it is expected that architects with access to computers will make use of those facilities. However, for architects in remote areas, a handbook which permits quantification of heat loads with the use of simple geometry and arithmetic is of value.

Another design aid which has been produced by the Department of Architecture at the University of Newcastle is a computer program which will produce charts for summer, winter and the equinox of the direct and diffuse components of solar radiation and the quantity of each which will be transmitted through clear glass of any nominated orientation. Figures 19, 20, 21 and 22 show this data for Newcastle (latitude 32.9°S) for glazing facing North, South, East and West.

In these graphs the transmissivity of clear glass for specified angles of incidence has been taken into account. The graphical presentation of this information enables the architect to see at a glance:

(a) the good sense in avoiding orientating glazing to the east or west; and

(b) the order of magnitude of the heat load which can be controlled by completely shading the glazing against the direct component (using a non-redundant sunscreen); or

(c) the way in which external movable sunscreens can be used to exclude the summer direct and diffuse components or admit some or all of the direct and diffuse components at other times of the year.

Although the above aids give the architect a first order of magnitude upon which to base his initial design concepts, he would be well advised

VERTICAL SURFACE   DIRECT COMPONENT

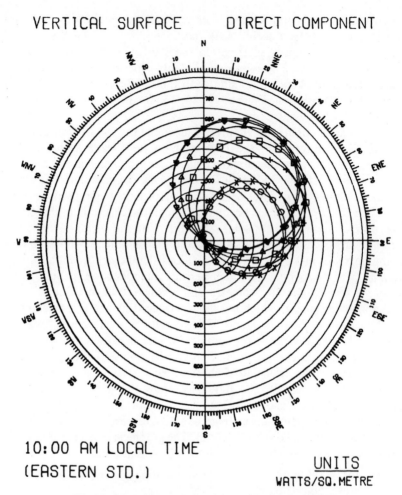

10:00 AM LOCAL TIME
(EASTERN STD.)

<u>UNITS</u>
WATTS/SQ.METRE

Fig. 17. Solar radiation intensities for Newcastle N.S.W.

to seek the aid of computer-design techniques to quantify the effects of his early design decisions on the internal thermal environment of his building. As with models, the computer should be considered a design tool to be used in the design process; not as a means of presenting the final solution.

VERTICAL SURFACE   DIFFUSE COMPONENT

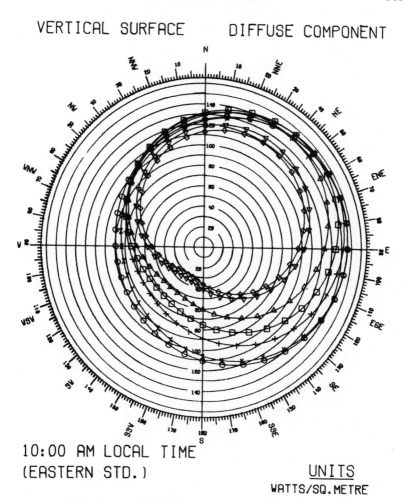

10:00 AM LOCAL TIME
(EASTERN STD.)   UNITS
                            WATTS/SQ.METRE

Fig. 18. Solar radiation intensities for Newcastle N.S.W.

13.5. DISCUSSION

In the future it is likely that a greater proportion of new buildings will
not be air-conditioned. In the future it is likely that existing buildings
which are at present air-conditioned might have the air-conditioning

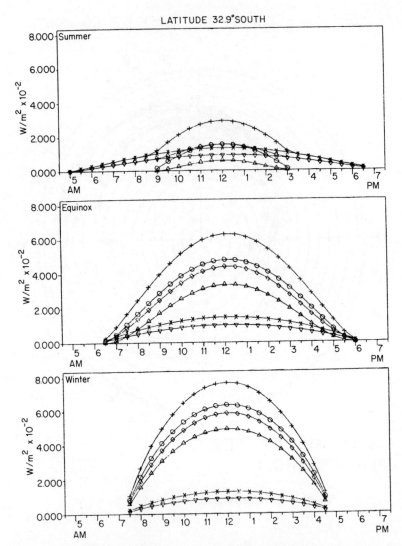

Fig. 19. Solar radiation intensities on a vertical surface. Orientation: North. The chart shows the heat load intensities transmitted through clear glass. Divisions on the vertical scale are in intervals of 200 watts/m². + Sum of direct plus diffuse components. ○ Direct component. ◇ Sum of direct plus diffuse components transmitted through clear glass. △ Direct component transmitted through clear glass. × Diffuse component. ▽ Diffuse component transmitted through clear glass.

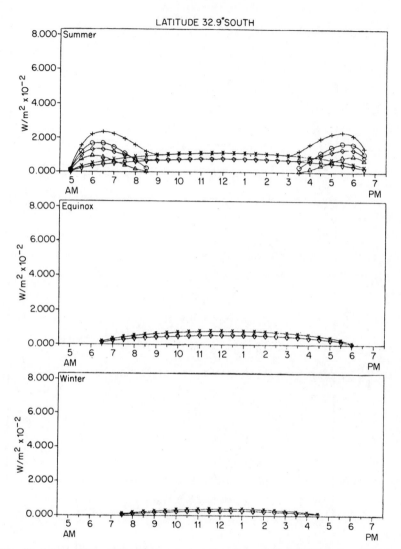

Fig. 20. Solar radiation intensities on a vertical surface. Orientation: South. The chart shows the heat load intensities transmitted through clear glass. Divisions on the vertical scale are in intervals of 200 watts/m². For key, see Fig. 19.

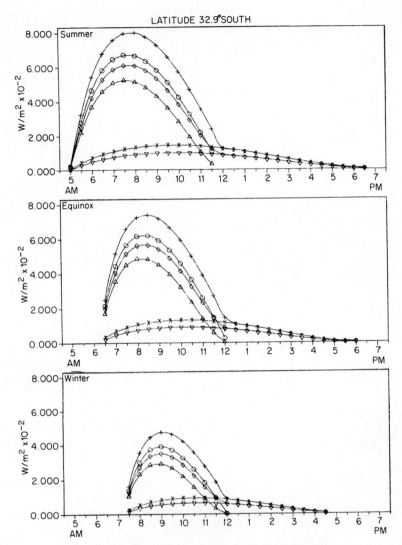

Fig. 21. Solar radiation intensities on a vertical surface. Orientation: East. The chart shows the heat load intensities transmitted through clear glass. Divisions on the vertical scale are in intervals of 200 watts/m². For key, see Fig. 19.

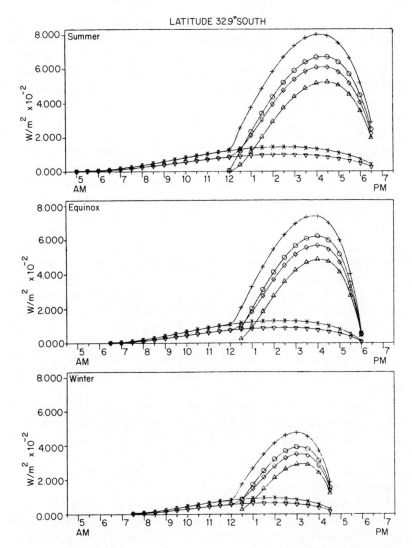

Fig. 22. Solar radiation intensities on a vertical surface. Orientation: West. The chart shows the heat load intensities transmitted through clear glass. Divisions on the vertical scale are in intervals of 200 watts/m². For key, see Fig. 19.

systems removed and the envelope of those buildings remodelled to provide thermal comfort using natural ventilation. The reason is that energy resources are finite and attention will have to be given to applying good passive design principles to buildings. In the future design of building envelopes—whether they be new envelopes or remodelled envelopes—will include either external movable sunscreens or fixed sunscreens designed to be non-redundant as explained in this chapter. Much of the remodelling of existing buildings will probably use movable sunscreens. Where movable sunscreens are used, architects and clients will have to accept the capital costs and the maintenance costs in the way that they today accept the capital cost of air-conditioning systems and their recurrent running costs. The space occupied within a building by the air-conditioning system is significant. It occupies rentable floor space and affects the floor-to-floor dimension more than any other service. The author has not taken out cost comparisons—his argument is based essentially upon the energy problem—but when one considers the initial cost of an air-conditioned building, rentable floor area occupied by the riser ducts, increased building height and volume to accommodate horizontal ducts within the building, costs of installation, skilled staff to maintain the system, energy costs of operating the system, the problem of recycled air quality, noise attenuation and designed obsolescence, an alternative might be attractive in the new-energy-value system which will almost certainly pervade in the near future.

It is likely that those buildings which in the future will have to be air-conditioned to achieve performance specifications of a narrow range of environmental temperatures, i.e. spaces to accommodate delicate equipment or documents, will be appropriately orientated or have sunscreens to reduce the size of their air-conditioning plants and consumption of energy through life.

In the western world contemporary architects do not have a ready familiarity with movable sunscreening systems. Failure of some systems on recently built large buildings will, no doubt, add doubts to architects' contemplation about using such systems. Mentioned above is the need to accept that maintenance of such mechanical devices will be a recurrent cost and that buildings will have to be designed for ready access to provide that maintenance. One country which could be used as a source of experience in the use of external movable sunscreening is Argentina. Local expertise in designing and manufacturing low-maintenance external movable sunscreens for high-rise buildings will develop as the market need develops.

The University of Newcastle hopes to have the perimeter offices in its proposed Clinical Sciences Building designed to be naturally ventilated. It is a particularly difficult problem because the offices face east and west. If successful, this building could herald a new trend towards naturally ventilated office buildings for the region.

13.6. CONCLUSION

Naturally ventilated buildings will likely be a trend in the near future. In order to achieve thermal comfort in those buildings it will be necessary to synthesise into the building design effective sunscreening devices, whether they be fixed or movable. Design procedures are available which the architect may use in producing functionally designed sunscreens. Computer programs are available which the architect may use to estimate the range of internal temperatures of the completed building. It is likely that in work environments a wider range of environmental temperatures will have to be tolerated in the future.

13.7. ACKNOWLEDGEMENTS

The sunscreens illustrated in Figs. 12, 13 and 14 were designed respectively by Peter Campbell, Stacey Jones and Philip Wiggs as part of their second-year studies in architecture at the University of Newcastle.

REFERENCES

1. Harkness, E. L., 'Some aspects of fenestration on design in modern buildings,' *Architectural Science Review*, **20,** 14–21, March, 1977.
2. Harkness, E. L., *Some Aspects of The Use of Models in Design for Sunlight Penetration Control, Daylight Illumination and Supplementary Lighting*, paper presented to a conference of the Australian and New Zealand Architectural Science Association, Canberra, August 1976.
3. Harkness E. L. and Mehta, M. L., *Solar Radiation Control in Buildings*, Applied Science Publishers, London, 1978.
4. Phillips, R. O., *Sunshine and Shade in Australasia*, Bulletin No. 8, Commonwealth Experimental Building Station, Sydney, 1969. (First published as Technical study No. 23 in 1948.)
5. Harkness, E. L. and Malcolm, D. J. *Solar Radiation Intensities in Newcastle: Charts of solar radiation intensities on the horizontal and vertical planes of any orientation at Newcastle, N.S.W., latitude 32.9°S for each month of the year at half hourly intervals in the Australian Eastern Standard Time Zone*, September, 1978.

Bibliography

K. G. DUNSTAN

Department of Architectural Science, University of Sydney, Australia

JOURNALS

1. *Applied Solar Energy* (a cover-to-cover translation of the Russian journal, *Geliotekhnika*), bi-monthly, Faraday Press, New York.
2. *Energy and Buildings,* an international journal of research applied to energy efficiency in the built environment, quarterly, Elsevier Sequoia S.A., Lausanne, Switzerland.
3. *Solar Age,* monthly, Solar Vision, New York.
4. *Solar Energy Intelligence Report,* Weekly, Business Publishers Inc., Silver Spring, Md.
5. *Solar Energy. The Journal of Solar Energy Science and Technology,* published monthly for the International Solar Energy Society, Pergamon, Oxford.
6. *Solar Energy Progress in Australia and New Zealand,* publication of the Australian and New Zealand Section of the International Solar Energy Society, published annually.
7. *Sun World,* published quarterly for the International Solar Energy Society (Melbourne). Pergamon, Oxford.

BOOKS

8. Anderson, B. N., *The Solar Home Book: Heating, Cooling and Designing with the Sun,* Cheshire Books, Harrisville (NH), 1976, 297 pp.
9. Anderson, B. N., *Solar Energy: Fundamentals in Building Design,* McGraw-Hill, New York, 1977, 374 pp.

10. Backus, C. E., (ed.), *Solar Cells,* IEEE Press, New York, 1976, 504 pp.
11. Barber, E. M. and Watson, D. A., *Design Criteria for Solar-Heated Buildings,* Sunworks, Guilford (Conn.), 1975.
12. Barrett, D., Epstein, P. and Haar, C. M., *Financing the Solar Home: Understanding and Improving Mortage—Market Receptivity to Energy Conservation and Housing Innovation,* Lexington Books, Lexington (Mass.), 1977, 201 pp.
13. Beckman, W. A., Klein, S. A. and Duffie, J. A., *Solar Heating by the f-Chart Method,* Wiley, New York, 1977, 200 pp.
14. Behrman, D., *Solar Energy: The Awakening Science,* Little, Brown and Co., Boston, 1976, 408 pp.
15. Berkowitz, M. K., *Implementing Solar Energy in Canada: The Costs Benefits and Role of Government,* for the Renewable Energy Resources Branch of the Canadian Department of Energy, Mines and Resources, Supply and Services Canada, Ottawa, 1977, 239 pp.
16. Bockris, J. O'M., *Energy, The Solar-Hydrogen Alternative,* Architectural Press, London, 1976, 365 pp.
17. Brinkworth, B. J., *Solar Energy for Man,* Compton Press, Salisbury, 1972, 251 pp.
18. Burberry, P., Building for Energy Conservation, Architectural Press, London, 1978, 60 pp.
19. Clegg, P., *New Low-Cost Sources of Energy for the Home,* Garden Way Pub., Charlotte (Vermont), 1975, 252 pp.
20. Daniels, F., *Direct Use of the Sun's Energy,* Yale U.P., New Haven, 1964, 374 pp.
21. Daniels, G. E., *Solar Homes and Sun Heating,* Harper and Row, New York, 1976, 178 pp.
22. Danz, E., *Architecture and the Sun: An International Survey of Sun Protection Methods,* Thames and Hudson, London, 1967, 149 pp.
23. Duffie, J. A. and Beckman, W. A., *Solar Energy Thermal Processes,* Wiley, New York, 1974, 386 pp.
24. Ewers, W. L., *Solar Energy, A Biased Guide,* Australia and New Zealand Book Co., Brookvale (NSW), 1977, 95 pp.
25. Fanger, P. O., *Thermal Comfort,* Danish Technical Press, Copenhagen, 1970, 244 pp.
26. Fisher, J. C., *Energy Crisis in Perspective,* Wiley, New York, 1974, 196 pp.
27. Foster, W. M., *Homeowner's Guide to Solar Heating and Cooling,*

G/L Tab Books, Blue Ridge Summit (Pa.), 1977, 196 pp.

28. Givoni, B., *Man, Climate and Architecture,* Second ed., Applied Science, London, 1976, 483 pp.

29. Gropp, L., *Solar Houses—48 Energy-saving Designs,* A House and Garden Book, Pantheon, New York, 1978.

30. Groundwater, I. S., *Solar Radiation in Air conditioning,* Crosby Lockwood, London, 1957, 125 pp.

31. Halacy, D. S., *The Coming Age of Solar Energy,* Harper and Row, New York, 1963, 249 pp.

32. Halacy, D. S., *The Coming Age of Solar Energy,* Avon paperback, New York, 1975, 248 pp.

33. Hammond, A. L., Metz, W. D. and Maugh II, T. H., *Energy and the Future,* American Association for the Advancement of Science, Washington (D.C.), 1973, 184 pp.

34. Harkness, E. L. and Mehta, M. L., *Solar Radiation Control in Buildings,* Applied Science Publishers, London, 1978, 271 pp.

35. Hayes, D., *Rays of Hope: the Transition to a Post-Petroleum World,* Norton, New York, 1977, 240 pp.

36. Hickok, F., *Handbook of Solar and Wind Energy,* Cahners Books, Boston (Mass.), 1975, 125 pp.

37. Howell, D., *Your Solar Energy Home, Including Wind and Methane Applications,* Pergamon, Oxford, 1979, 200 pp.

38. Illich, I. D., *Energy and Equity,* Calder and Boyars, London, 1974, 96 pp.

39. Jenkins, H. R., *Solar Heating: How to Construct a Solar Heater at Minimal Cost,* Wilson and Horton, Herald Dollar Book, Auckland, 1976, 38 pp.

40. Kestel, R. W. O., *Radiant Energy, a Working Power in the Mechanism of the Universe,* 1898.

41. Keyes, J. H., *Harnessing the Sun: a Practical No-Nonsense Approach to Home Solar Heating,* 2nd. ed., Morgan and Morgan, Dobbs Ferry (N.Y.), 1975, 196 pp.

42. Kreider, J. F. and Kreith, F., *Solar heating and cooling: engineering, practical design, and economics,* Hemisphere, Washington (D.C) 1977, 342 pp.

43. Lambeth, J. and Delap, J. D., *Solar Designing,* Fayetteville (Arkansas), 1977, 115 pp.

44. Landa, H. C., et al., *The Solar Energy Handbook: a practical engineering approach to the application of solar energy to the needs of man and environment,* including sections on terrestial cooling

and wind power. Research, engineering and designs by the Solar Energy Engineering Company of America, FICOA/SEECOA. 3rd. ed., Milwaukee (Wis.), 1975.

45. Lapedes, D. N. (editor in chief), *Encyclopedia of Energy,* McGraw-Hill, New York, 1976.

46. Lee, K. *Encyclopaedia of Energy Efficient Building Design: 391 Practical Case Studies,* Environmental Design and Research Center, Boston (Mass.), 1977, 2 volumes, 1023 pp.

47. Lucas, T., *How to Build a Solar Heater: a complete guide to building and buying solar panels, water heaters, pool heaters, barbecues, and power plants,* Ward Ritchie Press, Pasadena (Cal.), 1975, 236 pp.

48. McLaughlin, T., *A House for the Future,* Severn House Pub., London, 1976, 80 pp.

49. McVeigh, J. C., *Sun Power: An Introduction to the Application of Solar Energy,* Pergamon, Oxford, 1977, 208 pp.

50. Meador, R., *Future Energies,* Ann Arbor Science, Ann Arbor (Mich.), 1976, 63 pp.

51. Meinel A. B. and Meinel, M. P., *Applied Solar Energy, an introduction,* Addision-Wesley, Reading (Mass.), 1977, 651 pp.

52. Merrigan, J. A., *Sunlight to Electricity: Prospects for Solar Energy Conversion by Photovoltaics,* MIT Press, Cambridge (Mass.), 1975, 163 pp.

53. Messel, H. and Butler, S. T. (eds.), *Solar Energy,* Shakespeare Head Press, Sydney, 1974, 336 pp.

54. Mula, J. M., Ward, R. A., Thornton, B. S. and Malanos, C., *Solar Australia: Australia at the Crossroads,* A report on a project for the foundation for Australian resources evaluating Australia's solar energy policy alternatives, 1977, 122 pp.

55. Olgyay, A. and Olgyay, V., *Solar Control and Shading Devices,* Princeton University Press, Princeton, (N.J.), 1957.

56. Olgyay, V. G., *Design with Climate,* Princeton University Press, Princeton, (N.J.), 1963, 200 pp.

57. Palz, W., *Solar Electricity—An Economic Approach to Solar Energy,* UNESCO, Paris, and Butterworths, London, 1978, 292 pp.

58. Patton, A. R., *Solar Energy for Heating and Cooling of Buildings,* Noyes Data Corp, Park Ridge (N.J.), 1975, 328 pp.

59. Paul, J. K., *Solar Heating and Cooling: Recent Advances,* Noyes Data Corp., Park Ridge (N.J.), 1977, 495 pp.

60. Prenis, J. (ed.), *Energy Book 1—Natural Sources and Backyard Applications*, Running Press, Philadelphia, 1975, 112 pp.
61. Randell, J. E. (ed.), *Ambient Energy and Building Design*, The Construction Press, Lancaster, 1978, 166 pp.
62. Rau, H. and Duffin, D. J., *Solar Energy*, Macmillan, New York, 1964, 175 pp.
63. Sabady, P. R., *The Solar House: A Guide to Solar Energy Utilization in Domestic, Industrial and Commercial Building*, Newnes—Butterworths, London, 1978, 115 pp.
64. Schoen, R., Hirshberg, A., Weingart, J. and Stein, J. (ed.), *New Energy Technologies for Buildings: Institutional Problems and Solutions*, Ballinger Pub. Co., Cambridge (Mass.), 1975, 217 pp.
65. Shurcliff, W. A., *Solar Heated Buildings: a Brief Survey*, The Author, Cambridge (Mass.), 1977.
66. Steadman, P., *Energy, Environment and Building*, Cambridge University Press, Cambridge, 1975, 287 pp.
67. Stein, R. G., *Architecture and Energy: Conserving Energy Through Rational Design*, Anchor Press, New York, 1977, 322 pp.
68. Szokolay, S. V., *Solar Energy and Building*, 2nd. ed., Architectural Press, London, 1977.
69. Theodore, D., *Natural Energy in Your Home*, Ure Smith, Summit Books, Sydney, 1977, 79 pp.
70. Thomason, H. E., *Solar Houses and Solar House Models*, Edmund Scientific Company, Barrington (N.J.), 1972.
71. Thomason H. E. and Thomason, H. J. L., *Solar Greenhouse and Swimming Pool*, Edmund Scientific Co., N. J., 1974, 22 pp.
72. Vale, B. and Vale, R., *The Autonomous House, Design and Planning for Self-Sufficiency*; Thames and Hudson, London, 1975, 224 pp.
73. Watson, D., *Designing and Building a Solar House: Your Place in the Sun*, Garden Way Pub., Charlotte (Vt.), 1977, 281 pp.
74. Williams, J. R., *Solar Energy Technology and Applications*, Ann Arbor Science, Ann Arbor (Mich.), 1974, 120 pp.
75. Williams, J. R., *1976 Solar Update for Solar Energy Technology and Applications*, Ann Arbor Science Pub., Ann Arbor (Mich.), 1976, 47 pp.
76. Zarem, A. M. and Erway, D. D. (eds.), *Introduction to the Utilization of Solar Energy*, McGraw-Hill, New York, 1963, 410 pp.

PUBLICATIONS PREPARED BY VARIOUS ORGANIZATIONS

77. *Applications of Solar Energy for Heating and Cooling of Buildings,* American Society of Heating, Refrigerating and Air-Conditioning Engineers, Inc., 1977.

78. *Application of Solar Technology to Today's Energy Needs,* Congress of the United States, Office of Technology Assessment, Washington (D.C.), Volume 1, June 1978, 525 pp.

79. *ASHRAE Handbook: 1977, Fundamentals,* Chapter 26, published by the American Society of Heating, Refrigerating and Air-Conditioning Engineers, Inc., New York, 1977.

80. *ASHRAE Handbook and Product Directory: 1978, Applications,* Chapter 58: 'Solar Energy Utilization for Heating and Cooling', 26 p., published by the American Society of Heating, Refrigerating and Air-Conditioning Engineers, Inc., New York, 1978.

81. *Australian Academy of Science, Report 17,* Report of the Committee on Solar Energy Research in Australia, September 1973, 63 pp.

82. *Energy Conservation in Building Design, ASHRAE Standard 90–75,* The American Society of Heating, Refrigerating and Air-Conditioning Engineers Inc., New York, 1975, 53 pp.

83. *Energy Research and Technology.* Abstracts of NSF (National Science Foundation) /RANN (Research Applied to National Needs), October 1970–December 1974, RANN Document Center, Washington (D.C.), 319 pp.

84. *Here Comes the Sun 1981 (Solar Heated Multi-Family Housing),* Researched for the American Institute of Architects, Joint Venture Inc., Boulder (Colorado), 1975, 97 pp.

85. *Interim Performance Criteria for Solar Heating-Cooling Systems and Dwellings,* prepared by the National Bureau of Standards for the U.S. Department of Housing and Urban Development, Government Printing Office, Washington (D.C.), 1975, 110 pp.

86. *National Program for Solar Heating and Cooling: Residential and Commerical Applications,* issued by the Energy Research and Development Administration, Division of Solar Energy, Government Printing Office, Washington (D.C.), 1975, 83 pp.

87. *Passive Design Ideas for the Energy Conscious Architect,* National

Solar Heating and Cooling Information Center, Rockville (Md.), USA, 1977.

88. *Passive Design Ideas for the Energy Conscious Builder,* National Solar Heating and Cooling Information Center, Rockville (Md.), USA, 1977, 52 pp.

89. *Recommendations for an Energy Policy for Australia,* Summary Report and Recommendations, The Task Force on Energy, The Institution of Engineers, Australia, Canberra, October 1977, 28 pp.

90. *Report on Solar Energy,* Senate Standing Committee on National Resources, The Parliament of the Commonwealth of Australia, Canberra, Parliamentary Paper No. 68/1977, 92 pp.

91. *Solar Dwelling Design Concepts,* By the AIA Research Corporation, Washington, D.C., for the US Department of Housing and Urban Development, Office of Policy Development and Research. Washington (D.C.), 1976, 146 pp.

92. *Solar-Energy,* Prepared for Air Force Office of Scientific Research by Informatics Inc. Author: V. A. Stevovich. Distributed by: NTIS (National Technical Information Service), US Department of Commerce, Washington (D.C.), 1974, 441 pp.

93. *Solar Energy and Housing, Design Concepts,* Prepared by Giffels Associates, Inc. for AIA Research Corporation, Washington (D.C.), 1975, 145 pp.

94. *Solar Energy: A UK Assessment.* Report of the panel convened by the UK section of International Solar Energy Society to analyse all aspects of solar energy systems and to assess the potential for solar energy utilization and research and development needs in the UK and for export. Prepared by the UK. section of the ISES, London, 1976, 375 pp.

95. *Solar Energy for Earth.* American Institute for Aeronautics and Astronautics, 1290 Avenue of the Americas, New York, 1975, 113 pp.

96. *Solar Energy Home Design in Four Climates,* prepared and published by Total Environmental Action, Harrisville (N.H.), 1976, 198 pp.

97. *Solar Energy in America's Future: A Preliminary Assessment,* prepared by J. S. Reuyl and others of the Stanford Research Institute for the Environmental and Resource Studies Branch, Division of Solar Energy, Energy Research and Development

Administration, 2nd. ed., Government Printing Office, Washington, (D.C.), 1977, 106 pp.

98. *Solar Energy: Official Hansard Report,* Senate Standing Committee on National Resources, Commonwealth Government Printer, Canberra, 1976, 3 vols.

99. *Solar Energy Utilization for Heating and Cooling,* J. I. Yellott (compiler), C. W. MacPhee (principal investigator), prepared for the American Society of Heating, Refrigerating and Air-Conditioning Engineers, Inc., Government Printing Office, Washington (D.C.), 1974, 20 pp.

100. *Solar Heat and the Overheating of Buildings,* Dept of the Environment, Directorate of Building Development, Property Services Agency, HMSO, London, 1975, 44 pp.

101. *Solar Heating and Cooling Demonstration Program.* A descriptive summary of H.U.D. solar residential demonstrations cycle 1. US Department of Housing and Urban Development, Washington, (D.C.), 1976, 53 pp.

102. *Solar Heating and Cooling Experiment for a School in Atlanta, Design Report.* Prepared for the National Science Foundation. Georgia Institute of Technology, Atlanta (Ga.), 1974, paging: various.

103. *Solar Radiation Considerations in Building Planning and Design,* National Academy of Sciences, Washington (D.C.), 1976, 179 pp.

104. *Sunlight and Daylight: Planning Criteria and Design of Buildings,* Department of the Environment, HMSO, London, 1971, 56 pp.

CONFERENCES

105. *Conferences on Energy 1977. Towards an Energy Policy for Australia.* Report of the Task force on energy of the Institution of Engineers, Australia. Submissions of Working Parties. Canberra, 20–22 July 1977, 242 pp.

106 *Energy and Housing,* A symposium held at the Open University, Milton Keynes, October 1974. *Building Science Special Supplement,* Pergamon, Oxford, 1975, 158 pp.

107. *Energy Conservation in Buildings,* Symposium papers, Sydney, November 1978.

108. *European Solar Houses,* Proceedings of a Conference of the

International Solar Energy Society, UK Section, held at the North East London Polytechnic, London, April 1976, 64 pp.

109. *International Solar Energy Society Conference, 1970, Melbourne.* Preprints of papers, published by the Australian and New Zealand Section of the Society, Melbourne, 1970.

110. *Passive Solar Heating and Cooling,* Conference and Workshop Proceedings, May 18–19, 1976, University of New Mexico, Albuquerque (New Mexico), 355 pp.

111. *Proceedings of the ASC/AIA* (Association of Student Chapters/ American Institute of Architects) *Forum 75, Solar Architecture,* Arizona State University, G. Franta ed., Government Printing Office, Washington (D.C.), 1976.

112. *Proceedings of the Solar Heating and Cooling for Buildings Workshop,* held in Washington D.C., in March 1973. Prepared for the National Science Foundation, Research Applied to National Needs, by the Department of Mechanical Engineering, University of Maryland. R. Allen ed., Government Printing Office, Washington (D.C.), 1974.

113. *Seminar on Energy Resources for Domestic Use,* Bentley, Western Australia, 1975, Papers Presented. Organised by the W.A. Div. of the Inst. of Engrs., Aust., W. A. Chapter of the Royal Aust. Inst. of Architects, and the W.A. Inst. of Technology, Perth (W.A.), 1975.

114. *Sharing the Sun: Solar Technology in the Seventies,* Proceedings of a Joint Conference of the American Section, International Solar Energy Society and the Solar Energy Society of Canada, Inc., August 15–20, 1976, Winnipeg, Canada, (K.W. Böer editor), 10 vols.

Vol. 1, International and US programs, solar flux.
Vol. 2, Solar collectors.
Vol. 3, Solar heating and cooling of buildings.
Vol. 4, Solar systems, simulation, design.
Vol. 5, Solar thermal and ocean thermal.
Vol. 6, Photovoltaics and materials.
Vol. 7, Agriculture, biomass, wind, new developments.
Vol. 8, Storage, water heater, data communication, education.
Vol. 9, Socio-economics and cultural.
Vol.10, Business, commerical, poster session, miscellaneous.

115. *Solar Cooling for Buildings,* Proceedings of a workshop held in conjunction with a meeting of the American Society of Heating,

Refrigerating and Air Conditioning Engineers, Inc., Los Angeles, February 1974, F. de Winter (ed.), sponsored by the National Science Foundation, Research Applied to National Needs, Government Printing Office, Washington (D.C.), 1974, 231 pp.

116. *Solar Effects on Building Design,* Report of a program held as part of the 1962 conferences of the Building Research Institute of the USA, Washington (D.C.), 1963, 173 pp.

117. *Solar Energy Applications,* Papers presented at the Symposium held at the annual meeting of the American Society of Heating, Refrigerating and Air-Conditioning Engineers, Inc., June 1974, 52 pp.

118. *Solar Energy, Architecture, and Planning,* Conference held at the Polytechnic of North London, April 1975, pub. by International Solar Energy Society, UK Section, London, 1975, 54 pp.

119. *Solar Energy—for Buildings?* Building Science Forum of Australia, 31st Conference, Sydney 1978.

120. *Solar Energy Today,* Proceedings of Victorian Government Conference, Melbourne, February 1979.

121. *Solar Energy Utilization,* Conference held at the Brighton Polytechnic, pub. by International Solar Energy Society, UK Section, London 1974, 79 pp.

122. *Solar Energy Utilization in USA, France, Italy and Australia,* Conference held at the Brighton Polytechnic, pub. by International Solar Energy Society, UK Section, 1974, 21 pp.

123. *Solar Radiation Considerations in Building Planning and Design:* Proceedings of a Working Conference on Solar Energy in the Heating and Cooling of Buildings, April 1975, in Washington. Convened by the Committee on Solar Energy in the Heating and Cooling of Buildings, National Research Council. National Academy of Sciences, Washington (D.C.), 1976, 179 pp.

124. *Symposium on Applications of Solar Energy Research and Development in Australia,* Proceedings of a technical meeting held at the National Science Centre, Parkville, Melbourne, July 1975. Sponsored and published by the International Solar Energy Society, Australian and New Zealand Section, Melbourne, 1975.

125. *Testing of Solar Collectors and Systems,* Proceedings of a Conference held at the Royal Institution, April 1977, London, pub. by the International Solar Energy Society, UK Section, London 1977, 82 pp.

REPORTS AND MONOGRAPHS

126. *Architectural Control of Sunlight Penetration,* Industrial Services Division, Department of Labor and National Service, Australia, Sydney, 1957, 42 pp.

127. Ballantyne, E. R., *Solar Energy—the Resource and its Availability,* Report 47, Division of Building Research, CSIRO, Melbourne, 1976, 18 pp.

128. BRE Working Party Report, *Energy Conservation: A Study of Energy Consumption in Buildings and Possible Means of Saving Energy in Housing,* Building Research Establishment Current Paper 56/75, Watford (England), 1975.

129. *CSIRO Solar Energy Studies: Reports.* Irregularly published by the Commonwealth Scientific and Industrial Research Organization, Melbourne.

130. Chinnery, D. N. W., *Solar Water Heating in South Africa,* Bulletin 44, National Building Research Institute, Pretoria, 1971, 79 pp.

131. Christie, E. A., *A Method of Measuring the Performance Characteristics of Flat-Plate Solar Collectors,* CSIRO Technical Report No. TR6, Melbourne, 1976.

132. Commonwealth Scientific and Industrial Research Organisation, Division of Mechanical Engineering, Melbourne. Information Service (pamphlets).
Solar Heating of Swimming Pools, No. 12/A/3, Aug. 1977.
Guidelines for Prospective Purchasers of Domestic Solar Water Heaters, No. 12/A/2, September 1977.
Domestic Solar Water Heating, No. 12/A/1, November 1977.
Solar Heating and Cooling of Buildings, No. 12/A/6, April 1978.
CSIRO Low Energy Consumption House, Bulletin Number 1, No. 12/B/4, August 1978.

133. Courtney, R. G., *An Appraisal of Solar Water Heating in the UK,* Building Research Establishment Current Paper 7/76, Watford (England), 1976.

134. Courtney, R. G., *Solar Energy Utilization in the U.K.: Current Research and Future Prospects,* Building Research Establishment Current Paper 64/76, Watford (England), 1976.

135. Crisp, V.H.C. *Energy Conservation in Buildings: A Preliminary Study of Automatic Daylight Control of Artificial Lighting,* Building Research Establishment Current Paper 20/77, Watford (England), 1977.

136. *Domestic Solar Water Heating,* Commonwealth Scientific and Industrial Research Organization, Division of Mechanical Engineering, Melbourne, 1976, 8 pp.

137. Geue, P. J., *Solar Energy: a select bibliography of general references, reviews, bibliographies and conferences, 1965–1973.* Australian Atomic Energy Commission, Research Establishment, Lucas Heights (N.S.W), 1974, 34 pp.

138. Hill, R. K., *Utilization of Solar Energy for an Improved Environment Within Housing for the Humid Tropics,* Report 30, CSIRO Division of Building Research, Melbourne, 1974, 20 pp.

139. *How to Build a Solar Water Heater,* Brace Research Institute, McGill University, Montreal, 1973.

140. *Introductory Guide to Solar Energy,* National Building Research Institute, Pretoria, 1976, 39 pp.

141. Isakson, P. and Ofverholm, E., *Reporting format for solar energy buildings; and outline,* Swedish Council for Building Research, Stockholm, 1976, 39 pp.

142. Loudon, A. G., *Summertime Temperatures in Buildings Without Air-Conditioning,* Building Research Establishment Current Paper 47/68, Watford (England), 1968.

143. Milbank, N. O., *A New Approach to Predicting the Thermal Environment in Buildings at the Early Design Stage,* Building Research Establishment Current Paper 2/74, Watford (England), 1974.

144. Morse, R. N., *Solar Water Heaters for Domestic and Farm Use,* Engineering Section, CSIRO, Report ED 3, Melbourne, 1956, 28 pp.

145. Morse, R. N., Cooper, P. I. and Proctor, D. (prepared by), *Report on the Status of Solar Energy Utilization in Australia for Industrial Commerical and Domestic Purposes,* CSIRO Solar Energy Studies Report No. 74/1, Melbourne, 1974, 45 pp.

146. Morse, R. N. and Morse, F. H. (compilers), *US/Australia Agreement for Scientific and Technical Co-operation; Joint Meetings on Solar Energy Utilization, February-March 1974*; CSIRO Solar Energy Studies Report No. 74/2, sponsored by Department of Science, Australia and National Science Foundation, USA, Melbourne, 118 pp.

147. Phillips, R. O., *Sunshine and Shade in Australasia,* Commonwealth Experimental Building Station Technical Study No. 23, Sydney, 1951.

322 K. G. DUNSTAN

148. Quirouette, R. L., *Solar Heating—the State of the Art,* Building Research Note No. 102, Division of Building Research, National Research Council Canada, Ottawa, 1975, 11 pp.
149. Salt, H., *Progress Report on the Performance of Three Australian Solar Hot Water Systems,* CSIRO Solar Energy Studies Report No. 8, Melbourne 1976, 25 pp.
150. Salt, H., *Final Report on the Performance of Three Australian Solar Hot Water Systems,* CSIRO Solar Energy Studies Report No. 9, Melbourne, 1977, 11 pp.
151. Sheridan, N. R., *The Simple Domestic Solar Water Heater,* Department of Mechanical Engineering, University of Queensland, Brisbane, 1973.
152. Smith, G. E., *Economics of Solar Collectors, Heat Pumps and Wind Generators,* Technical Research Division, Department of Architecture, University of Cambridge, Cambridge, 1973, 40 pp.
153. Smith, P. R., *Windows and Sunlight Penetration,* Physical Environment Report No. 5, Department of Architectural Science, University of Sydney, Sydney, 1973, 6 pp.
154. *Solarch Experimental House Mark 1 Progress Report,* Faculty of Architecture Research Group, University of New South Wales, Sydney, No. 1, 1976.
155. Spencer, J. W., *Calculation of Solar Position for Building Purposes,* CSIRO Division of Building Research Technical Paper No. 14, Melbourne, 1965, 16 pp.
156. Spencer, J. W., *Estimation of Solar Radiation in Australasian Localities on Clear Days,* CSIRO Division of Building Research Technical Paper No. 15, Melbourne, 1965, 19 pp.
157. Spencer, J. W., *Solar Position and Radiation Tables for Adelaide (Latitude 35°s.),* CSIRO Division of Building Research Technical Paper No. 18, Melbourne, 1965, 79 pp.
158. Spencer, J. W., *Solar Position and Radiation Tables for Darwin (Latitude 12.5°s.),* CSIRO Division of Building Research Technical Paper No. 19, Melbourne, 1965, 79 pp.
159. Spencer, J. W., *Solar Position and Radiation Tables for Brisbane (Latitude 27.5°s.),* CSIRO Division of Building Research Technical Paper No. 28, Melbourne, 1971, 75 pp.
160. Spencer, J. W., *Melbourne Solar Tables: Tables for Solar Position and Radiation for Melbourne (Latitude 38.0°s.) in SI Units,* CSIRO Division of Building Research Technical Paper (Second Series) No. 7, Melbourne, 1974, 91 pp.

161. Spencer, J. W., *Perth Solar Tables: Tables for Solar Position and Radiation for Perth (Latitude 32.0°s.) in S1 Units*, CSIRO Division of Building Research Technical Paper (Second Series) No. 10, Melbourne, 1976, 91 pp.

162. Spencer, J. W., *Hobart Solar Tables: Tables for Solar Position and Radiation for Hobart (Latitude 43° s) in S1 Units*, CSIRO Division of Building Research Technical Paper (Second Series) No. 14, Melbourne, 1977, 91 pp.

163. Spencer, J. W., *Canberra Solar Tables: Tables of Solar Position and Radiation for Canberra (Latitude 35.3°s.) in S1 Units*, CSIRO Division of Building Research Technical Paper (Second Series) No. 22, Melbourne, 1978, 91 pp.

164. Vale, R. J. D., *Analysis of Forms for an Autonomous House*, Working Paper No. 10, University of Cambridge, Department of Architecture, Cambridge, 1973, 24 pp.

165. Vale, R. J. D., *Results of Solar Collector Study*, Technical Research Division, Department of Architecture, University of Cambridge, Cambridge, 1973, 24 pp.

DIRECTORIES AND BIBLIOGRAPHIES

166. Bone, D. (compiler), *Solar Energy*, Access Information Package No. 3, Greater London Council Department of Architecture and Civic Design, London, 1975, 26 pp.

167. *Energy Information Locator.* Environment Information Center Inc., New York, 1975, 187 pp.

168. Harrah, B. K. and Harrah, D. F., *Alternate Sources of Energy: A Bibliography of Solar, Geothermal, Wind and Tidal Energy, and Environmental Architecture*, Scarecrow Press, Metuchen (N.J.), 1975, 201 pp.

169. Hundemann A. S. (ed.), National Technical Information Service, *Solar Space Heating and Air Conditioning: Citations from the NTIS Data Base*, Springfield, 1976, 256 + various pp.

170. Jensen, J. S. (ed.), *Applied Solar Energy Research: A Directory of World Activities and Bibliography of Significant Literature*, 2nd. ed., published by the Association for Applied Solar Energy, now International Solar Energy Association, Phoenix (Arizona), 1959.

171. Khuman, R. and Burgess, S., *Solar Energy: Two Bibliographies*, University of New South Wales Library, Sydney, 1975, 36 pp.

172. Lee, K., *Bibliography of Energy Conservation in Architecture: Keyword Searched,* Environmental Design and Research Center, Boston (Mass.), 1977, 214 pp.

173. Loyd, S. and Starling, C., *Heat and Power from the Sun: An Annotated Bibliography with a Survey of Available Products and their Suppliers,* third ed., Building Services Research and Information Association, Bracknell, 1977, 70 pp.

174. Pesko, C. (ed.), *Solar Directory,* Ann Arbor Science, Ann Arbor (Mich.), 1975, 667 pp.

175. Shurcliff, W. A., *Informal Directory of the Organisations and People Involved in the Solar Heating of Buildings,* third ed., Cambridge (Mass.), 1977, 243 pp.

176. *Solar Energy: A Select Bibliography,* Supp. 1, Birmingham Public Libraries Technical Bibliographies, no. 4a, Birmingham, 1975.

177. *Solar Energy Directory. A Directory of Domestic and International Firms Involved in Solar Energy.* Centreline Corp. pub., Phoenix (Arizona), 1976, 108 pp.

178. *Spectrum: An Alternate Technology Equipment Directory,* Prepared by *Alternative Sources of Energy,* Milaca (Minn.), 1975, 63 pp.

PAPERS

179. *Architectural Forum:* Architecture and Energy number, New York, July/August, 1973.

180. Close, D. J., Dunkle, R. V. and Robeson, K. A. Design and performance of a thermal storage air conditioning system, *Mechanical and Chemical Transactions, Institution of Engineers, Australia,* Vol. **MC-4,** No. 1, 45, May 1968.

181. Courtney, R. G., Solar energy utilisation in UK Buildings —current research and future prospects, *Architectural Science Review,* Vol. **19,** No. 2, 44–49, June 1976.

182. Forwood, B., Some thoughts on the use of energy codes to control the use of energy in buildings, *Architectural Science Review,* Vol. **20,** No. 1, 7–9, March 1977.

183. Harnessing heat from the sun, *Ecos, CSIRO Environmental Research,* No. 8, 11–16, May 1976.

184. Kimura, Ken-Ichi, Present technologies of solar heating, cooling and hot water supply in Japan, *Architectural Science Review, Vol.* **19,** No. 2, 41–44 June 1976.

185. Lynes, J. H., The optimisation of flat-plate solar collectors, *Architectural Science Review,* Vol. **17,** No. 4, 70–71, December 1974.
186. Prospects for solar air-conditioning, *Ecos, CSIRO Environmental Research,* No. 12, 19–23 May 1977.
187. Read, W. R. and Wooldridge, M. J., Solar Heating—Domestic Applications, *Architectural Science Review,* Vol. **19,** No. 2, 31–34, June 1976.
188. Roger, A., Software and hardware solutions to energy problems in the built environment, *Architectural Science Review,* Vol. **20,** No. 1, 3–6, March 1977.
189. Saini, B. S., Housing in Northern Australia, *Architectural Science Review,* Vol. **19,** No. 3, 55–57, September 1976.
190. Sheridan, N. R., Solar energy for tropical residences, *Architectural Science Review,* Vol. **19,** No. 2, 34–40, June 1976.
191. Sheridan, N. R., Review of solar cooling, *Proceedings of Symposium on Solar Cooling,* International Solar Energy Society, Brisbane, 1977.
192. Sheridan, N. R., Developments in solar energy for buildings, *Architectural Science Review,* Vol. **21,** Nos. 1 and 2, 10–19, March–June 1978.
193. Sheridan, N. R. and Duffie, J. A., Solar absorption refrigeration, *Australian Refrigeration, Air Conditioning, and Heating,* Vol. **18,** No. 8, 14–20, August 1964.
194. Smith, P. R., Solar energy in buildings—is it worth the trouble?, *Architectural Science Review,* Vol. **17,** No. 4, 72–74, December 1974.
195. Solar air-conditioned house, Brisbane, *Architecture in Australia,* 122–125, March 1965.
196. *Solar Energy in Architecture and Engineering.* A Special issue of the *Architectural Science Review,* Vol. **19,** No. 2, June 1976.
197. Szokolay, S. V., Thermal controls in Northern Australian housing, *Architectural Science Review,* Vol. **19,** No. 3, 58–60, September 1976.
198. Thau, A. Architectural and town planning aspects of domestic solar water heaters, *Architectural Science Review,* Vol. **16,** No. 1, 89–104, March 1973.

Index